고급 최상위

VOCA
2400

TOEFL · SAT · IELTS 보카바이블

고급 최상위 VOCA **2400**

저 자 최예름
발행인 고본화
발 행 반석출판사
2023년 9월 10일 초판 2쇄 인쇄
2023년 9월 15일 초판 2쇄 발행
홈페이지 www.bansok.co.kr
이메일 bansok@bansok.co.kr
블로그 blog.naver.com/bansokbooks

157-779 서울시 강서구 양천로 583. B동 1007호
　　　　　(서울시 강서구 염창동 240-21번지 우림블루나인 비즈니스센터 B동 1007호)
대표전화 02) 2093-3399 **팩 스** 02) 2093-3393
출 판 부 02) 2093-3395 **영업부** 02) 2093-3396
등록번호 제315-2008-000033호

ISBN 978-89-7172-854-3 (13740)

고급 최상위

VOCA
2400

반석출판사
Bansok

Survival of the Fittest!

현대사회를 살아가는 데 있어서 가장 중요한 경쟁력 중 하나는 주어진 환경을 적절하게 활용하고 적응하는 능력입니다. 이러한 적응력에는 최소의 시간을 투자하여 최대의 효과를 거둘 수 있는 효율적인 시간 안배와 관련 정보 습득을 기본으로 합니다. 특히 시험을 준비하는 과정에서 이러한 적응력에 따라 그 결과는 판이하게 달라집니다. 단순히 남보다 더 열심히 노력하고 많은 시간을 투자하여 공부하는 것만이 능사가 아닌 것입니다.

TOEFL, SAT, IELTS, 편입시험, 공무원시험 등 그 어떤 시험도 크게 다르지 않습니다. 시험들마다 특징이 조금씩 다른 만큼 완전히 같지는 않지만, 결국은 어느 정도는 영어 실력을 평가하는 시험인 만큼 출제되는 단어가 서로 동떨어져 있지도 않습니다. 정말 중요한 단어, 반드시 알아야 하는 단어는 시험 종류와 상관없이 자주 출제되는 것이지요. 따라서 단어를 효율적으로 공부하려면 무작정 단어를 외우는 것이 아니라 빈출되는 단어를 위주로 공부해 나가야 합니다.

필자는 단순히 단어만 나열하지 않고 보다 적은 시간을 투자하되 최대의 효과를 거둘 수 있도록 각종 시험에 출제되는 빈도에 따라 단어를 정리하였습니다. Ranking 1~6으로 구분하고 빈출되는 단어를 앞쪽으로 배치하였습니다. 고득점을 노린다면 처음부터 끝까지 단어를 충분히 익히고, 시간이 촉박하다면 Ranking 1~2 혹은 1~3 부분을 위주로 반복해서 공부하는 것도 괜찮습니다.

거의 모든 영어 시험에서 가장 기본이 되고 결국 마지막까지 수험생을 힘들게 하는 것이 바로 Vocabulary라 할 수 있습니다. 특히 단어 공부는 비단 독해(Reading) 파트뿐 아니라 작문(Writing) 파트를 대비하는 데에도 큰 도움을 줍니다. 작문 파트가 있는 IELTS나 SAT 등의 시험을 준비하는 학생들이라면 더더욱 이 책에 수록되어 있는 단어들을 꼼꼼하게 공부하는 것이 도움이 됩니다.

지피지기면 백전백승이라는 말이 있습니다. 각종 시험에 자주 출제되는 유형과 패턴을 사전에 알고 적절하게 대처해야 소기의 목적을 달성할 수 있습니다. 이 책은 시험에 출제된 실전문제를 바탕으로 주요 어휘를 선별하였기 때문에 빈출 어휘를 짧은 시간 안에 공략할 수 있습니다. 이 책으로 공부하는 모든 수험생들의 건승을 기원합니다.

저자 최 예 름

5

PART 1

PART 2

PART 3

PART 4

PART 5

PART 6

acclaim.
intermitte
LONG
accommodate
static
inhibit
arbitrary
facult
PURCHASE
discourse
anony
rhetoric
viction
champion
renown
anecdote
render
eccentric
dema
indignation
oke
predecessor
grandiose
zeal
EMENT
ambiguou
implement
ep
figurative
dent
superficial
METICULOUS
conse
ancillary
espouse pragmatic

Look here!

| 차 례 |

7

PART 1

PART 2

PART 3

PART 4

PART 5

PART 6

1. 2,400여 개의 단어 엄선 수록

시험에 자주 출제되는 단어는 정해져 있습니다. 이 책은 각종 시험에서 빈출되는 2,400여 개의 단어를 수록하고 있기 때문에 본 책의 수록 어휘를 암기한다면 기본 실력은 갖추게 됩니다.

2. 기출 빈도순 정리

목차에서 이미 확인했듯이 표제어는 시험에 출제되는 빈도에 따라 정리되었습니다. Ranking 01(★★★★★)이 시험에 가장 자주 출제되는 중요한 단어들입니다. 빈출되는 단어일수록 랭킹이 높고 별이 많은 앞부분에 배치되어 있어 전략적인 공부가 가능합니다. 간단한 셀프 테스트(각 페이지 하단에 위치)를 통해 공부한 단어를 체크할 수 있도록 꾸몄습니다.

3. 효과만점의 페이지 구성

본 책은 어휘학습의 효율성을 높이기 위해 단어를 횡적으로 배치했습니다. 즉, 왼쪽 페이지에는 표제어와 영어예문을 오른쪽 페이지에는 한글 뜻과 영영해설을 제공하기 때문에 단어를 찾기 쉬울 뿐 아니라 공부할 때 시간을 절약할 수 있습니다.

그리고 어휘는 관련 예문을 통해 암기하는 것이 효율적일 뿐 아니라 기억에도 오래 남습니다. 특히 본 책에 제시된 예문은 기출문장을 변형시켜서 만들었기 때문에 실전감각을 익히는 데 큰 도움이 됩니다. 자투리 시간을 이용하여 본 책과 함께 제공된 mp3파일을 반복 청취하여 완전히 자신의 것으로 소화시키시기 바랍니다.(단어의 효율적인 암기를 위해 표제어의 철자,** 예문***을 녹음했습니다)

9

PART 1

PART 2

PART 3

PART 4

PART 5

PART 6

최상위 영단어

★★★★★

Ranking 1

1 ☐☐	**abstract** [æbstrǽkt]	Her works are abstract. 그녀의 작품들은 추상 예술이다. Her head's full of abstract ideas about justice and revolution. 그녀의 머리는 온통 정의와 혁명에 관한 추상적인 생각들로 꽉 차있다.
2 ☐☐	**accord** [əkɔ́ːrd]	His principles and practice do not accord well together. 그의 신념과 실천은 딱 일치하지 않는다. They accorded praise to him for his good work. 그들은 그의 선행에 대해 그를 칭찬했다.
3 ☐☐	**acknowledge** [əknɑ́lidʒ]	I acknowledge him as my superior. 그가 나보다 우수하다는 것을 인정한다. We should acknowledge the rights of others. 우리는 다른 사람의 권리를 인정해야 한다.
4 ☐☐	**acute** [əkjúːt]	He is an acute observer. 그는 예리한 관찰자이다. Their sensitivity to the moods, expectations, and needs of other people was so acute that at times they seemed to be almost clairvoyant. 다른 사람들의 기분과 기대와 필요에 대한 그들의 감각이 너무나 예민해서 때로 그들은 거의 천리안을 가진 것 같았다.
5 ☐☐	**adapt** [ədǽpt]	The teachers adapt their understanding and method to suit the child. 교사들은 자신들의 이해력과 지도 방법을 아동에 맞춘다. When you go to a new country, you must adapt yourself to new customs. 낯선 나라에 가면 새로운 관습에 적응해야 한다.
6 ☐☐	**address** [ədrés]	On the first day of college, the Dean addressed the students, pointing out some of the rules. 대학 입학 첫 날, 학생처장이 학생들 앞에서 연설하는 중에 몇 가지 규칙을 지적했다. Over the next couple of days, we hope to address this issue. 앞으로 며칠 간 우리는 이 문제를 집중적으로 다루었으면 합니다.
7 ☐☐	**advent** [ǽdvent]	Semaphore was widely used at sea, before the advent of electricity. 신호기는 전기가 등장하기 전 바다에서 널리 이용되었다. Most Americans were unaware of the advent of the Nuclear Age until the news of Hiroshima reached them. 대부분의 미국인들은 히로시마의 원자탄 투하 소식을 들은 후에야 핵시대의 도래를 알았다.

☐ vindicate _____ ☐ volatile _____ ☐ voluminous _____

1_7 13

PART 1

PART 2

PART 3

PART 4

PART 5

PART 6

Definition	Meaning/Relation
추상적인	ⓐ considered apart from concrete existence
일치시키다; 주다	ⓥ to cause to conform or agree; to grant, especially as being due or appropriate **accord with** …와 일치하다
인정하다	ⓥ to admit the existence, reality, or truth of **acknowledge frankly[openly]** 솔직히 인정하다 **acknowledge gratefully** 감사를 표명하다 **acknowledge as** …라고 인정하다
예리한, 날카로운	ⓐ having a sharp point or tip **an acute accent** 양음(揚音) 부호 acute [deep, great, indescribable, untold] **agony** 극심한(도저히 말로 다 할 수 없는) 고통 **acute alcoholism** 급성 알코올 중독 **an acute angle** 예각 **acute anguish** 모진 고통 **acute anxiety** 극심한 불안 an acute **attack** 급작스런 발병 **an acute case** 급성 환자 **an acute condition** 급성질환 **an acute [grave, serious] crisis** 심각한(중대한) 위기
적응시키다	ⓥ to make suitable to or fit for a specific use or situation **adapt for** …용으로 개작하다 **adapt from** …에서 개작하다 **adapt to** …에 적응하다(시키다)
말하다; 연설하다	ⓥ to speak to; to make a formal speech to **address to** …앞으로 보내다 **address oneself to** (숙고하여)다루다
출현, 도래	ⓝ the coming or arrival, especially of something extremely important

☐ wily _____   ☐ wither _____

NO.	Entry Word	Example Sentence
8 ☐☐	**advocate** [ǽdvəkit]	Although at this time he was advocating a policy of neutrality, one could usually find him adopting a more militant attitude. 이번에는 그가 중립 정책을 주장하였지만 보통 때는 아주 호전적인 태도를 취한다는 것을 알 수 있었다. He incurred the animosity of the ruling class because he advocated limitations of their power. 그는 지배계급의 권력을 제한하기를 주장했기 때문에 그들로부터 적대감을 일으켰다.
9 ☐☐	**aesthetic** [esθétik]	The committee laid stress on aesthetic elements of the works. 그 위원회는 작품의 미적인 요소에 중점을 두었다. This chair may be aesthetic but it's not very comfortable. 이 의자는 미학적일지는 몰라도 별로 편하지 않다.
10 ☐☐	**appreciate** [əprí:ʃièit]	I appreciate your difficulty. 나는 네 어려움을 이해한다. I appreciate your concern. 걱정해 주셔서 감사해요.
11 ☐☐	**appropriate** [əpróuprièit]	Do you think this an appropriate gift? 이것이면 적당한 선물이 될까요? Your clothes are not appropriate for the party. 네 옷은 파티용으로는 적당하지 않다.
12 ☐☐	**arid** [ǽrid]	This two foot tall shrub likes hot, arid climates. 키가 2피트 되는 이 관목은 뜨겁고 건조한 기후를 좋아한다. Nomads travel these arid regions with their camel herds. 유목민들은 낙타 떼를 몰고 이 건조한 지역을 돌아다닌다.
13 ☐☐	**assert** [əsə́:rt]	He asserted his innocence. 그는 자기의 결백을 강력히 주장했다. More and more countries are interacting with each other and struggling to assert national interests. 점점 더 많은 나라들이 서로 교류하며 자국의 이익을 위해 강한 주장을 펴고 있다.
14 ☐☐	**attribute** [ətríbju:t]	The decline in test scores has been attributed to poor reading skills. 시험 점수가 내려간 것은 독해력이 떨어지기 때문이다. The rise was attributed by many analysts to expectations of a rise in U.S. interest rates. 많은 분석가들에 의하면 이런 상승은 미국의 금리 상승에 대한 기대 심리탓이라고 합니다.

☐ abstract _____ ☐ accord _____ ☐ acknowledge _____

Definition	Meaning/Relation
주장하다	ⓥ to speak, plead, or argue in favor of **advocate strongly** 강력하게 주장하다
미적인, 미학의	ⓐ relating to the philosophy or theories of aesthetics
평가하다; 감사하다	ⓥ to recognize the quality, significance, or magnitude of; to be thankful or show gratitude for **appreciate deeply[greatly, keenly, sincerely, very much]** 깊이 감사하다
적합한	ⓐ suitable for a particular person, condition, occasion, or place **highly appropriate** 대단히 적절한 **appropriate for[to]** ⋯에 적합한(적당한)
건조한	ⓐ lacking moisture, especially having insufficient rainfall to support trees or woody plants **an arid desert** 건조한 사막
주장하다, 단언하다	ⓥ to state or express positively **assert boldly** 분명히 단언하다
⋯의 탓으로 하다	ⓥ to relate to a particular cause or source **attribute to** ⋯에 돌리다

8_14 15

PART 1

PART 2

PART 3

PART 4

PART 5

PART 6

☐ acute _____ ☐ adapt _____ ☐ address _____ ☐ advent _____

NO.	Entry Word	Example Sentence	
15 ☐☐	**awe** [ɔ́ː]	His knees smote together in awe. 그는 두려워서 무릎이 덜덜 떨렸다. They are in awe of their teacher. 그들은 선생님을 무서워한다.	
16 ☐☐	**civil** [sívəl]	They were deprived of their civil rights. 그들은 시민권을 빼앗겼다. In wartime, people get together under the flag for national independence and civil rights. 전쟁 시에는 사람들이 국가의 독립과 민권을 위해 깃발 아래 함께 모인다.	
17 ☐☐	**cohere** [kouhíər]	Brick and mortar cohere. 벽돌과 무르타르는 밀착한다. His story does not cohere. 그의 이야기는 조리가 서지 않는다.	
18 ☐☐	**comprehensive** [kὰmprihénsiv]	He initiated a comprehensive review of industrial policy. 그는 산업정책에 대한 포괄적인 조사를 시작했다. This book provides a comprehensive review of verbal and math skills for the SAT. 이 책은 SAT(미 학력고사)를 대비하여 언어 및 수학 능력의 포괄적인 복습을 제공한다.	
19 ☐☐	**compromise** [kάmprəmàiz]	They reached a satisfactory compromise. 그들은 만족할 만한 타협을 보았다. A compromise has been duly effected between the two. 양자 사이에 정당하게 타협이 이루어졌다.	
20 ☐☐	**contempt** [kəntémpt]	She showed him contempt. 그녀는 그를 경멸했다. At school, she had complete contempt for all her teachers. 학교에서 그녀는 자신의 교사들을 전부 경멸했다.	
21 ☐☐	**contend** [kənténd]	There are three world-class tennis players contending for this title. 이 타이틀을 얻기 위해 경쟁하는 세계적인 테니스 선수들이 세 명이나 있다. Each day at the docks, the fishermen must contend with birds who try to steal their catch. 부두에서는 매일같이 어부들이 물고기를 훔쳐가려는 새들과 싸워야만 한다.	

☐ advocate _____   ☐ aesthetic _____   ☐ appreciate _____

Definition	Meaning/Relation
두려움, 경외	ⓝ a mixed emotion of reverence, respect, dread, and wonder inspired by authority, genius, great beauty, sublimity, or might **inspire awe in** …에게 경외심을 갖게 하다 **hold** *sb* **in awe** …에 대해 경외심을 갖다 **deep awe** 깊은 경외심 **in awe of** …을 경외하여 **stand in awe of** *sb* …을 경외하다 **awe into** 경외감에 …하게 하다
시민의	ⓐ of or relating to citizens and their interrelations with one another or with the state **civil to** …에게 예의 바른
밀착하다; 논리가 서다	ⓥ to stick or hold together in a mass that resists separation; to have internal elements or parts logically connected so that aesthetic consistency results
포괄적인	ⓐ so large in scope or content as to include much **a comprehensive bibliography** 포괄적인 참고 문헌 목록 **comprehensive[full] coverage** 완전보상 **a comprehensive examination** 종합 시험
타협	ⓝ a settlement of differences in which each side makes concessions **agree 【英】[agree on, agree to, arrive at, come to, reach, work out] a compromise** 타협에 이르다, 타협을 보다 **reject a compromise** 타협안을 거부하다 **compromise on[over]** …에 대해 타협하다 **compromise with** …와 타협하다
경멸, 멸시	ⓝ disparaging or haughty disdain, as for something base or unworthy; scorn **demonstrate[display, show, express] contempt for** …에 대한 경멸을 드러내다
싸우다	ⓥ to strive in opposition or against difficulties **contend for** …을 두고 다투다

PART 1 PART 2 PART 3 PART 4 PART 5 PART 6

☐ appropriate _____ ☐ arid _____ ☐ assert _____ ☐ attribute _____

NO.	Entry Word	Example Sentence
22 ☐☐	**contest** [kántest]	He won the swimming contest. 그는 수영 대회에서 우승했다. The oven design was originally developed for a contest sponsored by the Swedish National Energy Administration. 그 오븐 디자인은 당초 스웨덴 국가 에너지 관리국이 후원한 콘테스트에 출품하기 위해 개발되었다.
23 ☐☐	**conventional** [kənvénʃənəl]	He took a stand opposed to conventional wisdom. 그는 통설과 정반대의 입장을 취했다. Today's desktop publishing systems offer a very good emulation of conventional printing methods. 오늘날의 데스크탑 컴퓨터를 이용한 출판 체계는 전통적인 인쇄 방식을 훌륭하게 대신하고 있다.
24 ☐☐	**cynic** [sínik]	I'm too much of a cynic to believe that he'll keep his promise. 그가 약속을 지킬 거라고 믿기에는 나는 너무 냉소적이다. A cynic might say that women increased their labor force participation so men can retire early. 어떤 냉소가는 여성 노동 인구가 증가해서 남자들이 일찍 은퇴할 수 있다고 말한다.
25 ☐☐	**deliberate** [dilíbərèit]	Richard Golub says the difference is deliberate. 리차드 골럽에 의하면 다르게 만든 건 의도적이었다고 합니다. The making of a tennis player is a deliberate process. 한 명의 테니스 선수를 만들어 내는 것은 아주 신중한 과정입니다.
26 ☐☐	**depict** [dipíkt]	Her novel depicts the life of country people. 그녀의 소설은 시골 사람들의 삶을 묘사한다. They depicted the situation to us in great detail. 그들은 우리에게 상황을 매우 상세하게 설명했다
27 ☐☐	**deride** [diráid]	They derided his efforts (as childish). 그들은 그의 노력을 (유치하다고) 비웃었다. The people derided his grandiose schemes. 국민들은 그의 과장된 계획을 조롱했다.
28 ☐☐	**die** [dai]	Man must die. 인간은 반드시 죽는 법이다. He does not hesitate even to die. 그는 죽음도 사양치 않는다.

☐ awe _____ ☐ civil _____ ☐ cohere _____ ☐ comprehensive _____

PART 1

PART 2

PART 3

PART 4

PART 5

PART 6

Definition	Meaning/Relation
대회	ⓝ a struggle for superiority or victory between rivals **have[hold, organize, stage] a contest** 대회를 개최하다 **judge a contest** 대회를 심판하다 **contest bitterly** 심하게 반박하다
전통(인습)적인	ⓐ based on or in accordance with general agreement, use, or practice **conventional in (one's tastes)** (기호)에 있어 인습적인
냉소가	ⓝ a person who believes all people are motivated by selfishness
의도적인, 신중한	ⓐ done with or marked by full consciousness of the nature and effects arising from or marked by careful consideration **deliberate in** …에서 신중한
묘사하다	ⓥ to represent in a picture or sculpture
비웃다, 조롱하다	ⓥ to speak of or treat with contemptuous mirth
죽다	ⓥ to cease living

☐ compromise _____   ☐ contempt _____   ☐ contend _____

NO.	Entry Word	Example Sentence	
29 ☐☐	**disdain** [disdéin]	She disdains flattery. 그녀는 아첨을 경멸한다. He strums the nylon strings of this instrument with his fingers, disdaining the plastic pick, the tool of jazz guitarists. 그는 재즈 기타리스트의 도구인 플라스틱 픽을 무시하고 이 악기의 나일론 현을 직접 손가락으로 연주합니다.	
30 ☐☐	**dismiss** [dismís]	Long dismissed as primitive, African music is actually extremely complex. 오랫동안 원시적이라는 이유로 도외시 됐던 아프리카 음악은 사실상 아주 복잡하다. These are findings we should not dismiss without exhaustive testing. 이것들은 철저한 검증 없이는 기각시킬 수 없는 조사 결과들이다.	
31 ☐☐	**diverse** [divə́:rs]	Linguistics embraces a diverse range of subjects such as phoneitcs and stylistics. 언어학은 음성학이나 문체론 같은 다양한 과목을 포함한다. A select group of sociology professors will contribute essays analyzing the diverse aspects of societal transformation during the past two decades. 선택된 한 그룹의 한국 사회학 교수들이 지난 20년 동안 사회 변혁의 다양한 측면을 분석하는 에세이를 쓸 것이다.	
32 ☐☐	**evoke** [ivóuk]	That smell always evokes memories of my old school. 저 냄새는 언제나 내가 옛날에 다닌 학교의 추억을 불러 일으킨다. The question evoked much controversy among the publicists. 그 문제는 논단을 떠들썩하게 하였다.	
33 ☐☐	**exacting** [igzǽktiŋ]	He is exacting even in trifles. 그는 사소한 일까지도 매우 딱딱하게 군다 His work schedule is exacting. 그의 작업 일정이 힘들다.	
34 ☐☐	**exploit** [éksplɔit]	Everybody is trying to establish a brand and exploit it. 모두가 브랜드를 만들어서 이용하려 하고 있어요. Some of the early explorers thought of the local people as benighted savages who could be exploited. 초창기 탐험가 중 몇 사람은 현지인을 이용해도 되는 미개한 야만인이라고 생각했다.	
35 ☐☐	**foster** [fɔ́(:)stər]	Europe's new economic climate has largely fostered the trend toward independence. 유럽의 새로운 경제적 풍토는 많은 독립생활의 추세를 부추기고 있다. Dedicated and enthusiastic teachers are essential to foster a love of learning in children. 아이들의 학습 의욕을 길러주는 데는 헌신적이고 열정적인 교사가 필수적이다.	

☐ contest _____   ☐ conventional _____   ☐ cynic _____

Definition	Meaning/Relation
경멸하다, 멸시하다	ⓥ to regard or treat with haughty contempt despise
무시하다	ⓥ to refuse to consider or accept **dismiss curtly[summarily]** 일언지하에 물리치다〔퇴짜놓다〕, 즉결 해고하다 **dismiss lightly** 간단히 물리치다〔제쳐놓다〕
다양한	ⓐ made up of distinct characteristics **diverse elements** 여러 구성원 **a diverse view** 다양한 의견
불러일으키다	ⓥ to summon or call forth **evoke[bring up, call up] an association** 연상을 불러 일으키다 **evoke[arouse, cause, create, excite] comment** 물의를 일으키다 **evoke[bring back, call up, conjure up, dredge up, stir up] a memory** 추억을 일깨우다, 기억을 되살리다 **evoke[call forth, draw, elicit] a response** 답변을 유도해 내다〔끌어내다〕 **evoke a smile** 미소를 자아내다
엄하게 요구하는; 힘든	ⓐ making severe demands; requiring great care, effort, or attention
이용하다; 개발하다	ⓥ to make use of selfishly or unethically; to employ to the greatest possible advantage **exploit ruthlessly** 무자비하게 착취하다
촉진하다	ⓥ to promote the growth and development of **foster[promote] (good) fellowship** 연대감〔친목〕을 조성하다 **foster[promote, stimulate] growth** 성장을 촉진하다

☐ deliberate _____ ☐ depict _____ ☐ deride _____ ☐ die _____

29_35 21

PART 1

PART 2

PART 3

PART 4

PART 5

PART 6

36 ☐☐	**fundamental** [fʌndəméntl]	That is a fundamental change in politics. 그것은 정치상의 근본적인 변화이다. The right of petition is one of the fundamental privileges of free people. 탄원의 권리는 자유민의 기본 특권 중 하나이다.	
37 ☐☐	**genre** [ʒɑ́:nrə]	The novel and the short story are different genres. 소설과 단편소설은 다른 장르이다. This romance is her first attempt at writing genre fiction. 이 로맨스는 그녀가 처음으로 집필을 시도한 장르 소설이다.	
38 ☐☐	**integrity** [intégrəti]	He is a person of integrity and is respected by everyone. 그는 성실한 사람이라 모든 사람들에게 존경받고 있다. Nobody doubted his integrity and knowledge of countryside matters. 아무도 그의 성실함과 시골의 사정에 대한 지식을 의심하지 않았다.	
39 ☐☐	**lament** [ləmént]	We all lamented the death of our friend. 우리들은 모두 친구의 죽음을 애도했다. The nation lamented the passing of its great war leader. 온 나라는 그들의 위대한 전쟁 지도자를 잃은 슬픔에 빠졌다.	
40 ☐☐	**minute** [mínit]	It's a few minutes' walk from here to the station. 여기서 역까지 몇 분 걸린다. It just passed by about five minutes ago. 약 5분 전에 지나갔다.	
41 ☐☐	**mundane** [mʌ́ndein]	The former president just began to ignore mundane affairs. 전직 대통령은 세속적인 일을 무시하기 시작했다. He was concerned only with mundane matters, especially the daily stock market quotations. 그는 세속적인 문제 특히 증권 시장의 주식 시세들에만 관심이 있었다.	
42 ☐☐	**obscure** [əbskjúər]	Their real intention is obscure. 그들의 진정한 의도는 애매하다. Like many sports, this has obscure origins. 다른 스포츠처럼, 이것은 애매모호한 기원을 가지고 있다.	

☐ disdain _____   ☐ dismiss _____   ☐ diverse _____   ☐ evoke _____

Definition	Meaning/Relation
근본적인, 기본이 되는	ⓐ of or relating to the foundation or base **fundamental to** …에 기본적인
장르	ⓝ a category of artistic composition, as in music or literature, marked by a distinctive style, form, or content
성실, 고결	ⓝ steadfast adherence to a strict moral or ethical code **display[show] integrity** 청렴함을 보이다 **have integrity** 청렴함(고결성)을 지니다
슬퍼하다	ⓥ to express grief for or about **lament bitterly[deeply]** 깊이 애도하다 **lament over** …에 대해 비탄하다
분	ⓝ a unit of time equal to one sixtieth of an hour, or 60 seconds **in a minute** 금방
세속의	ⓐ of, relating go, or typical of this world **an mundane[everyday] subject** 일상적인 주제
애매한	ⓐ not clearly understood or expressed **obscure to** …에게 있어서 애매한

□ exacting _____   □ exploit _____   □ foster _____

NO.	Entry Word	Example Sentence
43 ☐☐	**potential** [poʊténʃəl]	The boy is a potential actor. 그 소년은 가능성 있는 배우다. But declines on Wall Street and concerns about a potential war between the U.S. and Iraq took the KOSPI sharply lower on this trading day. 그러나 미국 월가의 증시 하락과, 미국과 이라크의 전쟁 발생 가능성으로 KOSPI가 오늘 급격한 하락세를 보였습니다.
44 ☐☐	**profound** [prəfáund]	The child fell into a profound sleep. 그 아이는 깊은 잠에 빠졌다. Opera uses the profound power of music to communicate feelings and to express emotions. 오페라는 음악의 심오한 효과를 이용하여 감동을 전달하고 감정을 표현합니다.
45 ☐☐	**random** [rǽndəm]	He asked random questions. 그는 닥치는 대로 질문을 했다. He made a random collection of old stamps. 그는 옛날 우표를 닥치는 대로 수집했다.
46 ☐☐	**satire** [sǽtaiər]	Her play was a cruel satire on life in the 80s. 그녀가 보여준 연극은 80년대의 삶에 관한 신랄한 풍자였다. His plays, including Tartuffe and The Misanthrope are recognized today as classics of comic satire. 「타르튀프」와 「미상트로프」를 비롯한 그의 희곡들은 오늘날 희극적 풍자의 고전으로 알려져 있다.
47 ☐☐	**scale** [skeil]	Mary stands on the scale. 메리는 저울 위에 서 있다. His invention is a microcomputer and display screen connected to a scale that weighs a vehicle's driver. 그가 발명한 것은 저울과 연결된 마이크로컴퓨터와 모니터인데 이 저울은 운전자의 무게를 잰다.
48 ☐☐	**sustain** [səstéin]	We do not have sufficient resources to sustain our campaign for long. 우리에게는 우리의 캠페인을 오랫동안 지속할 만한 충분한 재력이 없다. The process requires sustaining temperatures of nearly 600 degrees C for over an hour. 그 공정은 섭씨 600도에 달하는 온도를 한 시간 이상 유지할 것을 요한다.
49 ☐☐	**ultimate** [ʌ́ltəmit]	Peace was the ultimate goal of the meeting. 평화가 그 모임의 궁극적인 목표였다. The ultimate solution to this problem is getting all of our people productive. 이 문제에 대한 궁극적 해결책은 우리 국민 모두를 생산성 있게 만드는 거예요.

☐ fundamental _____ ☐ genre _____ ☐ integrity _____

PART 1

PART 2

PART 3

PART 4

PART 5

PART 6

Definition	Meaning/Relation
가능성 있는	ⓐ capable of being but not yet in existence develop one's potential 가능성을 키우다 realize one's potential 가능성을 실현하다
깊은, 심오한	ⓐ situated at, extending to, or coming from a great depth
닥치는 대로의, 임의로	ⓐ having no specific pattern, purpose, or objective at random 무작위로
풍자	ⓝ a literary work in which human vice or folly is attacked through irony, derision, or wit (a) biting[scathing] satire 통렬한〔호된〕 풍자 political satire 정치적 풍자 a satire on …에 대한 풍자
저울	ⓝ a device bearing marks used as a reference standard in measurement a bathroom scale 욕실의 체중계 a kitchen scale 부엌〔요리〕용 저울 a spring scale 용수철 저울 a table scale 탁상 저울 on a scale 저울로
유지하다; 지속하다	ⓥ to keep in existence; maintain sustain[get, have, receive] a concussion 충격을 받다 sustain[suffer] damage 손해를 입다 sustain[receive, suffer] an injury 부상을 당하다
최종의, 궁극적인	ⓐ being last in a series, process, or progression the ultimate in …의 궁극점

☐ lament _____ ☐ minute _____ ☐ mundane _____ ☐ obscure _____

NO.	Entry Word	Example Sentence
50 ☐☐	**undermine** [ʌ̀ndərmáin]	He complained that there had been a campaign to undermine his credibility as leader. 그는 지도자로서의 자신의 신용을 은밀히 해치려는 운동이 있었다고 불평했다. As a junior officer you have no right to undermine my authority by countermanding my orders. 하급 장교인 당신은 내 명령을 취소함으로써 내 권위를 훼손할 권리가 없다.
51 ☐☐	**universal** [jùːnəvə́ːrsəl]	It is a universal truth. 그것은 보편적인 진리다. The project received universal approval. 그 계획은 널리 승인을 얻었다.
52 ☐☐	**valid** [vǽlid]	He raised valid objections to the scheme. 그는 ㄱ 계획에 대해 타당한 이의를 제기했다. There is still no valid research that supports your theory. 당신의 이론을 뒷받침할 유효한 연구가 여전히 이루어지지 않고 있습니다.
53 ☐☐	**verge** [vəːrdʒ]	All the plates have chipped verges. 모든 접시들의 가장자리는 이가 빠져 있다. His firm was on the verge of bankruptcy. 그의 회사는 파산 직전에 있었다.
54 ☐☐	**virtual** [və́ːrtʃuəl]	The helmet is connected to the virtual reality computer. 이 헬멧은 가상 현실 컴퓨터에 연결됩니다. A visitor walks inside the multimedia spaceball 'Geome', a virtual soccer arena next to the Burgtheater theatre building in Vienna, Austria. 방문객은 오스트리아 비엔나에 Burgtheater 영화관 건물 옆에 있는 가상 축구장인 멀티미디어 스페이스볼 'Geome'안에서 걸을 수 있다.
55 ☐☐	**vital** [váitl]	Air is vital to man. 공기는 사람에게 중요하다. The heart is a vital organ. 심장은 매우 중요한 기관이다.
56 ☐☐	**wary** [wɛ́əri]	He is wary of strangers. 그는 낯선 사람을 경계한다. All authors need to be wary of inadvertent plagiarism of other people's work. 모든 저자들은 부주의로 인해 다른 사람들의 작품을 표절하지 않도록 조심해야 한다.

☐ potential _____ ☐ profound _____ ☐ random _____

50_56   27

PART 1

PART 2

PART 3

PART 4

PART 5

PART 6

Definition	Meaning/Relation
은밀히 손상시키다	ⓥ to weaken, injure, or impair, often by degrees or imperceptibly **undermine authority** 권위를 손상시키다〔훼손하다〕 **confidence** …의 신용〔신뢰〕을 손상시키다 **damage[undermine]** *sb's* **credibility** 신뢰성를 떨어뜨리다
보편적인	ⓐ applicable or common to all purpose, conditions or situations **universal peace** 세계 평화
타당한, 유효한	ⓐ well grounded **valid for** …동안 유효한
가장자리; 직전	ⓝ an enclosing boundary; the point beyond which an action, a state, or a condition is likely to begin or occur **on the verge of** …하기 직전에, …에 직면하여
가상의	ⓐ existing in the mind, especially as a product of the imagination **a virtual image** 컴퓨터 가상기억 이미지, 허상 **virtual memory** 가상 메모리 **virtual reality** 가상 현실
(생존에) 중요한	ⓐ necessary to continued existence or effectiveness
경계하는; 조심하는	ⓐ on guard; watchful

☐ satire _____   ☐ scale _____   ☐ sustain _____   ☐ ultimate _____

우선순위 영단어

★★★★

Ranking 2

NO.	Entry Word	Example Sentence	
57 ☐☐	**absolute** [ǽbsəlùːt]	I have absolute trust in him. 나는 그를 절대적으로 믿는다. King Gyanendra dismissed the government and took absolute power in February 2005. 2005년 2월 Gyanendra 국왕은 국회를 해산하고 절대권력을 장악했습니다.	
58 ☐☐	**acclaim** [əkléim]	The people acclaimed him (as) king. 민중은 환호 속에 그를 왕으로 맞이하였다. The new drug has been acclaimed as the most important discovery for years. 그 신약은 수년 동안 가장 중요한 발견물로 갈채를 받았다.	
59 ☐☐	**accommodate** [əkámədèit]	Section managers will make every effort to accommodate their employees' preferences. 부서장들은 부서 직원들이 원하는 바를 최대한 수용하도록 노력할 것이다. I'm looking for a tent that can accommodate two adults and two children. 어른 두 명과 어린이 두 명이 쓸 수 있는 텐트를 찾고 있어요.	
60 ☐☐	**alienate** [éiljənèit]	Many artists feel alienated from society. 많은 예술가들이 사회에서 이질감을 느낀다. The prime minister's policy has alienated many of his supporters. 수상의 정책은 많은 그의 지지자들을 멀리하게 했다.	
61 ☐☐	**ambiguous** [æmbígjuəs]	That sentence is ambiguous. 그 문장은 애매하다. Her speech was deliberately ambiguous to avoid offending either side. 그녀의 연설은 어느 쪽도 자극하지 않으려고 의도적으로 애매했다.	
62 ☐☐	**ancillary** [ǽnsəlèri]	This includes students, teachers, administrators, ancillary employees, and even parents. 이것은 학생, 교사, 행정관, 보조 직원, 및 부모까지를 포함한다. Other fuel saving enhancements have been made courtesy of various ancillary devices. 다른 연료 절약 장치들이 다양한 보조 장치들을 위해서 만들어졌다.	
63 ☐☐	**anecdote** [ǽnikdòut]	He spiced his conversation with humorous anecdotes. 그는 재미있는 일화를 넣어 이야기에 흥취를 더했다. Mr. Jumperwala told her some amusing anecdotes about the English aristocracy. Jumperwala 씨는 그녀에게 영국의 귀족정치에 관한 재미있는 일화들을 들려주었다.	

☐ undermine _____ ☐ universal _____ ☐ valid _____ ☐ verge _____

Definition	Meaning/Relation
절대적인	ⓐ perfect in quality or nature **absolute[complete, full, supreme, unquestioned] authority** 절대적인 권한(권위) **absolute[complete, sheer, utter] bedlam** 완전 아수라장 **an absolute[complete, rank] beginner** 완전 초심자
갈채(환호)하다	ⓥ to praise enthusiastically and often publicly
돌보다; (숙박처를) 제공하다	ⓥ to do a favor or service for; to provide for
멀리하다, 소원하게 하다	ⓥ to cause to become unfriendly or hostile estrange **alienate from** …와 소원하게 만들다
애매한	ⓐ doubtful or uncertain
보조의	ⓐ auxiliary **ancillary staff/duties/services/equipment** 보조직원/임무/서비스/장비 **poorly paid ancillary workers in the health service** 박한 보수를 받는 공공의료계의 보조 구조자들
일화	ⓝ a short account of an interesting or humorous incident **relate[tell] an anecdote** 일화를 이야기하다 **an amusing[funny, witty] anecdote** 재미있는 일화 **an anecdote about** …에 관한 일화

PART 1

PART 2

PART 3

PART 4

PART 5

PART 6

☐ virtual _____ ☐ vital _____ ☐ wary _____

NO.	Entry Word	Example Sentence	
64 ☐☐	**anonymous** [ənánəməs]	He tried to ascertain the identity of the writer of the anonymous letter. 그는 익명의 편지를 쓴 사람의 신원을 밝히려고 노력했다. We want to express our heartfelt gratitude to the anonymous donor who gave this generous gift to our Building Fund. 우리는 건축기금에 이러한 관대한 기부를 한 익명의 기증자에게 진심에서 우러나온 감사를 표하고 싶다.	
65 ☐☐	**apathetic** [æ̀pəθétik]	He is apathetic to delicate women's feelings. 그는 여자의 미묘한 감정에 대해서 무신경하다 The general public was apathetic as to whether Scotland Yard would solve the mystery. 일반 대중들은 런던 경찰국이 그 미해결 사건을 풀 것인가 하는 데는 관심이 없었다.	
66 ☐☐	**arbitrary** [ɑ́ːrbətrèri]	She does not make an arbitrary decision. 그녀는 멋대로 결정을 내리지 않는다. She made an arbitrary choice of the black shoes instead of the brown ones. 그녀는 멋대로 갈색 구두 대신 검정색 구두를 선택했다.	
67 ☐☐	**articulate** [ɑːrtíkjəlèit]	The baby cries and gurgles but does not use articulate speech. 아기는 울고 갸르륵 소리를 내지만 명료한 말은 하지 못한다. At the age of 93, he was still sharp-witted and articulate. 93세의 나이에도 그는 여전히 기지가 예리하며 발음이 명료했다.	
68 ☐☐	**astute** [əstjúːt]	It was an astute move to sell just before the prices went down. 가격이 폭락하기 직전에 판매한 것은 기민한 동작이었다. His astute handling of this difficult situation saved her from disaster. 그가 이 어려운 상황을 기민하게 처리해서 그녀는 재난을 면했다.	
69 ☐☐	**censure** [sénʃər]	His dishonest behavior came under severe censure. 그의 부정직한 행동은 호된 비난을 받았다. It is a controversial policy which has attracted international censure. 그것은 국제적인 비난을 야기한 논쟁의 여지가 있는 정책이다.	
70 ☐☐	**champion** [tʃǽmpiən]	The swimming champion is very young. 그 수영 우승자는 매우 어리다. This last game will decide who is to be a champion. 이 마지막 경기가 누가 챔피언이 될 것인지를 결정할 것이다.	

☐ absolute _____ ☐ acclaim _____ ☐ accommodate _____ ☐ alienate _____

| --- | --- |
익명의	ⓐ having an unknown or unacknowledged name Alcoholics Anonymous 금주회, 알코올 중독자 갱생회(약어 AA) Recipients remain anonymous. 도움 받은 사람의 이름은 밝히지 않습니다. remain anonymous 익명으로 남다, 이름이 밝혀지지 않다
무관심의	ⓐ feeling or showing a lack of interest or concern
임의의, 멋대로인	ⓐ determined by chance, whim, or impulse, and not necessity, reason, or principle
명료한	ⓐ composed of distinct, meaningful syllables or words, as human speech an articulate idea 논리 정연한 생각 articulate speech 뜻을 알 수 있는 말, 인간의 말
기민한	ⓐ having or showing shrewdness and discernment, especially with respect to one's own concerns astute at …에 빈틈없는
비난	ⓝ an expression of strong disapproval or harsh criticism bitter[strong] censure 통렬한 비난 public censure 사회의 비난
우승자	ⓝ one that wins first place or first prize in a competition a swimming champion 수영 우승자 a champion of peace 평화의 옹호자 a champion at singing 노래를 잘 부르는 사람

64_70 33

PART 1

PART 2

PART 3

PART 4

PART 5

PART 6

☐ ambiguous _____　☐ ancillary _____　☐ anecdote _____

NO.	Entry Word	Example Sentence	
71 ☐☐	**charisma** [kərízmə]	People with charisma tend to lead the van of riots. 카리스마가 있는 사람들이 소동의 선두를 맡는 경향이 있다. Stella is a person with charisma who keeps the weather of the organization. 스텔라는 조직을 좌지우지하는 카리스마 있는 사람이다.	
72 ☐☐	**compatible** [kəmpǽtəbəl]	His interests are not compatible with mine. 그의 이해(利害)는 나의 이해와 양립하지 않는다. Do you think that your unwillingness to study foreign language is compatible with your ambition to get a job in the Foreign Service? 외국어 공부를 꺼리는 당신의 태도가 외무부서에서 일자리를 구하려는 당신의 야망과 양립할 수 있다고 생각하십니까?	
73 ☐☐	**complement** [kámpləmənt]	This is an indispensable complement. 이것은 불가결한 보충물이다. A good wine is a complement to a good meal. 좋은 술은 훌륭한 식사를 더욱 빛나게 해준다.	
74 ☐☐	**concise** [kənsáis]	The essay is written in a concise style. 그 수필은 간결한 문체로 쓰여 있다. What you need to keep in mind is to be clear and concise when you write the monthly reports. 당신이 월례 보고서를 쓸 때 명심할 필요가 있는 것은 명확하고 간결해야 한다는 것입니다.	
75 ☐☐	**concord** [káŋkɔːrd]	His speech did nothing for racial concord. 그의 연설은 인종적 일치(조화)를 조성하는 데 아무것도 한 일이 없다. There was complete concord among the delegates. 대표들 간에 완전한 의견의 일치를 보았다.	
76 ☐☐	**condescend** [kàndisénd]	He condescends to every woman he meets. 그는 만나는 모든 여자들에게 자기를 낮춘다. He condescended to their intellectual level in order to be understood. 그는 그들이 이해하기 좋도록 그들의 지적 수준에 맞추었다.	
77 ☐☐	**conjure** [kándʒər]	Her dream conjured up a scene of horror. 그녀의 꿈은 무서운 광경을 그려냈다. He conjured up an image of a reformed city and had the cotters completely under his spell. 그는 개혁된 도시의 모습을 그려냄으로써 완전히 유권자들을 사로잡았다	

☐ anonymous _____   ☐ apathetic _____   ☐ arbitrary _____

71_77 35

PART 1

PART 2

PART 3

PART 4

PART 5

PART 6

Definition	Meaning/Relation
남을 끌어당기는 강한 매력 (카리스마)	ⓝ a rare personal quality attributed to leaders who arouse fervent popular devotion and enthusiasm **have charisma** 카리스마〔권위〕가 있다 **personal charisma** 개인적인 카리스마 자질
양립할 수 있는	ⓐ capable of existing or performing in harmonious combination with another to others **perfectly compatible** 완벽하게 양립하는〔호환되는〕 **compatible with** …와 양립할 수 있는
보충물	ⓝ something that completes, makes up a whole, or brings to perfection **a full complement** 전체 정원 **a perfect complement** 완벽한 보완물 **a ship's complement** 해군 함선의 승무원 정원(=a crew) **a predicate complement** 문법 서술보어 **a complement to** …에 대한 보완물
간결한	ⓐ expressing much in few words **a concise dictionary** 간단한 소사전 **a brief[concise, simple, succinct] explanation** 간결한 설명 **a concise form** 간결한 형태
일치, 조화	ⓝ harmony or agreement of interests or feelings; accord **in concord with** …와 일치하는
자기를 낮추다	ⓥ to descend to the level of one considered inferior **condescend to** 체면을 버리고 …하다
그려내다	ⓥ to summon (a devil or spirit) by magical or supernatural power **a name to conjure with** 주문에 쓰는 이름, 유력한〔영향력 있는〕 이름 **conjure away** 마술로 쫓아 버리다 **conjure out** 마술〔요술〕로 …을 내놓다 **conjure up** 주문을 외어〔마술을 써서〕 〈죽은 이의 영혼 · 귀신 등을〉 나타나게 하다〔불러내다〕, 상상으로 나타나게 하다, 눈 깜짝할 사이에 …을 만들다

□ articulate _____   □ astute _____   □ censure _____   □ champion _____

NO.	Entry Word	Example Sentence	
78 ☐☐	**consensus** [kənsénsəs]	The consensus among the students was that the professor should be dismissed. 학생들간의 다수의 의견은 교수를 해임시켜야 한다는 것이었다. There is a broad consensus that the government should not slow down the pace of its drive to get rid of red tape and bureaucracy. 정부가 형식주의와 관료주의 청산 운동의 속도를 늦추지 말아야 한다는 데 폭넓은 합의가 모아지고 있다.	
79 ☐☐	**conviction** [kənvíkʃən]	His testimony shook my conviction of his innocence. 그의 증언으로 그가 무죄라는 나의 확신이 흔들렸다.	
80 ☐☐	**daunt** [dɔːnt]	The immensity of the task is daunting. 헤아릴 수 없이 엄청난 양의 일이 사람을 낙담하게 한다. He is not a man to be daunted by a single failure. 한 번 실패로 낙담할 사람이 아니다.	
81 ☐☐	**dearth** [dəːrθ]	There seems to be a dearth of good young players at the moment. 지금은 훌륭한 젊은 선수가 부족한 것 같다. The dearth of skilled labor compelled the employers to open trade schools. 숙련공이 부족하여 고용주들이 직업학교를 열게 되었다.	
82 ☐☐	**debunk** [diːbʌŋk]	Reporters debunked the candidate's claim that he was a fervent environmentalist. 기자들은 그가 과거에는 열렬한 환경보호론자라는 그 후보의 주장이 사실이 아님을 폭로했다. These climate scientists debunked mathematical models used to hype global warming. 기후학자들은 지구온난화를 감추기 위해 사용된 수학적 모델이 잘못되었음을 폭로했다.	
83 ☐☐	**delineate** [dilínièit]	Children like to delineate object in drawing. 어린이들은 사물을 그림으로 묘사하는 것을 좋아한다. Many Koreans still delineate the president as a hero. 많은 한국인들은 여전히 그 대통령을 영웅으로 묘사한다.	
84 ☐☐	**demagogue** [déməgɔ̀ːg]	Many people regard Hitler as having been a demagogue. 많은 사람들은 히틀러가 선동가였다고 생각한다. The demagogue incited the mob to take action into its own hands. 민중 선동가는 군중을 선동해서 직접 조치를 취하도록 했다.	

☐ charisma _____ ☐ compatible _____ ☐ complement _____

PART 1

PART 2

PART 3

PART 4

PART 5

PART 6

Definition	Meaning/Relation
다수의 의견	ⓝ an opinion or position reached by a group as a whole or by majority will **reach a consensus on** 합의에 이르다 **a general consensus** 전반적인 합의
확신; 유죄판결	ⓝ the state of being convinced; the judgement a jury or judge that a person is guilty of a crime as charged **carry conviction** 신념을 담고 있다
낙담시키다	ⓥ to abate the courage of
(…의) 부족	ⓝ a scarce supply
폭로하다	ⓥ to expose or ridicule the falseness, sham, or exaggerated claims of **debunk[discredit, disprove, explode, refute] a theory** 이론을 부정하다, 이론이 틀렸음을 증명하다
묘사하다	ⓥ to draw or trace the outline of **delineate[depict, draw] a character** 인물을 그리다(묘사하다)
선동가	ⓝ a leader who obtains power by means of impassioned appeals to the emotions and prejudices of the populace

☐ concise _____ ☐ concord _____ ☐ condescend _____ ☐ conjure _____

NO.	Entry Word	Example Sentence	
85 ☐☐	**demeanor** [dimíːnər]	She disliked his haughty demeanor. 그녀는 그의 거만한 태도가 싫었다. His sober demeanor quieted the noisy revelers. 그의 근엄한 태도 때문에 시끄러운 술꾼들이 조용해졌다.	
86 ☐☐	**denounce** [dináuns]	He denounced the U.S. pressure as an act of war. 그는 미국의 압력을 전쟁 행위라고 비난했습니다. The proposal was denounced immediately and called an unnecessary obstacle to peace. 그 제안은 즉시 비난을 받았고 평화를 막는 불필요한 걸림돌로 받아들여졌다.	
87 ☐☐	**discourse** [dískɔːrs]	The discourse of politicians is very hostile to immigration. 정치인들의 발언은 이민에 매우 적대적입니다. He discoursed on Greek mythology. 그는 그리스 신화에 관해서 강연했다.	
88 ☐☐	**disparage** [dispǽridʒ]	He asked them not to disparage his government by mentioning an anonymous scholar. 그는 익명의 학자를 언급함으로써 그들에게 그의 정부를 험담하지 않을 것을 요청했다. He was not trying to disparage the remarkable achievements and strengths of Korea. 그는 한국의 주목할 만한 업적과 힘을 험담하려 하지 않았다.	
89 ☐☐	**dubious** [djúːbiəs]	He's a dubious character. 그는 의심스러운 인물이다. This report is of dubious authenticity. 이 보고의 진위는 확실치가 않다.	
90 ☐☐	**eccentric** [ikséntrik]	There is something eccentric in his composition. 그의 성질에는 좀 유별난 데가 있다. She had an eccentric habit of collecting stray cats. 그녀는 집 없는 고양이들을 모으는 유별난 취미를 갖고 있었다.	
91 ☐☐	**empirical** [empírikəl]	Until recently, very little empirical work had been done, aside from Milgram's initial experiment. 최근까지도 milgram의 초기 실험을 제외하고는 실증 실험이 거의 이루어지지 않았다. He distrusted hunches and intuitive flashes; he placed his reliance entirely on empirical data. 그는 예감이나 직감을 불신하고 전적으로 실증적인 자료에 근거를 두었다.	

☐ consensus _____   ☐ conviction _____   ☐ daunt _____   ☐ dearth _____

Definition	Meaning/Relation
태도	ⓝ the way in which a person behaves **a cheerful[friendly] demeanor** 명랑한(다정한) 태도 **an unfriendly demeanor** 다정치 못한(비우호적) 태도
비난하다	ⓥ to condemn openly as being evil or reprehensible **denounce angrily[bitterly]** 심하게 비난하다 **denounce openly[publicly]** 공개적으로 비난하다
발언, 담론; 강연하다	ⓝ conversation; a formal discussion of a subject, either writer or speaker **direct discourse** 직접 화법 ⓥ to speak or write formally and at length
험담하다	ⓥ to speak of in a slighting way
의심스러운	ⓐ fraught with uncertainty or doubt
유별난	ⓐ departing from a recognized, conventional, or established norm or pattern **eccentric in** …이 괴상한
실증적인	ⓐ relying on or derived from observation or experiment **the empirical method** 경험적인 방법 **(an) empirical observation** 경험적 관찰 **empirical philosophy** 경험 철학 **an empirical study** 경험적 조사

☐ debunk _____ ☐ delineate _____ ☐ demagogue _____

NO.	Entry Word	Example Sentence	
92 ☐☐	**engage** [engéidʒ]	He actively engages in volunteer work. 그는 자원 활동에 적극적으로 참여하고 있다. Every day each of us engages in many types of complex activities. 매일 우리는 다양한 형태의 복잡한 활동을 하고 있다.	
93 ☐☐	**epilogue** [épilɔ̀g]	Fortinbras speaks the epilogue in Shakespeare's 'Hamlet.' Fortinbras가 셰익스피어의 햄릿에 나오는 끝맺음말을 말한다. The audience was so disappointed in the play that many did not remain to hear the epilogue. 청중들은 그 연극에 너무 실망한 나머지 상당수는 끝맺음말을 들을 때까지 남으려고 하지 않았다.	
94 ☐☐	**erroneous** [iróuniəs]	He had the erroneous impression that the more it cost the better it must be. 그는 값이 비쌀수록 더 좋을 것이라는 잘못된 생각을 가지고 있었다. It's erroneous to assume that the press always prints the truth. 언론이 항상 진실을 말한다는 생각은 그릇된 것이다.	
95 ☐☐	**espouse** [ispáuz]	Vegetarianism is one cause she does not espouse. 그녀는 채식주의라는 명분을 지지하지 않는다. There is one theory that no one seems to espouse. 어떤 사람도 지지하지 않는 듯한 이론이 있다.	
96 ☐☐	**esteem** [istíːm]	I esteem your advice highly. 나는 귀하의 충고를 매우 존중합니다. He was held in great esteem by his colleagues. 그는 동료들에게 크게 존경을 받았다.	
97 ☐☐	**exacerbate** [igzǽsərbèit]	This attack will exacerbate the already tense relations between the two communities. 이 공격 때문에 두 지역 사이에 있었던 긴장이 악화될 것이다. President's speech exacerbated the bad situation. 대통령의 연설이 이미 나쁜 상황을 악화시켰다.	
98 ☐☐	**faculty** [fǽkəlti]	She has a faculty for making friends. 그녀는 친구를 사귀는 재능이 있다. NYU faculty will teach two thirds of the courses and NUS faculty will teach one third. 뉴욕 대학교 교수진들은 과목들의 3분의 2를 가르치고 싱가포르의 교수진들은 3분의 1을 가르치게 됩니다.	

☐ demeanor _____ ☐ denounce _____ ☐ discourse _____ ☐ disparage _____

Definition	Meaning/Relation
참여하다	ⓥ to involve oneself or become occupied **engage in** …에 종사하다
끝맺음말	ⓝ a short poem or speech spoken directly to the audience following the conclusion of a play
잘못된	ⓐ containing or derived from error
지지하다	ⓥ to give one's loyalty or support to (a cause, for example)
존중[존경]하다	ⓥ to regard with respect **esteem greatly[highly]** 매우 존경하다
악화시키다	ⓥ to increase the severity, violence, or bitterness of **exacerbate the pain** 고통을 악화시키다 **exacerbate[heighten, increase] tension** 긴장을 높이다(더하다)
재능; 학부; 교수진	ⓝ an inherent power or ability; a division of learning at a college or university; the teachers in college, university, or school **a faculty for** …의 재능

☐ dubious _____ ☐ eccentric _____ ☐ empirical _____

NO.	Entry Word	Example Sentence	
99 ☐☐	**fathom** [fǽðəm]	It is impossible to fathom his real intention. 그의 셈속을 알 수 없다. I'm trying to fathom out the motives behind his proposal. 나는 그의 제안 이면에 있는 동기를 헤아리려고 노력하는 중이다.	
100 ☐☐	**figurative** [fígjərətiv]	'A sweet temper' is a figurative expression, but 'sweet coffee' is not. A sweet temper는 비유적인 표현이지만, sweet coffee는 아니다. As early as 1915 she pioneered abstract art in America but later moved towards a more figurative style. 1915년에 이미 그 여자는 미국에서 추상 예술을 개척했으나 나중에는 더욱 비유적인 스타일로 나아갔다.	
101 ☐☐	**florid** [flɔ́(ː)rid]	He played the piece in a very florid style. 그는 매우 화려한 스타일로 그 작품을 연기했다. If you go to Florida and get a sunburn, your complexion will look florid. 만약 네가 플로리다에 가서 일광욕을 한다면, 너의 안색은 홍조를 띨 것이다.	
102 ☐☐	**founder** [fáundər]	This monument was built for the founder. 이 기념비는 창립자를 기념해서 세워졌다. Decartes was the founder of modern philosophy. 데카르트는 현대 철학의 창시자였다.	
103 ☐☐	**grandiose** [grǽndiòus]	He is full of grandiose ambitions for the future. 그는 미래에 대해 웅장한 야망을 품고 있다. The people derided his grandiose schemes. 국민들은 그의 웅장한 계획을 조롱했다.	
104 ☐☐	**guise** [ɡaiz]	He traveled under[in] the guise of a priest. 그는 신부로 변복하고 여행했다. The men who arrived in the guise of drug dealers were actually undercover police officers. 마약상으로 변장하고 도착한 남자들은 실제로는 비밀 조사 활동을 하고 있는 경찰관들이었다.	
105 ☐☐	**hypothetical** [hàipəθétikəl]	For the moment the dangers are hypothetical. 당장은 그 위험들은 가상의 것이다. This is only a hypothetical example, but it will help us to consider the problem. 이것은 다만 가설에 기반을 둔 사례이지만 우리가 그 문제를 고려하는 데 도움을 줄 것이다.	

☐ engage _____   ☐ epilogue _____   ☐ erroneous _____   ☐ espouse _____

PART 1

PART 2

PART 3

PART 4

PART 5

PART 6

Definition	Meaning/Relation
헤아리다; 이해하다	ⓥ to penetrate to the meaning or nature of; comprehend
비유적인	ⓐ based on or making use of figures of speech; metaphorical **a figurative expression** 비유적 표현 **a figurative meaning** 비유적인 의미 **a figurative sense** 비유적인 의미
화려한; 불그레한	ⓐ very ornate; flushed with rosy color flowery **a florid[ruddy] complexion** 불그스레한 얼굴
창립자	ⓝ one who establishes something or formulates the basis for something
웅장한	ⓐ characterized by greatness of scope or intent **a grandiose[glorious, grand, magnificent, noble] gesture** 당당한(품위 있는) 태도 **a grandiose idea** 웅대한 사고 **a grandiose[sweeping] plan** 장대한(전반적인) 계획 **grandiose planning** 대규모의 계획 **a grandiose scheme** 장대한 계획
변장	ⓝ false appearance **in[under] the guise of** …을 가장하여
가설의	ⓐ of, relating to, or based on a hypothesis **a hypothetical case** 가상의 경우

☐ esteem _____ ☐ exacerbate _____ ☐ faculty _____

NO.	Entry Word	Example Sentence	
106 ☐☐	**implement** [ímpləmənt]	It is increasingly difficult to implement the agreement. 그 협약을 이행하기가 점점 더 어려워지고 있다. Plans to implement far-reaching financial reform include deregulation of certain banking practices. 포괄적인 경제 개혁의 실행안에는 일부 금융 관행의 규제 완화도 포함되어 있었다.	
107 ☐☐	**implication** [ìmpləkéiʃən]	Don't just take her offer at face value. Think of the implications. 그녀의 제안을 액면 그대로 받아들여서는 안됩니다. 그 함축적 의미 생각하십시오. Some of the fast trackers don't always notice the implications of what they do. 출세 가도를 달리는 일부 사람들은 그들이 현재 하고 있는 일의 함축적 의미를 항상 주목하는 것은 아니다.	
108 ☐☐	**incorporate** [inkɔ́ːrpərèit]	The new car design incorporates all the latest safety features. 그 새로운 차의 설계는 모든 최근의 안전장치의 특징을 통합시킨다. Many of your suggestions have been incorporated (in the new plan). 당신의 제안 중에서 많은 부분이 (새로운 계획에) 통합되었다.	
109 ☐☐	**indifferent** [indífərənt]	Dangers are indifferent to us. 우리는 위험에 무관심하다. He's completely indifferent to the sufferings of the poor. 그는 가난한 사람들의 고통에 전혀 무관심하다.	
110 ☐☐	**indignation** [ìndignéiʃən]	He simmered with indignation. 그는 분노를 참느라 속이 부글부글 끓었다. He bridled his indignation. 그는 분노를 억눌렀다.	
111 ☐☐	**induce** [indjúːs]	What induced you to do such a stupid thing? 무엇이 너로 하여금 그런 어리석은 짓을 하도록 했느냐? We couldn't induce him even to set foot on the boat. 우리는 그가 심지어 발조차도 배 위에 올려놓게 설득할 수 없었다.	
112 ☐☐	**inept** [inépt]	You are completely inept at writing. 너는 글씨가 완전히 엉망이다. His behavior at the meeting was inept. 회의에서의 그의 태도는 부적절했다.	

☐ fathom _____   ☐ figurative _____   ☐ florid _____   ☐ founder _____

Definition	Meaning/Relation
실행하다; 이행하다	ⓥ to put into practical effect; carry out implement an idea 생각을 실행에 옮기다 implement[carry out, execute] a plan 계획을 실행[결행]하다 implement[carry out] a policy 정책을 실행하다 implement[act on, carry out] a recommendation 권고를 따르다 implement the will (of the majority) (다수의) 뜻을 따르다
함축	ⓝ the act of implicating or the condition of being implicated have an implication 함축성이 있다 a derogatory implication 경멸적인 함축성 a negative implication 부정적인 함축성 a serious implication 심각한 함축성 a significant implication 중요한 함축성 a subtle implication 미묘한 함축성 an implication for …에 대한 함축성 by implication 함축적으로, 넌지시 realize the full implications of sth …의 속뜻을 완전히 깨닫다
통합시키다	ⓥ to cause to merge or combine together into a united whole incorporate into …에 통합시키다
무관심한	ⓐ having no particulas interest, concern remain indifferent 여전히 무관심하다 indifferent about[concerning] …에 관하여 무관심한
분노	ⓝ anger aroused by something unjust, mean, or unworthy arouse indignation (in sb) (…에게서) 분노를 불러 일으키다 fill sb with indignation …을 분노에 가득 차게 만들다
설득하다	ⓥ to lead or move, as to a course of action, by influence or persuasion
서투른; 부적당한	ⓐ displaying a lack of judgment, sense, or reason; not apt or fitting inept at[in] …에 부적절한

106_112 45

PART 1

PART 2

PART 3

PART 4

PART 5

PART 6

☐ grandiose _____ ☐ guise _____ ☐ hypothetical _____

NO.	Entry Word	Example Sentence	
113 ☐☐	**inherent** [inhíərənt]	I have an inherent distrust of lawyers. 나는 본래부터 변호사에 대한 불신감을 가지고 있다. Logistical problems are inherent in the distribution of perishable goods in tropical countries. 열대 국가에서 부패하기 쉬운 식품을 유통하는 데는 수송 문제가 항상 뒤따른다.	
114 ☐☐	**inhibit** [inhíbit]	This drug will inhibit the progress of the disease. 이 약은 병의 진전을 억제할 것이다. We all have aggressive impulses, but in most cases our early training and conditioning tend to inhibit the open expression of them. 우리 모두가 공격 본능을 갖고 있지만 대부분의 경우 어렸을 때의 훈련과 조절이 이 본능의 공개적인 표현을 억제하는 경향이 있다.	
115 ☐☐	**innate** [inéit]	A good comedian has an innate wit. 훌륭한 코미디언은 타고난 재치가 있다. Looking back over the many years, Cyril's most impressive quality, for me, was his innate goodness. 지난 여러 해를 뒤돌아보니, 나한테 Cyril의 가장 인상적인 성격은 그의 타고난 선량함이었다.	
116 ☐☐	**intermittent** [ìntərmítənt]	You cannot hope to make good at this job by exerting intermittent efforts. 간헐적인 노력으로 이 일에서 성공하기를 바랄 수는 없다. Tomorrow will be sunny in the south, but there will be intermittent rain in the north. 내일 남부 지방은 화창하겠으나, 북부 지방에는 간헐적으로 비가 내릴 것이다.	
117 ☐☐	**intuition** [ìntʃuíʃən]	My intuition told me that he was telling a lie. 나는 그가 거짓말을 하고 있다는 것을 직감으로 알았다. The right side of the brain is concerned with imagination and intuition. 뇌의 우측은 상상력과 직관에 연관 되어있다.	
118 ☐☐	**ironic** [airánik]	He gave an ironic comment on my work. 그는 내 작품에 대해 빈정대는 듯한 평을 했다. She took the passage seriously rather than humorously because she misconstrued the author's ironic tone. 그녀는 작가의 반어적인 어조를 잘못 해석하여 그 구절을 해학적이기보다는 심각하게 받아들였다.	
119 ☐☐	**lucid** [lúːsid]	She gave a clear and lucid account of her plan for the company's future. 그녀는 회사의 미래에 대한 자신의 계획을 분명하고 알기 쉽게 설명했다. The stream in the mountain is very lucid. 그 산의 시내는 아주 맑다.	

☐ implement _____ ☐ implication _____ ☐ incorporate _____

113_119 47

PART 1

PART 2

PART 3

PART 4

PART 5

PART 6

Definition	Meaning/Relation
타고난	ⓐ existing as an essential constituent or characteristic; intrinsic **inherent in[to]** …에 고유한
억제하다	ⓥ to hold back **inhibit from** …을 금하다
타고난	ⓐ possessed at birth **innate in** …을 타고난
간헐적인	ⓐ stopping and starting at intervals **an intermittent fever** (말라리아 따위의) 간헐적인 열 **(an) intermittent rain** 간헐적인 비 **intermittent showers** 간헐적으로 내리는 소나기
직감, 직관	ⓝ the act or faculty of knowing or sensing without the use of rational processes; immediate cognition
빈정대는, 반어적인	ⓐ characterized by or constituting irony
이해하기 쉬운; 맑은	ⓐ easily understood; translucent or transparent **lucid explanation** 명쾌한(분명한) 설명 **a lucid interval** (정신 장애자가 잠시 정신이 든) 의식 청명기, 폭풍우 중의 잠시 잠잠한 때

☐ indifferent _____ ☐ indignation _____ ☐ induce _____ ☐ inept _____

NO.	Entry Word	Example Sentence	
120 ☐☐	**malicious** [məlíʃəs]	His pranks are not malicious, only mischievous. 그의 농담은 악의가 아니라 단지 장난이었다.	
		Our advisers can help you if you are receiving malicious calls. 악의적인 전화를 받고 있다면 우리 상담자들이 당신을 도울 수 있을 것입니다.	
121 ☐☐	**meticulous** [mətíkjələs]	Many hours of meticulous preparation have gone into writing the book. 그 책을 쓰는 데에는 여러 시간에 걸친 꼼꼼한 준비가 들어갔다.	
		Throughout her career Georgia O'Keeffe paid meticulous attention to her craft. 그녀의 직업에서 처음부터 끝까지 Georgia O'Keeffe 는 자신의 미술 작업에 세심한 관심을 기울였다.	
122 ☐☐	**mode** [moud]	Heat is a mode of motion. 열은 운동의 한 형태이다.	
		They had a special mode of life. 그들은 특별한 생활 양식을 가지고 있었다.	
123 ☐☐	**momentous** [mouméntəs]	Choosing between peace and war is a momentous decision. 평화와 전쟁 중 택일하는 것은 중대한 결정이다.	
		Any one of these things could be momentous and might require a whole new approach to life. 이런 것들은 중요할 수 있으며 삶에 완전히 새로운 접근법을 요구할지도 모른다.	
124 ☐☐	**monetary** [mánətəri]	Meanwhile the debate on European political and monetary union continues. 그동안 유럽의 정치 및 화폐의 통합에 관한 논의가 계속되고 있다.	
		Lately the main focus of monetary policy has shifted to interest rates. 최근 통화 정책의 주요 초점은 이자율로 옮겨갔다.	
125 ☐☐	**nostalgia** [nɑstǽldʒiə]	Some people feel nostalgia for their school days. 어떤 이들은 학창 시절을 그리워한다.	
		South Korean President Roh Moo-hyun has accused Japan of clinging to what he called a "dark nostalgia" for its imperial past. 한국의 노무현 대통령은 일본이 과거 제국주의 시대의 "어두운 향수"에 매달리고 있다고 비판했습니다.	
126 ☐☐	**objective** [əbdʒéktiv]	It's an admirably objective and impartial report. 그것은 존경스러울만큼 객관적이고 공정한 보도이다.	
		The policeman gave an objective report of the accident. 그 경관은 그 사고에 대한 객관적 보고를 했다.	

☐ inherent _____ ☐ inhibit _____ ☐ innate _____ ☐ intermittent _____

Definition	Meaning/Relation
악의적인	ⓐ having the nature of or resulting from malice **malicious towards** …에 대해 악감정이 있는
꼼꼼한	ⓐ extremely careful and precise **meticulous about [in]** …에 세심한
방법, 양식	ⓝ a manner, way, or method of doing or acting **the latest mode** 최신 유행
중요[중대]한	ⓐ of utmost importance **a momentous change** 커다란 변화 **a momentous decision** 중요한 결정 **a momentous occasion** 중요한 행사
화폐의, 통화의	ⓐ of or relating to money **a monetary contribution** 금전적 기부 **a monetary inducement** 재정적 동인 **monetary policy** 금융 정책, 재정 정책
향수, 그리움	ⓝ a bittersweet longing for things, persons, or situations of the past **feel nostalgia** 향수를 느끼다 **nostalgia for** …에 대한 향수
객관적인	ⓐ uninfluenced by emotions or personal prejudices

□ intuition _____   □ ironic _____   □ lucid _____

120_126 49

PART 1

PART 2

PART 3

PART 4

PART 5

PART 6

127 ☐☐	**offensive** [əfénsiv]	He told some really offensive racist and sexist jokes. 그는 정말로 불쾌하게 인종 차별적이고 성 차별적인 농담을 했다. U.S. intelligence officials are worried that China may have revived and expanded its offensive germ warfare program. 미국 정보 당국자들은 중국이 공격용 세균전 계획을 부활시켜 확장했을 가능성이 있는 것으로 우려하고 있다.	
128 ☐☐	**orthodox** [ɔ́ːrθədɑ̀ks]	We would prefer a more orthodox approach to the problem. 우리는 그 문제에 대해 좀 더 정통적인 접근법을 선호한다. They ignored the orthodox theory. 그들은 종래의 정설의 이론을 무시했다.	
129 ☐☐	**outspoken** [àutspóukən]	I ask your outspoken views of you. 나는 솔직한 견해를 듣고 싶다. He is an outspoken critic of the government. 그는 거리낌없이 정부를 비판한다.	
130 ☐☐	**partisan** [pɑ́ːrtəzən]	He was a passionate partisan of these people. 그는 이 사람들의 열렬한 지지자였다. Senior Bush aides believe the first partisan dust-up could come within weeks. 부시 대통령의 고위 보좌관들은 양당간의 첫 갈등은 몇 주안에 일어날 수도 있다고 보고 있다.	
131 ☐☐	**passive** [pǽsiv]	The government took a passive action. 정부는 소극적인 조치를 취했다. They accepted their defeat with passive resignation. 그들은 수동적인 체념으로 자기네 패배를 받아들였다.	
132 ☐☐	**patent** [pǽtənt]	When does the patent expire? 그 특허는 언제 기한이 만료되는가? China has vowed to punish officials who ignore copyright, trademark, and patent violations. 중국은 저작권과 상표권, 특허를 위반하는 관리들을 처벌하겠다고 약속하고 있습니다.	
133 ☐☐	**pathos** [péiθɑs]	It was a performance full of pathos and anger. 그것은 비애감과 분노가 가득한 공연이었다. There is pathos in his novels. 그의 소설에는 비애가 있다.	

☐ malicious _____ ☐ meticulous _____ ☐ mode _____ ☐ momentous _____

Definition	Meaning/Relation
불쾌감을 주는; 공격적인	ⓐ causing anger, displeasure, resentment, or affront; making or atteck **offensive to** …에게 무례한 **assume[go on, go over to, start (up), take] the offensive** 공세를 취하다 **launch[mount] an offensive** 공격을 개시하다
정통의	ⓐ adhering to what is commonly accepted, customary, or traditional **an Orthodox bishop** 정통파 주교 **the (Eastern) Orthodox church** (동방) 정교회 **Orthodox Judaism** 정통파 유대교
솔직한; 거리낌없는	ⓐ spoken without reserve; candid **outspoken in** …에 있어서 솔직한
지지자(당원)	ⓝ a fervent, sometimes militant supporter or proponent of a party, cause, faction, person, or idea **partisan politics** 파벌 정치 **partisan spirit** 당파심
소극적인, 수동적인	ⓐ receiving or subjected to an action without responding or initiating an action in return; inactive **a passive audience** 냉담한 청중 **passive immunity** 수동 면역 **passive immunization** 수동적 예방
특허(권)	ⓝ a grant made by a government that confers upon the creator of an invention the sole right to make, use, and sell that invention for a set period of time **grant[issue] a patent** 특허를 주다 **apply for a patent** 특허를 신청하다
비애	ⓝ a quality, as of an experience or a work of art, that arouses feelings of pity, sympathy, tenderness, or sorrow

☐ monetary ＿＿＿＿＿＿＿   ☐ nostalgia ＿＿＿＿＿＿＿   ☐ objective ＿＿＿＿＿＿＿

PART 1

PART 2

PART 3

PART 4

PART 5

PART 6

NO.	Entry Word	Example Sentence	
134 ☐☐	**placid** [plǽsid]	On a warm sunny day the river seems placid and benign. 따뜻하고 햇빛 나는 날에는 그 강은 평온하고 온화해 보인다. His father, normally a placid man, had become enraged at the sight of the damaged car. 그의 아버지는 평소에는 조용한 사람인데, 차가 부서진 광경을 보고는 몹시 화를 냈다.	
135 ☐☐	**pragmatic** [prægmǽtik]	A pragmatic politician, he was guided by what was expedient rather than by what was ethical. 실용주의 노선의 정치가인 그는 도덕적인 것보다는 편리한 것에 의해 이끌렸다. What point is there in dwelling on far-ranging theories when we are faced with a pragmatic problem of actual survival? 당장 살아 남느냐라는 실제적인 문제에 직면해 있으면서 광범위한 이론을 길게 논하는 것이 무슨 의미가 있습니까?	
136 ☐☐	**precise** [prisáis]	The bunker's precise location is a closely guarded secret. 벙커의 정확한 위치는 엄격히 비밀에 부쳐지고 있다. Our train leaves at about half past nine – 09:33 to be precise. 우리 기차는 9시 30분경, 정확히 말하면 9시 33분에 떠난다.	
137 ☐☐	**predecessor** [prédisèsər]	Our new doctor is much younger than his predecessor. 우리의 새 의사는 전임자보다 훨씬 젊다. The new prison governor is much more humane than her predecessor. 새로운 간수장은 전임자보다 훨씬 더 인간적이다.	
138 ☐☐	**prevail** [privéil]	Good will prevail. 선은 언제인가는 이긴다. That fashion will not prevail long. 그 유행은 오래가지 않을 것이다.	
139 ☐☐	**prolong** [proulɔ́ːŋ]	Good care may prolong a sick person's life. 간호를 잘 하면 환자의 생명이 연장될 수 있다. We were having such a good time that we decided to prolong our stay by another week. 우리는 너무나도 즐거운 시간을 보내서 한 주 더 머무르기로 하였다.	
140 ☐☐	**provoke** [prəvóuk]	He was provoked out of patience. 그는 화가 나서 참을 수 없었다. That dog is very dangerous when provoked. 그 개는 화났을 때 매우 위험하다.	

☐ offensive _____   ☐ orthodox _____   ☐ outspoken _____

Definition	Meaning/Relation
평온한	ⓐ undisturbed by tumult or disorder **a placid nature** 차분한 성격
실용적인	ⓐ dealing or concerned with facts or actual occurrences **a politician with a pragmatic approach** 실용적으로 접근하는 정치인 **a pragmatic solution to the problem** 그 문제에 대한 실용적인 해결책
정확한	ⓐ clearly expressed or delineated **precise about** …에 대해 정확한 **precise in** …에 있어 정확한〔꼼꼼한〕
전임자	ⓝ one who precedes another in time, especially in holding an office or a position *sb's* **immediate predecessor** …의 바로 전임자
우세하다; 유행하다	ⓥ to be greater in strength or influence; to be most common or frequent, be predominant **prevail against[over]** …을 압도하다〔이기다〕
연장하다	ⓥ to lengthen in duration **prolong the agony** 고민을 오래 끌다 **prolong a life** 생명을 연장하다
화나게 하다	ⓥ to incite to anger or resentment **provoke into** 자극해서 …하게 하다

☐ partisan _____ ☐ passive _____ ☐ patent _____ ☐ pathos _____

NO.	Entry Word	Example Sentence
141 ☐☐	**prudent** [prú:dənt]	The prudent way is to bet with the odds. 신중한 방법은 승산이 있는 쪽에 거는 것이다. It would be prudent to read the contract properly before signing it. 계약서에 서명하기 전에 제대로 읽어보는 것은 신중한 일일 것이다.
142 ☐☐	**purchase** [pə́:rtʃəs]	If you purchase more than ten thousand units, we can reduce it to twelve dollars. 만일 만 개 이상 구매하시면 12달러로 가격을 낮출 수 있습니다. Please return it to the store where it was purchased for a complete refund of the purchase price. 구입하신 상점에 가지고 가셔서 구입 가격으로 환불받으십시오.
143 ☐☐	**refute** [rifjú:t]	She refuted his argument. 그녀는 그의 주장을 반박했다. The barrister used new evidence to refute the charges and clear the defendant. 그 변호사는 피고에게 씌워진 혐의를 반박하고 그의 결백을 증명하기 위해 새로운 증거를 이용했다.
144 ☐☐	**regime** [reiʒí:m]	The regime itself is in an advanced dry rot. 그 정권 자체가 이미 상당히 부패되었다. The regime persists in the unwelcome education policy. 그 정권은 인기 없는 교육 정책을 고집하고 있다.
145 ☐☐	**reiterate** [ri:ítərèit]	I shall reiterate this message until all have understood it. 모든 사람이 이해할 때까지 나는 메시지를 반복할 것이다. The government has reiterated its refusal to compromise with terrorists. 정부는 테러리스트들과의 협상 거부를 되풀이했다.
146 ☐☐	**render** [réndər]	I'll render back your money. 네 돈을 갚겠다. His high position renders him immune from criticism. 그는 지위가 높아서 비판받지 않는다.
147 ☐☐	**renown** [rináun]	He won renown as a painter. 그는 화가로서 명성을 얻었다. Neil Armstrong won great renown for being the first man on the moon. 닐 암스트롱은 달에 도착한 최초의 사람으로 큰 명성을 얻었다.

☐ placid _____   ☐ pragmatic _____   ☐ precise _____   ☐ predecessor _____

Definition	Meaning/Relation
신중한	ⓐ wise in handling practical matters
구매하다; 구매	ⓥ to obtain in exchange for money or its equivalent ⓝ the act of an instanre of buying **purchase for** ···때문에 구입하다 **purchase from** ···에서 구입하다
반박하다	ⓥ to prove to be false or erroneous **refute completely** 전적으로 반박하다, 꼼짝 못하게 하다
정권	ⓝ a form of government **establish a regime** 정권을 세우다 **bring down[overthrow] a regime** 정권을 전복시키다 **an authoritarian [dictatorial, totalitarian] regime** 전체주의 체제 **puppet regime** 허수아비[괴뢰] 정권 **repressive regime** 압제 정권 **under a regime** 정권 아래
되풀이하다	ⓥ to say or do repeatedly
주다	ⓥ to give
명성	ⓝ the quality of being widely honored and acclaimed **achieve[attain, win] renown** 명성을 얻다, 유명해지다 **wide[great] renown** 대단한 명성 **international[worldwide] renown** 국제적 명성 **national renown** 국가적인[전국적인] 명성 **of renown** 유명한

☐ prevail _____ ☐ prolong _____ ☐ provoke _____

NO.	Entry Word	Example Sentence	
148 ☐☐	**rent** [rent]	Do I have to pay any rent in advance? 집세는 선불로 지불합니까? How much would it cost to rent a compact car for a week? 일주일 간 소형차를 빌리는 데 얼마나 들죠?	
149 ☐☐	**rhetoric** [rétərik]	He was spouting political rhetoric. 그는 정치적 발언을 끊임없이 내뱉었어. Rhetoric is the art of using language effectively. 웅변술은 설득력 있게 말하는 기술이다.	
150 ☐☐	**sarcasm** [sάːrkæzəm]	The sarcasm is overdone. 풍자가 지나쳤다 The critic's caustic remarks angered the hapless actors who were the subjects of his sarcasm. 비평가의 신랄한 비판은 그의 비판의 대상이 된 운 나쁜 배우들을 화나게 했다.	
151 ☐☐	**static** [stǽtik]	Prices on the stock market are rather static at the moment. 주식의 가격이 현재에는 큰 변동이 없다. The characters in his movels seem rather static. 그의 소설 속의 주인공들은 다소 정적인 인물로 보인다.	
152 ☐☐	**superficial** [sùːpərfíʃəl]	His knowledge is superficial. 그의 지식은 피상적이다. His cut was superficial. 그의 베인 상처는 깊지 않았다.	
153 ☐☐	**transparent** [trænspέərənt]	Window glass is transparent. 유리창은 투명하다. Wolfowitz says the key is to improve investor confidence by developing government institutions that deliver services in a transparent and accountable way. Wolfowitz는 개발도상국 기관들의 투명성과 신뢰도를 높여 투자자 자신감을 높이는 것이 열쇠라고 말했습니다.	
154 ☐☐	**underscore** [ʌ̀ndərskɔ́ːr]	The recent violence underscores the sensitivity of the issue of Jerusalem. 최근의 폭력사태는 예루살렘 문제가 얼마나 민감한지를 강조하고 있다. Our recent experience with a computer virus has underscored the need to back up the system on a regular schedule. 최근의 컴퓨터 바이러스 감염은 우리에게 시스템을 정기적으로 백업할 필요성을 강조해 주었다.	

☐ prudent _____   ☐ purchase _____   ☐ refute _____   ☐ regime _____

Definition	Meaning/Relation
임대료; 임대하다	ⓝ payment, usually of an amount fixed by contract, made by a tenant ⓥ to obtain occupancy or use of (another property) in return for regular payments **pay rent for a house** 집세를 내다 **raise the rent** 임대료를 올리다((美)) **for rent** 임대의 **rent control** (정부의) 집세 통제
수사(修辭), 웅변술	ⓝ a speech using language effectively and persuasively **spout[resort to] rhetoric** 미사여구를 늘어놓다 **eloquent rhetoric** 거창한 웅변 **impassioned[passionate] rhetoric** 열정적인 미사여구 **soothing rhetoric** 듣기 좋게 달래는 말
풍자	ⓝ a cutting, often ironic remark intended to wound **biting[devastating, keen, piercing, scathing, withering] sarcasm** 통렬한〔신랄한〕야유 **mild sarcasm** 가벼운 야유 **veiled sarcasm** (살짝) 가려진〔분명치 않은〕야유 **sarcasm about** …에 대한 야유 **dripping with sarcasm** 야유로 가득 찬
정적인	ⓐ having no motion
피상적인, 얕은	ⓐ shallow, not serious **a superficial[slight] acquaintance** 약간의〔피상적인〕지식 **a superficial analogy** 표면적인 유사 **a superficial[mild,minor] burn** 가벼운〔대단치 않은〕화상
투명한	ⓐ capable of transmitting light so that objects or images can be seen as if there were no intervening material **a transparent[downright, monstrous, outright, whopping] lie** 엄청난〔명백한〕 거짓말 **a transparent[blatant, deliberate] untruth** 뻔한 거짓말
강조하다	ⓥ to emphasize or stress **underscore a point** …의 문제를 강조하다

☐ reiterate _____ ☐ render _____ ☐ renown _____

NO.	Entry Word	Example Sentence
155 ☐☐	**vehement** [víːəmənt]	He has a vehement dislike of loud pop music. 그는 시끄러운 팝 음악을 매우 싫어한다. They launched a vehement attack on the government's handling of environmental issues. 그들은 정부가 환경 문제를 다루는 방식에 대해 맹렬한 공격을 시작했다.
156 ☐☐	**virtue** [vɜ́ːrtʃuː]	Patience is a virtue. 인내는 미덕이다. She is a pattern of virtue. 그녀는 부덕(婦德)의 귀감이다.
157 ☐☐	**wallow** [wálou]	The man is wallowing in mud. 남자가 진흙탕 속에서 뒹굴고 있다. Don't just wallow in self-pity; do something about your problems! 자기 연민에 빠지지 말고 문제를 해결하기 위해 무언가를 해라!
158 ☐☐	**warrant** [wɔ́ːrənt]	The circumstances warrant such measures. 사정상 그런 수단이 용납된다. Nothing warranted his behaving like that. 그 무엇도 그의 그 같은 행위를 정당화시키지는 못했다.
159 ☐☐	**yield** [jiːld]	He yielded me his property. 그는 나에게 재산을 양도해 주었다. We plan to mine the near-surface ore deposits, which we estimate will yield 80,000 ounces of gold per year. 우리는 지표 가까이 위치한 광산을 채굴할 계획인데, 이곳에서 연간 80,000온스의 금이 산출될 것으로 보고 있다.
160 ☐☐	**zeal** [ziːl]	They prepared for the party with zeal. 그들은 열정적으로 파티를 준비했다. They are pursuing their aims with a determined zeal. 그들은 결연한 열정으로 자신들의 목표를 추구하고 있다.

☐ rent _____   ☐ rhetoric _____   ☐ sarcasm _____   ☐ ststic _____

Definition	Meaning/Relation
맹렬한, 격렬한	ⓐ marked by or full of vigor or energy; strong **a vehement attack** 격렬한(맹렬한) 비난, 맹공 **a vehement denial** 강력한 부정 **vehement denunciation** 강력한 비난
미덕	ⓝ moral excellence and righteousness **have a virtue** 장점을 가지고 있다
뒹굴다; 빠지다	ⓥ to roll the body about indolently or clumsily in or as if in water, snow, or mud; to indulge excessively **wallow in** …의 속에서 뒹굴다
용납되다, 정당화하다	ⓥ to make the action seem necessary or appripriate for the circumstances
양도하다; 산출하다	ⓥ to give up (an advantage, for example) to another; to give forth by or as if by a natural process, especially by cultivation
열심, 열의	ⓝ enthusiastic devotion to a cause, an ideal, or a goal and tireless diligence in its furtherance **demonstrate zeal** 열의를 보이다 **great zeal** 대단한 열의

155_160 59

PART 1

PART 2

PART 3

PART 4

PART 5

PART 6

☐ superficial _____ ☐ transparent _____ ☐ underscore _____

핵심 영단어
★★★

Ranking 3

NO.	Entry Word	Example Sentence	
161 ☐☐	**abet** [əbét]	He abetted his friend in crime. 그는 친구에게 범죄를 교사했다. She was unwilling to abet him in the swindle he had planned. 그녀는 계획했던 사기행위를 저지르라고 그를 부추기고 싶지 않았다.	
162 ☐☐	**abhor** [æbhɔ́ːr]	Nature abhors a vacuum. 자연은 진공을 싫어한다. They abhor all forms of racism. 그들은 모든 종류의 인종 차별주의를 혐오한다.	
163 ☐☐	**abstruse** [əbstrúːs]	I found her argument very abstruse. 나는 그녀의 주장이 매우 난해하다고 알았다. He tried to conceal his lack of true scholarship and intellectual depth by making use of unnecessarily abstruse language. 쓸데없이 난해한 말을 사용함으로써 그는 참다운 학식과 지적인 깊이의 부족을 감추려고 애썼다.	
164 ☐☐	**accelerate** [æksélərèit]	This car can accelerate from 0 to 60 mph in 7 seconds. 이 차는 7초 이내에 시속 0에서 60마일까지 가속할 수 있다. Do her efforts to accelerate our departure mean that she is trying to help us, or just get rid of us? 우리의 출발을 재촉하려고 그녀가 애쓰는 것은 우리를 돕겠다는 뜻일까 아니면 우리를 떨쳐버리겠다는 뜻일까?	
165 ☐☐	**acumen** [əkjúːmən]	She has considerable business acumen. 그녀는 상당한 사업 통찰력을 가지고 있다. His business acumen helped him to succeed where others had failed. 그의 사업적인 통찰력은 남들이 실패하는 곳에서 그가 성공하는데 도움이 되었다.	
166 ☐☐	**adhere** [ædhíər]	He adheres too closely to the regulations. 그는 너무 고지식하게 규칙을 고수한다. I will adhere to this opinion until proof that I am wrong is presented. 나는 내가 잘못되었다는 증거가 제시될 때까지 이 견해를 고수할 것이다.	
167 ☐☐	**adroit** [ədrɔ́it]	It requires very adroit management. 그것은 아주 능숙한 솜씨를 필요로 한다. She became adroit at dealing with difficult questions. 그녀는 어려운 질문을 다루는 데에 능숙해졌다.	

☐ vehement _____ ☐ virtue _____ ☐ wallow _____

Definition	Meaning/Relation
부추기다	ⓥ to approve, encourage, and support (an action or a plan of action) aid and abet 교사하다 being a party to a death pact ; aiding and abetting suicide 자살 방조죄
혐오하다, 싫어하다	ⓥ to regard with horror or loathing be utterly abhorrent to / have a deadly abhorrence of / have a strong aversion to/ abhor[detest, hate, loathe] absolutely 죽기보다 싫다.
난해한	ⓐ difficult to understand
촉진하다	ⓥ to increase the speed of accelerate[step up] the arms race 군비 경쟁을 가속화하다
통찰력	ⓝ quickness, accuracy, and keenness of judgment or insight display[demonstrate] acumen 수완을 보이다 business[financial] acumen 사업적인 수완 legal acumen 뛰어난 법률적인 안목 political acumen 정치적 통찰력
고수하다	ⓥ to follow exactly adhere closely[doggedly, stubbornly, strictly, tenaciously] 단단히〔끈질기게, 완강히, 집요하게〕 들러붙다 adhere to …을 고수하다
능숙한	ⓐ dexterous adroit at[in] …에 능숙한

161_167 63

PART 1

PART 2

PART 3

PART 4

PART 5

PART 6

☐ warrant _____ ☐ yield _____ ☐ zeal _____

NO.	Entry Word	Example Sentence
168 ☐☐	**adulation** [ædʒəléiʃən]	He thrived on the adulation of his henchmen. 그는 그의 추종자들의 아첨으로 행복에 젖었다. Durante is an born performer — she loves excitement and she loves the adulation. Durante는 타고난 연기자이다. 그녀는 흥분과 아첨을 좋아한다.
169 ☐☐	**agenda** [ədʒéndə]	What's on the agenda for tomorrow's meeting? 내일 회의 의제가 뭐예요? There were several important items on the agenda. 그 의제에는 몇 가지 중요한 항목이 있었다.
170 ☐☐	**aggrandize** [əgrǽndaiz]	They hoped to aggrandize the student's knowledge scope. 그들은 학생들의 지식 영역을 확대시키길 희망했다. The president aggrandized his power to act aggressively in international affairs. 대통령이 국제 문제를 강력하게 조치를 취하기 위해 권력을 확대했다.
171 ☐☐	**alacrity** [əlǽkrəti]	The United Nations has acted with alacrity and determination in this crisis. UN은 이 위기에 민첩하고 결단력 있게 대처했다. He demonstrated his eagerness to serve by his alacity in executing the orders of his master. 그는 주인의 명령을 민첩하게 실행함으로써 그의 봉사에 대한 열정을 나타내었다.
172 ☐☐	**allocate** [ǽləkèit]	The government is allocating $10 million for health education. 정부는 보건 교육에 천 만 달러를 할당하고 있다. This report says we need to allocate more space to production, and the sooner the better. 이 보고서의 내용은 우리가 생산 공간을 더 확보해야 하는데, 빠를수록 좋다는 것이다.
173 ☐☐	**altruism** [ǽltruìzəm]	He has abandoned all ambition to become president and is now actuated wholly by altruism. 그는 대통령이 되려는 모든 야망을 버리고 지금은 완전히 이타주의에 따라서 행동한다. Empathy, as we have seen, leads to caring, altruism, and compassion. 앞에서도 보았듯이 감정이입은 배려심, 이타주의 그리고 동정심으로 이르게 된다.
174 ☐☐	**amiable** [éimiəbəl]	She is an amiable girl and gets along with everyone. 그녀는 호감을 주는 소녀이며 누구와도 사이좋게 지낸다. He is unlikely to be remembered as a great president, but rather more as an amiable transition figure. 그는 위대한 대통령이 아니라 오히려 온화한 과도기적 인물로 기억될 가능성이 있다.

☐ abet _____   ☐ abhor _____   ☐ abstruse _____   ☐ accelerate _____

Definition	Meaning/Relation
아첨	ⓝ excessive flattery or admiration **bask in the adulation[love] of one's followers** 추종자들의 아부(사랑)를 받다
의제	ⓝ a list or program of things to be done or considered **draw up[make up, put together] an agenda** 의사록을 작성하다 **place[put]** *sth.* **on the agenda** …을 상정하다 **a hidden agenda** 비밀 의제(=a secret plan) **an item on the agenda** 의제록의 안건한 항목 **high on the agenda** 중요한 안건
확대하다	ⓥ to increase the scope of
민첩	ⓝ speed or quickness **with alacrity** 민첩하게
할당하다	ⓥ to distribute according to a plan
이타주의	ⓝ unselfish concern for the welfare of others
호감을 주는; 온화한	ⓐ friendly and agreeable in disposition; good-natured and likable

168_174   65

PART 1

PART 2

PART 3

PART 4

PART 5

PART 6

☐ acumen _____ ☐ adhere _____ ☐ adroit _____

NO.	Entry Word	Example Sentence	
175 ☐☐	**analogy** [ənǽlədʒi]	There is an analogy between human heart and pump. 인간의 심장과 펌프 사이에는 유사점이 있다. By the analogy with their figure, I can tell they are sisters. 그들이 외모가 유사한 것을 보아서, 나는 그들이 자매라는 것을 알 수 있다.	
176 ☐☐	**appease** [əpíːz]	He tried to appease the crying child by giving him candy. 그는 우는 아이에게 사탕을 주어 달래려 했다. In ancient times, people sacrificed animals, and even human beings, to appease the gods. 옛날에 사람들은 신들을 달래느라 동물 심지어 사람까지도 제물로 바쳤다.	
177 ☐☐	**apprehensive** [æprihénsiv]	This may make a sensitive child tense and apprehensive. 민감한 아이에겐 이것이 긴장과 걱정을 안겨줄 수도 있다. Those students who have been doing their work all term need not feel apprehensive about the final examination. 전 학기에 걸쳐 꾸준히 공부를 해왔던 학생들은 학기말 시험에 대해 걱정을 할 필요가 없다.	
178 ☐☐	**archaic** [ɑːrkéiik]	The meaning of some archaic forms of writing is not always well understood today. 일부 고대 문자의 의미를 오늘날 언제나 잘 해독할 수 있는 것은 아니다. Methinks, thee, and thou are archaic words which are no longer part of our normal vocabulary. Methinks, thee, thou은 지금은 더 이상 통상적인 어휘에 포함되지 않는 고어들이다.	
179 ☐☐	**ascertain** [æsərtéin]	The detective tried to ascertain the facts about the robbery. 형사는 강도 사건에 대한 여러 사실을 확인하려 했다. The police have so far been unable to ascertain the cause of the explosion. 경찰은 아직까지 그 폭발의 원인을 확실하게 규명할 수 없었다.	
180 ☐☐	**augment** [ɔːgmént]	Vicious crimes augment in an alarming way. 악질 범죄가 놀랄만큼 증가한다. New York City draws water from the Hudson River to augment reservoirs when they are low. 뉴욕 시는 저수지 수위가 낮을 때 수량을 늘리기 위해 허드슨 강에서 물을 끌어 온다.	
181 ☐☐	**autonomous** [ɔːtánəməs]	The local groups are autonomous of the national organization. 그 지역 단체들은 국가 조직으로부터 독립해 있다. The majority of Scots favors an autonomous Scotland involving devolution or complete independence. 대다수 스코틀랜드 사람들은 자치권을 가진 스코틀랜드가 중앙 정부로부터의 권한 이양이나 완전한 독립을 포함하는 것에 찬성한다.	

☐ adulation _____　　☐ agenda _____　　☐ aggrandize _____　　☐ alacrity _____

PART 1

PART 2

PART 3

PART 4

PART 5

PART 6

Definition	Meaning/Relation
유사	ⓝ similarity in some respects between things that are otherwise dissimilar **draw[make] an analogy** 유사성을 밝히다 **a close analogy** 밀접한 유사성 **an analogy between** ⋯사이의 유사성 **an analogy to[with]** ⋯와의 유사성 **by analogy** 유추에 의해 **on the analogy of** ⋯에서 유추하여
달래다	ⓥ to bring peace, quiet, or calm to **appease one's anger** 화를 달래다 **appease one's curiosity[hunger]** 호기심〔시장기〕을 달래다
걱정하는	ⓐ anxious or fearful about the future **apprehensive about[for]** ⋯을 우려하여〔염려하여〕
고대의	ⓐ of, relating to, or characteristic of a much earlier, often more primitive period **an archaic word** 고어 **an archaic expression** 예스러운 말투
확인하다, 규명하다	ⓥ to discover with certainty, as through examination or experimentation
증가시키다, 늘리다	ⓥ to make (something already developed or well under way) greater, as in size, extent, or quantity
자치권이 있는	ⓐ not controlled by others or by outside forces **an autonomous province** 자치주 **an autonomous region** 자치 구역〔지역〕 **an autonomous republic** 자치 공화국

☐ allocate _____ ☐ altruism _____ ☐ amiable _____

NO.	Entry Word	Example Sentence
182 ☐☐	**belligerent** [bəlídʒərənt]	I don't know why she always seems so belligerent towards me. 왜 그녀가 늘 나에게 그렇게 호전적인지 모르겠다. Giving the ticket collector a belligerent look, he said he wouldn't pay his fare. 그는 표 수집원에게 호전적인 표정을 지어 보이면서 요금을 내지 않겠다고 말했다.
183 ☐☐	**brevity** [brévəti]	Brevity is the soul of wit. 간결함이 기지의 생명이다. Ambiguity resulted from the extreme brevity of the message. 그 말은 매우 짧아서 애매했다.
184 ☐☐	**brood** [bru:d]	Don't brood over such trifles. 그런 하찮은 일에 신경 쓰지 말아라. He sat at his desk, brooding over why she had left him. 그는 책상 앞에 앉아서 왜 그녀가 자기 곁을 떠났을까 곰곰이 생각했다.
185 ☐☐	**callous** [kǽləs]	He is callous about the distress of his neighbors. 그는 이웃 사람의 고통에 대하여 무신경하다. He had worked in the hospital for so many years that he was callous to the suffering in the wards. 그는 병원에서 너무 오랫동안 일을 해서 병실에서 고통스러워 하는 사람들에 대해 무감각해져 있다.
186 ☐☐	**capricious** [kəprí∫əs]	She's very capricious. 그녀는 아주 변덕스럽다. He was a cruel and capricious tyrant. 그는 잔인하고 변덕스러운 폭군이었다.
187 ☐☐	**catalyst** [kǽtəlist]	The First World War served as a catalyst for major social changes in Europe. 세계 1차 대전은 유럽 사회가 크게 변화하는데 촉매제 역할을 했다. The spate of suicides acted as a catalyst for change in the prison system. 자살의 범람은 감옥 체계의 변화를 위한 촉매로 작용했다.
188 ☐☐	**cerebral** [sérəbrəl]	He had an attack of cerebral anemia. 그는 뇌빈혈을 일으켰다. The main part of the brain is divided into the left and right cerebral hemispheres. 뇌의 주요 부분은 좌뇌와 우뇌로 나뉘어 있다.

☐ analogy _____   ☐ appease _____   ☐ apprehensive _____   ☐ archaic _____

PART 1

PART 2

PART 3

PART 4

PART 5

PART 6

Definition	Meaning/Relation
호전적인	ⓐ inclined or eager to fight; hostile or aggressive **belligerent towards** ···에 대해 호전적인
간결함, (시간, 기간등이) 짧음	ⓝ concise expression; the quality or state of being brief in duration
곰곰히 생각하다	ⓥ to be deep in thought **brood about[on, over]** ···에 대해 곰곰이 생각하다
무감각한	ⓐ having calluses **callous to** ···에 냉담한
변덕스러운	ⓐ characterized by or subject to whim
촉매(제)	ⓝ something that precipitates a process or event, especially without being involved in or changed by the consequences
뇌의	ⓐ of or relating to the brain or cerebrum **the cerebral cortex** 대뇌 피질 **a cerebral embolism** 뇌색전증 **a brain[cerebral] hemorrhage** 뇌출혈 **cerebral palsy** 뇌성마비

☐ ascertain _____ ☐ augment _____ ☐ autonomous _____

NO.	Entry Word	Example Sentence	
189 ☐☐	**chronic** [kránik]	There is a chronic shortage of teachers. 만성적으로 교사가 부족하다. Back or neck problems, or chronic pain? 등이나 목에 이상이 있다거나, 만성적인 통증이 있습니까?	
190 ☐☐	**circumscribe** [sə́ːrkəmskràib]	It was necessary to circumscribe the toddler's play area. 그 아장 걸음 아기의 노는 범위의 한계를 정하는 것이 필요했다. I do not wish to circumscribe your activities. 나는 당신의 행위를 제한하고 싶지 않다.	
191 ☐☐	**complacent** [kəmpléisənt]	He likes his job and has a complacent attitude toward life. 그는 자기 일을 좋아하며 인생에 대해 자족하는 태도를 가지고 있다. We are all much too complacent about the quality of our water-supply. 우리는 모두 우리의 상수도의 질에 대해 너무 만족해 있다.	
192 ☐☐	**component** [kəmpóunənt]	Decoding the paintings is not difficult once you know what the component parts symbolize. 구성 요소들이 무엇을 상징하는지 알기만 하면 회화 작품을 이해하는 것은 어렵지 않다. Most electronic components use silicon chips. 대부분의 전자 부품들은 실리콘 칩을 사용한다.	
193 ☐☐	**comprise** [kəmpráiz]	The committee comprises six members. 그 위원회는 여섯 명의 위원으로 이루어져 있다. Shias comprise 10 to 15 percent of the population. 시아파는 전체 인구의 10~15퍼센트를 차지한다.	
194 ☐☐	**conceit** [kənsíːt]	She has a great conceit regarding her own beauty. 그녀는 자신의 미모에 큰 자부심을 가지고 있다. The idea is a conceit that won't fool anyone over the age of about 35. 그 계획은 대략 35세 이상의 사람은 전혀 속일 수 없는 공상이다.	
195 ☐☐	**conciliatory** [kənsíliətɔ̀ːri]	His letter was couched in conciliatory terms. 그의 편지는 회유적인 말들로 표현되어 있었다. She was still angry despite his conciliatory words. 그녀는 그가 달래도 여전히 화를 내었다.	

☐ belligerent _____　☐ brevity _____　☐ brood _____　☐ callous _____

Definition	Meaning/Relation
만성적인	ⓐ of long duration **chronic addiction** 만성 중독 **a chronic ailment** 만성 질환 **a chronic alcoholic** 만성 알코올 중독자
제한하다	ⓥ to limit narrowly
자기만족의	ⓐ self-satisfied and unconcerned **become[get, grow] complacent** 안주하게 되다 **complacent about** …에 대해 안주하는
성분, 구성요소	ⓝ a constituent element, as of a system **a basic[essential, key, main, principal] component** 기본 성분
…으로 이루어지다	ⓥ to consist of
자부심; 공상	ⓝ a favorable and especially unduly high opinion of one's own abilities or worth; a fanciful thought **insufferable conceit** 참아줄 수 없는 자만심 **overwhelming conceit** 지나친 자부심 **Be out of conceit with** ─에 싫증이 나다
회유적인	ⓐ trying to conciliate or intended to conciliate **a conciliatory attitude** 회유적인 태도 **a conciliatory gesture** 달래는 듯한 몸짓, 유화〔타협〕적인 태도 **a conciliatory policy** 회유 정책

PART 1

PART 2

PART 3

PART 4

PART 5

PART 6

☐ capricious _____ ☐ catalyst _____ ☐ cerebral _____

NO.	Entry Word	Example Sentence	
196 ☐☐	**concoct** [kankákt]	How did the inventive chef ever concoct such a strange dish? 그 기발한 요리사가 어떻게 그런 이상한 음식을 만들어 냈을까? She'd concocted some unlikely tale about the train being held up by cows on the line. 그녀는 줄지어 가는 소들 때문에 기차가 멈췄다는 별 말 같지 않은 이야기를 지어냈다.	
197 ☐☐	**conducive** [kəndjúːsiv]	Temperance is conducive to long life. 절제는 장수를 가져온다. Rest and proper diet are conducive to good health. 휴식과 적절한 식사는 건강에 도움이 된다.	
198 ☐☐	**confound** [kənfáund]	I was very confounded by the sight. 그 광경을 보고 매우 당황하였다. The extraordinary election results confounded his critics. 예상 밖의 선거결과에 그를 비판한 사람들이 당황했다.	
199 ☐☐	**conscientious** [kànʃiénʃəs]	Conscientious parents sometimes worry so much about jealousy. 양심적인 부모는 때로 시기심에 대해 너무 많은 걱정을 한다. He is offered another job in management, but turns it down out of conscientious scruples. 그는 관리직 일자리를 제의 받지만 양심의 가책을 느껴 거절한다.	
200 ☐☐	**consummate** [kánsəmèit]	We have to consummate this deal by the end of the month. 우리는 이달 말까지 이 계약을 완료시켜야 한다. All that I needed to consummate the most important deal of my career was Mr. Elson's signature on the dotted line. 내 출세의 가장 중요한 부분을 성취하기 위해 내가 필요로 하는 모든 것은 점선 위에다 Elson 씨의 서명을 받는 일이었다.	
201 ☐☐	**contaminate** [kəntǽmənèit]	Flies contaminate food. 파리는 음식물을 오염시킨다. They are contaminating the minds of our young people with these subversive ideas. 그들은 이런 파괴적인 생각들로 우리의 젊은이들의 마음을 오염시키고 있다.	
202 ☐☐	**culpable** [kʌ́lpəbl]	He was held culpable for all that had happened. 그는 일어난 모든 일에 대해 과실이 있다는 판결을 받았다. Corrupt politicians who condone the activities of the gamblers are equally culpable. 도박 행위를 눈감아 주는 타락한 정치인들도 똑같이 비난받아 마땅하다.	

☐ chronic _____ ☐ circumscribe _____ ☐ complacent _____

Definition	Meaning/Relation
섞어서 만들다; 지어내다	ⓥ to prepare by mixing ingredients, as in cooking; to devise, using skill and intelligence concoct[cook up, fabricate, trump up] a charge 혐의를 날조하다 conceive[concoct, devise] a plan 계획을 꾸미다(짜다) concoct[cook up, devise, think up] a scheme 음모를 꾸미다, 계략을 짜내다
(…에) 도움이 되는	ⓐ tending to cause conducive to …에 도움이 되는 《단독 사용 불가》
당황하게 하다	ⓥ to cause to become confused or perplexed confound means with end 수단과 목적을 혼동하다
양심적인	ⓐ guided by or in accordance with the dictates of conscience conscientious about …에 성심을 다하는
완성하다	ⓥ to bring to completion or fruition consummate[wanton] cruelty 교묘한(이유없는) 학대 a consummate liar 굉장한 거짓말쟁이
오염시키다	ⓥ to make impure or unclean by contact or mixture contaminate by[with] …으로 오염시키다 contaminate *sb.* with *sth.* …을 …으로 오염시키다
과실이 있는	ⓐ deserving of blame or censure as being wrong, evil, improper, or injurious

196_202 73

PART 1

PART 2

PART 3

PART 4

PART 5

PART 6

☐ component _____ ☐ comprise _____ ☐ conceit _____ ☐ conciliatory _____

NO.	Entry Word	Example Sentence	
203 ☐☐	**debacle** [deibáːkl]	The collapse of the company was described as the greatest financial debacle in US history. 그 회사의 붕괴는 미국 역사상 가장 큰 재정적 재난으로 묘사되었다. This debacle in the government can only result in anarchy. 이 같은 정부의 와해는 무정부 상태를 초래할 수 있다.	
204 ☐☐	**debilitate** [dibílətèit]	We were all debilitated by the extreme heat. 우리 모두는 극심한 열에 의해 쇠약하게 되었다. Parkinson's disease is a debilitating and incurable disease of the nervous system. 파킨슨씨병은 사람을 쇠약하게 하는 신경계통의 불치병이다.	
205 ☐☐	**decorous** [dékərəs]	He explained the problem in his careful and decorous way. 그는 주의 깊고 예의 바르게 그 문제를 설명했다. They should try to behave in a more decorous manner and refrain from actions that may be harmful to the party. 그들은 예의 바르게 행동해야 하며 그 당에 해를 끼칠 수 있는 행동은 자제해야 한다.	
206 ☐☐	**deluge** [déljuːdʒ]	Few people survived the deluge. 그 대홍수에서 살아남은 사람은 거의 없었다. The white House is deluged with a great inpouring of mail. 백악관에는 우편물이 홍수처럼 밀려든다.	
207 ☐☐	**deplore** [diplɔ́ːr]	The philosothers deplored the crass commercialism. 철학자들은 천박한 상업주의를 비판했다. The president said he deplored the killings. 대통령의 그 죽음들을 애도한다고 말했다.	
208 ☐☐	**derelict** [dérəlikt]	There are plans to redevelop an area of derelict land near the station. 기차역 근처에 버려진 땅이 있는 지역을 재개발할 계획이 있다. There used to be a derelict old house on the hill. 언덕위에 오래된 버려진 집 한채가 있었다.	
209 ☐☐	**dilemma** [dilémə]	I went through sort of an elongated confidence dilemma. 전 오랫동안 자신감을 잃고 딜레마에 빠졌었죠. The Cruzan petition marks the first time the U.S. Supreme Court has grappled with the right-to-die dilemma. 크루잔 청원은 미국 대법원이 죽을 권리의 딜레마를 다룬 첫 사례이다.	

☐ concoct _____ ☐ conducive _____ ☐ confound _____ ☐ conscientious _____

Definition	Meaning/Relation
붕괴, 와해	ⓝ a sudden, disastrous collapse, downfall, or defeat
쇠약하게 하다	ⓥ to sap the strength or energy of
예의 바른	ⓐ characterized by or exhibiting decorum
대홍수; 쇄도하다	ⓝ a great flood ⓥ to overwhelm with a large number or amount **deluge with** …이 쇄도하다
비난하다; 애도하다	ⓥ to feel or express strong disapproval of; to express sorrow or grief over **deplore deeply[strongly, thoroughly]** 크게 한탄하다[몹시 유감스럽게 생각하다]
버려진	ⓐ deserted or abandoned by an owner or keeper **derelict in** …에 있어 임무 태만의, 무책임한
진퇴 양난	ⓝ a situation that requires a choice between options that are or seem equally unfavorable or mutually exclusive **confront a dilemma** 딜레마에 맞서다 **face a dilemma** 딜레마에 직면하다

☐ consummate _____ ☐ contaminate _____ ☐ culpable _____

203_209 75

PART 1

PART 2

PART 3

PART 4

PART 5

PART 6

NO.	Entry Word	Example Sentence	
210 ☐☐	**dilettante** [dìlətάːnt]	He's a bit of a dilettante as far as wine is concerned. 포도주에 관한 한 그는 어느 정도는 애호가인 셈이다. Edgar Jr. has reinforced his image as dilettante. Edgar Jr는 애호가로서의 그의 이미지를 강화했다.	
211 ☐☐	**discernible** [disə́ːʌnəbəl]	The influence of Rodin is discernible in the younger artist. 로댕의 영향을 그 젊은 화가에게서 볼 수 있다. The ships in the harbor were not discernible in the fog. 항구에 있는 선박들은 안개 때문에 분간이 되지 않았다.	
212 ☐☐	**discrepancy** [diskrépənsi]	There is some discrepancy between the two accounts. 두 설명에 서로 어긋나는 점이 있다. When both versions of the story were collated, major discrepancies were found. 그 이야기의 두 판본이 대조되면서 일치하지 않는 중요한 부분들이 발견되었다.	
213 ☐☐	**dispassionate** [dispǽʃənit]	You must try to subdue the natural emotions of a parent and make a dispassionate decision that will be in the best interests of your son. 당신은 부모로서의 자연발생적인 감정을 억제하고 당신의 아들에게 가장 이로울 수 있는 냉정한 결정을 내리도록 노력해야 합니다.	
214 ☐☐	**dissemble** [disémbəl]	Politicians frequently have to dissemble so as not to admit that mistakes have been made. 정치가들은 실수를 저질렀다는 것을 인정하지 않기 위해 자주 시치미를 떼야만 한다. When she went into her all too familiar act of the uncomplaining martyr, I could not dissemble my annoyance. 그녀가 참고 견디는 너무나 친숙한 행동을 했을 때 나는 괴로움을 감출 수가 없었다.	
215 ☐☐	**disseminate** [disémənèit]	One of the organization's aims is to disseminate information about the spread of the disease. 그 기구의 목표 중 하나는 그 질병의 전파에 대한 정보를 유포하는 것이다. Perhaps he did not originate that vicious rumor, but he certainly shares the responsibility for having disseminated it. 확실히 그가 그 악성 유언비어를 만들어내지는 않았지만 그것을 퍼뜨린데 대한 책임이 일부 있을 것은 확실하다.	
216 ☐☐	**divulge** [divʌ́ldʒ]	Journalists do not divulge their sources. 기자들은 기사의 출처를 누설하지 않는다. I will not tell you this news because I am sure you will divulge it prematurely. 나는 당신이 이 소식을 서둘러 밝힐 것이라고 확신하기 때문에 당신에게 말하지 않을 것이다.	

☐ debacle _____   ☐ debilitate _____   ☐ decorous _____   ☐ deluge _____

Definition	Meaning/Relation
애호가	ⓝ a lover of the fine arts
알아볼 수 있는	ⓐ perceptible, as by the faculty of vision or the intellect **a discernible[visible] change** 분명한〔뚜렷한〕변화 **discernible[noticeable] trend** 확실한 경향
불일치	ⓝ divergence or disagreement, as between facts or claims
냉정한	ⓐ devoid of or unaffected by passion, emotion, or bias
시치미떼다; 숨기다	ⓥ to make a false show of; to disguise or conceal behind a false appearance
유포하다, 퍼뜨리다	ⓥ to scatter widely, as in sowing seed **disseminate[foster, spread] culture** 교양〔지식〕을 보급시키다 **disseminate[communicate] ideas** 생각을 전하다〔퍼뜨리다〕 **disseminate[furnish, give, offer, provide] information** 정보를 제공하다
누설하다	ⓥ to make known (something private or secret) **divulge information to the press** 정보를 언론에 폭로하다

210_216 77

PART 1

PART 2

PART 3

PART 4

PART 5

PART 6

☐ deplore _____ ☐ derelict _____ ☐ dilemma _____

NO.	Entry Word	Example Sentence	
217 ☐☐	**docile** [dásəl]	He was an intelligent and docile pupil. 그는 총명하고 유순한 학생이었다. The young man who seemed so quiet and docile turned out to be very well-informed and to have strong opinions of his own. 그렇게 말이 없고 유순해 보이던 그 청년은 매우 박식하고 자기 나름의 확고한 견해를 갖고 있음이 드러났다.	
218 ☐☐	**eclectic** [eklέktik]	While it's not quite as big as many other international festivals, the Chicago showings reflect an eclectic mix of cinema. 그것은 다른 국제(國制) 영화제 만큼 규모가 크지는 않지만, 시카고 출품작들은 다양하게 잘 정선된 영화들이라는 걸 알 수 있습니다. The painter's style is very eclectic. 그 화가의 스타일은 다양하다.	
219 ☐☐	**elusive** [ilúːsiv]	Chronic fatigue syndrome was first identified in the 1980s, but the cause has been elusive. 만성피로증후군은 1980년대에 처음으로 규명됐지만 그 원인은 아직도 정의되지 않았다. His elusive dreams of wealth were costly to those of his friends who supported him financially. 부에 대한 그의 종잡을 수 없는 꿈은 그를 재정적으로 지원했던 친구들의 꿈에 희생을 가져다 주었다.	
220 ☐☐	**empathy** [émpəθi]	The writer's imaginative empathy with his subject is clear. 그 작가가 상상력 속에서 대상에게 감정이입을 하고 있음이 분명하다. There is a natural love and empathy between them. 그들 사이에는 자연스런 사랑과 감정이입이 있다.	
221 ☐☐	**emulate** [émjəlèit]	He now emulates his teacher in scholarship. 이제 그는 학문에서 스승에게 뒤지지 않는다. People often try to emulate their favorite pop singers or movie stars. 사람들은 종종 자기가 좋아하는 가수나 영화배우를 닮으려고 한다.	
222 ☐☐	**equitable** [ékwətəbəl]	There's a great need for a more equitable tax system. 좀 더 공정한 조세 제도가 절실히 필요하다. We must find a way of achieving a more equitable distribution of resources. 우리는 좀더 공정한 자원의 분배를 이루기 위한 방법을 찾아내야만 한다.	
223 ☐☐	**equivocal** [ikwívəkəl]	He gave an equivocal answer, typical of a politician. 그는 정치가들의 전형인 모호한 답변을 했다. I received an equivocal reply from her. 나는 그 여자로부터 애매한 대답을 받았다.	

☐ dilettante _____   ☐ discernible _____   ☐ discrepancy _____

PART 1

PART 2

PART 3

PART 4

PART 5

PART 6

Definition	Meaning/Relation
유순한	ⓐ yielding to supervision, direction or management
다방면에 걸친	ⓐ made up of combining elements from a bariety of sources
정의하기 어려운	ⓐ difficult to define or describe
감정이입	ⓝ identification with and understanding of another's situation, feelings, and motives **feel empathy** 공감하다 **show empathy** 공감을 나타내다 **empathy with** …와의 공감
우열을 다투다; 모방하다	ⓥ to striveto equal or excel; to approach or attain equality with
공정한	ⓐ marked by or having equity **(an) equitable[fair] distribution** 공평한 분배 **an equitable division** 공평한 배당 **an equitable solution** 공정한 해결책 **equitable[equal] treatment** 공평한 취급
애매모호한	ⓐ open to two or more interpretations and often intended to mislead

☐ divulge _____   ☐ dispassionate _____   ☐ dissemble _____   ☐ disseminate _____

NO.	Entry Word	Example Sentence
224 □□	**estrange** [istréindʒ]	He had estranged the party leadership. 그는 당 지도부와 소원해졌다. His impolite behavior estranged his friends. 그의 무례한 행동으로 친구들이 그에게서 떠나 버렸다.
225 □□	**eulogy** [júːlədʒi]	His brother delivered the eulogy at the funeral. 장례식에서 그의 형이 송덕사를 했다. The song was a eulogy to the joys of travelling. 그 노래는 여행의 기쁨에 대한 찬사였다.
226 □□	**exemplify** [igzémpləfài]	Her pictures nicely exemplify the sort of painting that was being done at that period. 그녀의 그림은 그 시기에 그렸던 그림의 종류를 예증한다. He exemplified himself for the world. 그는 세상에 귀감이 되었다.
227 □□	**exorbitant** [igzɔ́ːrbətənt]	The price of food here is exorbitant. 여기 식품 값은 터무니없다. It's illegal for them to raise your rent to such an exorbitant level. 그들이 집세를 그렇게 마구 올리는 것은 위법이다.
228 □□	**explicit** [iksplísit]	It was an explicit threat. 그것은 명백한 위협이었다. He was quite explicit on that point. 그는 그 점에 대해서 조금도 숨김이 없었다.
229 □□	**extol** [ikstóul]	He was extolled as a hero. 그는 영웅으로 칭송을 받았다. Government ministers began to extol the virtues of British technology. 정부 장관들이 영국 기술의 장점들을 격찬하기 시작했다.
230 □□	**exuberant** [igzúːbərənt]	He is a classical dancer with an exuberant, flamboyant style. 그는 원기왕성하고 현란한 스타일의 고전 무용수였다. His ebullient nature could not be repressed; he was always exuberant. 그의 열광적인 성격은 억제될 수 없었다. 언제나 그는 원기왕성했다.

□ docile _____ □ eclectic _____ □ elusive _____ □ empathy _____

Definition	Meaning/Relation
소원하게 하다	ⓥ to make hostile, unsympathetic, or indifferent
추도연설; 찬사	ⓝ a laudatory speech or written tribute, especially one praising someone who has died; high praise or commendation **deliver a eulogy for** …에 찬사를 보내다 **a touching eulogy** 감동적인 찬사
예증하다	ⓥ to illustrate by example
터무니 없는, 과도한	ⓐ exceeding all bounds, as of custom or fairness **an exorbitant[unreasonable] charge** 터무니없는 요금 **an exorbitant[excessive, unrealistic] demand** 터무니없는〔부당한〕요구 **a exorbitant[high, inflated, outrageous, prohibitive, steep, stiff] price** 엄청나게 비싼 가격, 고가 **an exorbitant[excess, windfall] profit** 엄청난〔막대한〕이익
명백한; 숨김없는	ⓐ fully and clearly expressed; forthright and unreserved in expression **sexually explicit** 성에 관하여 노골적으로 표현한 **explicit about** …에 대해 명료한
칭송하다, 격찬하다	ⓥ to praise or exalt highly **extol as** …이라고 격찬하다
원기왕성한	ⓐ full of unrestrained enthusiasm or joy

224_230

81

PART 1

PART 2

PART 3

PART 4

PART 5

PART 6

☐ emulate _____   ☐ equitable _____   ☐ equivocal _____

NO.	Entry Word	Example Sentence
231 ☐☐	**facet** [fǽsit]	The facets of a precious stone are the small flat surfaces cut on to it. 보석의 단면이란 보석을 자르고 난 작고 편평한 표면을 말한다. One needs to consider the various facets of the problem. 그 문제의 다양한 면들을 고려할 필요가 있다.
232 ☐☐	**facetious** [fəsíːʃəs]	We grew tired of his frequent facetious remarks. 우리는 그가 빈번하게 하는 엉뚱한 소리에 싫증이 나게 되었다. Some of them seemed shocked while others laughed heartily at the facetious metaphor. 그들 중의 몇몇은 충격을 받은 듯 보였지만 다른 일부는 그 익살스러운 은유에 진심으로 웃었다.
233 ☐☐	**fastidious** [fæstídiəs]	Her odd table manners embarrassed some of her more fastidious friends. 그녀의 이상한 식사예절은 그녀의 보다 까다로운 친구늘을 당황케 했나. He is not fastidious about what he eats. 그는 먹는 것에 까다롭지 않다.
234 ☐☐	**fickle** [fíkəl]	Woman is as fickle as a reed. 여자의 마음은 갈대와 같이 변덕스럽다. The taste of the public is so fickle that a TV performer who is a big hit one season may be out of a job the next. 대중의 취향이 매우 변덕스러워서 한 시즌 크게 히트했던 TV 연기자도 그 다음 시즌에는 일자리를 잃을 수 있다.
235 ☐☐	**fidelity** [fidéləti]	This book has been written with strict fidelity to historical facts. 이 책은 역사적 사실에 아주 충실하게 쓰여졌다. A dog's fidelity to its owner is one of the reasons why that animal is a favorite household pet. 개를 가정 애완동물로 선호하는 이유 중의 하나는 주인에 대한 충성 때문이다.
236 ☐☐	**flagrant** [fléigrənt]	The commission blasted the flagrant violation of human rights. 위원회는 명백한 인권침해를 규탄했다. Telling the story was a flagrant breach of trust. 그 이야기를 하는 것은 명백하게 신뢰를 파괴하는 일이었다.
237 ☐☐	**flaunt** [flɔːnt]	He's always flaunting his wealth. 그는 항상 자신의 부를 과시한다. They openly flaunted their relationship. 그들은 자신들의 관계를 공공연히 과시했다.

☐ estrange _____ ☐ eulogy _____ ☐ exemplify _____

Definition	Meaning/Relation
(보석 등의) 작은평면; (일의) 한 면	ⓝ one of the flat polished surfaces cut on a gemstone or occurring naturally on a crystal; any of the many parts of a subject to be considered
엉뚱한; 익살스러운	ⓐ playfully jocular; humorous **a facetious remark** 엉뚱한 말
(기호가) 까다로운	ⓐ possessing or displaying careful, meticulous attention to detail **fastidious about** …에 대해 까다로운
변덕스러운	ⓐ characterized by erratic changeableness or instability, especially with regard to affections or attachments **(as) fickle as fortune** 몹시 변덕스러운 **Fortune's fickle wheel** 변하기 쉬운 운명의 수레바퀴
충실, 충성	ⓝ faithfulness to obligations, duties, or observances **pledge[swear] fidelity** 충성을 맹세하다 **fidelity to** …에의 충성 **high fidelity** 고충실도 **reproduce sth. with complete fidelity** …을 실물 그대로 복제[복사]하다
명백한	ⓐ conspicuously bad, offensive, or reprehensible **flagrant[brazen, naked, outright, stark] aggression** 노골적인 침해[공격] **an flagrant[egregious] breach** 엄청난[터무니없는] 위반 **(a) flagrant[blatant, callous, complete, total] disregard** 완전 무시, 노골적인 무시 **a flagrant[cardinal, costly, egregious, glaring, grievous, gross, major, serious] error** 엄청난 잘못 **a flagrant[brazen, gross] violation** 엄청난 위반
과시하다	ⓥ to exhibit ostentatiously or shamelessly **flaunt one's erudition** 학식을 과시하다 **flaunt[parade] one's knowledge** 지식을 과시하다 **flaunt one's wealth** 재산을 과시하다

☐ exorbitant _____ ☐ explicit _____ ☐ extol _____ ☐ exuberant _____

NO.	Entry Word	Example Sentence	
238 □□	**flourish** [flə́ːriʃ]	This spring, packing companies will flourish. 이번 봄에 포장 회사들이 번성하게 될 것이다. Luckily for me and them, love did eventually grow and flourish. 나와 그들 모두에게 다행하게도 마침내 사랑은 커져서 풍성하게 되었다.	
239 □□	**flout** [flaut]	No one can flout the rules and get away with it. 아무도 규칙을 지키지 않으니 그것을 갖고 가라. The headstrong youth flouted all authority. 그 고집센 젊은이는 모든 권위를 경멸했다.	
240 □□	**formidable** [fɔ́ːrmidəbəl]	Benn had earned the reputation of being a formidable opponent. 벤은 무서운 적수라는 평판을 얻었다. It is a world of ferocious rivalry in which today's friends will turn out to be formidable foes tomorrow. 그것은 오늘의 친구가 내일 무서운 적이 되는 잔인한 경쟁의 세계이다.	
241 □□	**futile** [fjúːtl]	All my attempts to unlock the door were futile. 문을 열기 위한 나의 모든 시도는 헛되었다. She made some futile remark that I can't remember. 그녀는 내가 기억할 수 없는 쓸데없는 말을 했다.	
242 □□	**generic** [dʒənérik]	The plays all fit within the generic definition of comedy. 그 연극들은 희극이라는 포괄적 개념에 모두 들어 맞는다. A generic 'Made in the E·U' name dose not give any value to those products. 'Made in the E·U'라고 포괄적인 라벨을 붙여버리면 그런 상품들의 가치에 하나도 득이 될 게 없다.	
243 □□	**gravity** [grǽvəti]	Everything is under the gravity. 모든 것이 중력의 영향을 받는다. Things fall to the ground because of gravity. 물체는 중력 때문에 땅으로 떨어진다.	
244 □□	**hackneyed** [hǽknid]	The English teacher criticized her story because of its hackneyed and unoriginal plot. 영어 선생님께서는 진부하고 창의적이지 못한 구성 때문에 그녀의 이야기를 비판했다. She always tells a hackneyed idea at the meeting. 그녀는 회의 시에 항상 진부한 이야기를 한다.	

□ facet _____   □ facetious _____   □ fastidious _____

Definition	Meaning/Relation
번성(영)하다	ⓥ to grow well or luxuriantly
무시하다; 경멸하다	ⓥ to show contempt for; scorn **flout[defy] convention** 관례를 무시하다 **flout the law** 법을 무시하다
무서운	ⓐ arousing fear, dread, or alarm **a formidable[powerful] adversary** 무시무시한(강력한) (경쟁)상대 **a formidable antagonist** 만만치 않은 상대 **a formidable[real, serious] challenge** 심각한 도전 **a formidable[strong] challenger** 강력한 도전자 **formidable[bitter, close, fierce, heavy, intense, keen, stiff, strong, tough] competition** 치열한 경쟁 **a formidable[keen, strong] competitor** 강력한 경쟁 상대, 강적
헛된	ⓐ having no useful result
포괄적인	ⓐ relating to or descriptive of an entire group or class **a generic drug** 상표 등록에 의한 법적 보호를 받고 있지 않은 약 **a generic term** 속명
중력	ⓝ the natural force of attraction exerted by a celestial body, such as earth, upon objects at or near its surface, tending to draw them toward the center of the body **zero gravity** 무중력 상태 **the center of gravity** 무게중심 **the force of gravity** 인력
진부한	ⓐ overfamiliar through overuse **a hackneyed[trite] expression** 진부한 표현 **a hackneyed[stock, trite] phrase** 진부한(상투적인) 표현

☐ fickle _____ ☐ fidelity _____ ☐ flagrant _____ ☐ flaunt _____

NO.	Entry Word	Example Sentence
245 □□	**harbor** [háːrbər]	The harbor is closed to navigation. 그 항구는 선박 출입이 금지되어 있다. The harbor was glittering with lights. 항구는 불빛들로 반짝이고 있었다.
246 □□	**hardy** [háːrdi]	Farmers were interbreeding less hardy cattle with native breeds. 농부들은 좀 덜 강건한 소를 토종 소와 교배시키고 있었다. The pioneers who settled the West were hardy people who could cope with difficulties and dangers of all kinds. 서부에 정착한 개척자들은 온갖 어려움이나 위험과 싸울 수 있는 강인한 사람들이었다.
247 □□	**humility** [hjuːmíləti]	His pose of humility was a lie. 그의 겸손한 태도는 거짓이었다. The highest good consists in humility. 최고의 선은 겸손에 있다.
248 □□	**imbue** [imbjúː]	We expect to imbue them with pride as members of the Korean community. 우리는 한국인으로서의 자부심이 그들에게 스며들길 기대한다. There are not a few women who are imbued with these thoughts. 여자들 가운데는 왕왕 이러한 사상을 가진 사람이 있다.
249 □□	**impugn** [ìmpjúːn]	The lawyer impugned the witness's story. 변호사는 증인의 이야기에 이의를 제기했다. I cannot impugn your honesty without evidence. 나는 당신의 진실성을 증거도 없이 의심할 수는 없다
250 □□	**incompatible** [ìnkəmpǽtəbl]	Their interests were mutually incompatible. 그들의 이해관계는 서로 상반되었다. The married couple argued incessantly and finally decided to separate because they were incompatible. 결혼한 그 부부는 서로 화합하지 못했기 때문에 끊임없이 다투다가 마침내 별거하기로 했다.
251 □□	**indict** [indáit]	He was indicted for/on charges of corruption. 그는 매수혐의로 기소되었다. They indicted people they knew to be innocent. 그들은 그들이 무죄라고 알았던 사람들을 기소했다.

□ flourish _____   □ flout _____   □ formidable _____

|---|---|
항구	ⓝ a sheltered part of a body of water deep enough to provide anchorage for ships **clear a harbor** 항구를 떠나다 **dredge a harbor** 항구를 준설(浚渫)하다 **blockade a harbor** 항구를 봉쇄하다 **mine a harbor** 항구에 기뢰를 부설하다 **an artificial harbor** 인공 항구 **a natural harbor** 천연 항구 **a safe harbor** 안전한 항구, ((비유)) 피난처
강(건)한	ⓐ being in robust and sturdy good health **a hardy breed** 내한성(耐寒性) 품종 **a hardy perennial** 내한성(耐寒性) 다년생 식물
겸손	ⓝ the quality or condition of being humble **demonstrate[display, show] humility** 겸손함을 보이다 **in[with] humility** 겸손하게
스며들게 하다, 물들이다	ⓥ to inspire, permeate, or invade
이의를 제기하다, 의심하다	ⓥ to challenge in argument **impugn *sb's* honesty** …의 정직성을 의심하다
상반되는	ⓐ incapable of associating or blending or of being associated or blended because of disharmony, incongruity, or antagonism **mutually incompatible** 서로 상반되는, 양립할 수 없는 **incompatible with** …와 맞지 않는
기소하다	ⓥ to make a formal accusation or indictment against (a party) by the findings of a jury, especially a grand jury **indict for** …의 혐의로 기소하다

245_251 87

PART 1

PART 2

PART 3

PART 4

PART 5

PART 6

☐ futile _____ ☐ generic _____ ☐ gravity _____ ☐ hackneyed _____

NO.	Entry Word	Example Sentence	
252 ☐☐	**inexorable** [inéksərəbəl]	We begged him to reconsider his decision, but he remained inexorable. 그의 결정을 재고하도록 간청했지만 그는 계속 굽히지 않았다. After listening to the pleas for clemency, the judge was inexorable and gave the convicted man the maximum punishment allowed by law. 관대한 처분을 달라는 호소를 듣고 나서도 그 판사는 냉혹하게 법이 허용하는 최고형을 선고했다.	
253 ☐☐	**ingenious** [indʒíːnjəs]	The boy invented an ingenious excuse for being late. 그 소년은 늦은 데 대해 독창적인 변명을 꾸며댔다. Visitors to the show witness a simulation of an ingenious solution for diverting a possible impact. 쇼를 관람하는 사람들은 있을지도 모르는 충돌을 딴 곳으로 돌리는 독창적인 해결책에 관한 시뮬레이션을 보게 됩니다.	
254 ☐☐	**ingenuous** [indʒénjuːəs]	Children are more ingenuous than adults. 아이들은 어른들보다 솔직하다. Sally was so obviously sincere and ingenuous that everyone liked her. Sally는 너무나 성실하고 순진해서 모든 사람이 그녀를 좋아했다.	
255 ☐☐	**inundate** [ínəndèit]	If the dam breaks, it will inundate large parts of the town. 만약 댐이 무너지면 그 마을의 대부분 지역이 물에 잠길 것이다. When we asked for suggestions on how to raise money for the intramural sports program, we found ourselves inundated by bright ideas. 교내 운동경기를 위한 모금방법에 관해서 제안을 부탁했을 때 사방에서 훌륭한 아이디어가 쏟아져 나오는 것을 알았다.	
256 ☐☐	**juxtapose** [dʒʌkstəpóuz]	He liked to juxtapose colors to achieve visual effects. 그는 시각적인 효과를 얻기 위해 색을 나란히 배열하는 것을 좋아했다. We tried to juxtapose the sculptures to give the best effect. 우리는 가장 좋은 효과를 내기 위해 조각을 나란히 놓으려고 노력했다.	
257 ☐☐	**lavish** [lǽviʃ]	He is never lavish with his money. 그는 돈을 낭비하는 법이 결코 없다. Stories are told of corrupt government officials and of lavish living by aid workers amid dismal poverty. 참담한 빈곤이 만연되고 있는 가운데 정부관리의 부패와 원조 담당자들의 사치스러운 생활에 관한 이야기들이 나돌고 있다.	
258 ☐☐	**legacy** [légəsi]	Almost 128 years after abolition, Americans are still struggling with the costly political and social legacy of slavery. 노예 제도가 폐지된 지 거의 128년이 지났지만 미국인들은 여전히 노예제도의 값비싼 정치적 · 사회적 유산과 싸우고 있다. Disease and famine are often legacies of war. 질병과 기근은 흔히 전쟁이 남기는 유산이다.	

☐ harbor _____ ☐ hardy _____ ☐ humility _____ ☐ imbue _____

Definition	Meaning/Relation
굽힐 수 없는; 냉혹한	ⓐ not capable of being persuaded by entreaty; relentless **inexorable fate** 가차없는 운명 **inexorable[enormous, great, heavy, intense, maximum, relentless, severe, strong, unrelieved] pressure** 엄청난(극심한) 압력
독창적인	ⓐ marked by inventive skill and imagination; having or arising from an inventive or cunning mind
솔직한; 순진한	ⓐ lacking in sophistication or worldliness; artless
물에 잠기게 하다; 넘치다	ⓥ to cover with water, especially floodwaters; to overwhelm as if with a flood
배열하다, 나란히 놓다	ⓥ to place side by side, especially for comparison or contrast **juxtapose with** …와 나란히 하다
낭비하는, 사치스러운	ⓐ characterized by or produced with extravagance and profusion **lavish in[with]** …에 아낌없는
유산	ⓝ something handed down from an ancestor or a predecessor or from the past **hand down a legacy** 유산을 물려주다 **come into a legacy** 유산을 상속받다 **legacy duty** 유산 상속세

PART 1

PART 2

PART 3

PART 4

PART 5

PART 6

252_258
89

☐ impugn _____   ☐ incompatible _____   ☐ indict _____

NO.	Entry Word	Example Sentence
259	**lout** [laut]	He did not find it necessary to taunt or deprecate his opponents or behave like a lout inside or outside the ring. 그는 링 안에서나 밖에서나 그의 상대자를 비난하거나 시골뜨기처럼 행동하는 것이 필요하다는 것을 알지 못했다. He looked like a lager lout from a UK football match. 그는 영국 축구 게임에서 술취한 망나니처럼 보였다.
260	**luster** [lʌ́stər]	Her eyes lost their luster. 그녀의 눈은 광택을 잃었다. The company hopes that this prestigious publication will add new luster to their image. 그 회사는 출판물이 유명하기 때문에 회사 이미지에 득이 될 거라 희망한다.
261	**mandate** [mǽndeit]	He says Beijing is already struggling to have local governments implement its mandates in other areas. 그가 말하길 베이징은 지역정부의 명령에 따르기 위해 이미 열심히 노력하고 있다고 한다. The government does not have a mandate to introduce this new law. 정부는 이와 같은 새로운 법을 도입할 권한이 없다.
262	**manifest** [mǽnəfèst]	His guilt was manifest. 그의 유죄는 명백했다. The fears keep manifesting in ever-greater degrees until we deal with them. 그 두려움들에 대하여 대처하지 않으면 점점 더 증폭된 형태로 나타난다.
263	**maxim** [mǽksim]	He often preaches the maxim of 'use it or lose it.' 그는 '이용하지 않으면 잃는다'라는 격언을 설파하는 경우가 많다. It is a valid maxim that competition increases productivity. 경쟁이 생산성을 높인다는 것은 타당한 격언이다.
264	**mentor** [méntər]	My mentor is my good genius. 내 스승은 내게 좋은 감화를 준다. We need mentors for various components of your life. 우리는 삶의 다양한 측면에서 조언자가 될 사람이 필요하다
265	**myriad** [míriəd]	Each galaxy contains a myriad of stars. 각 은하계에는 무수한 별들이 있다. Myriads of followers joined Gandhi's cause. 무수한 추종자들은 Gandhi의 대의 명분에 합류했다.

☐ inexorable _____ ☐ ingenious _____ ☐ ingenuous _____

Definition	Meaning/Relation
시골뜨기, 얼간이	ⓝ a person regarded as awkward and stupid **a drunken lout** 술취한 망나니 **a stupid lout** 멍청한 망나니
(표면의) 빛	ⓝ soft reflected light **add luster to** …에 윤기를 내다, …에 윤기를 더하다 **take on a new luster** 새로운 윤기를 띠다
명령, 권한	ⓝ an authorization or a command given by a political electorate to its representative **seek a mandate** 명령을 구(求)하다
명백한; 나타나다	ⓐ clearly apparent to the sight or understanding ⓥ to show or display
격언	ⓝ a succinct formulation of a fundamental principle, general truth, or rule of conduct
스승, 조언자	ⓝ a wise and trusted counselor or teacher **a mentor to** …의 스승
무수(한 사람, 것)	ⓝ a vast number

259_265 91

PART 1

PART 2

PART 3

PART 4

PART 5

PART 6

☐ inundate _____　　☐ juxtapose _____　　☐ lavish _____　　☐ legacy _____

NO.	Entry Word	Example Sentence
266 ☐☐	**negligible** [néglidʒəbəl]	The damage to my car is negligible. 내 차의 피해는 무시해도 좋을 정도다. Since we are making negligible progress in our fight against pollution, the time has come for us to adopt completely new methods. 오염 퇴치에 있어서 별로 진전이 없기 때문에 우리는 전혀 새로운 방법을 채택할 때가 왔다.
267 ☐☐	**notorious** [noutɔ́:riəs]	She was a notorious character in London's underworld. 그녀는 런던 암흑가에서 악명 높은 인물이었다. London is notorious for its fog and rain. 런던은 안개와 비로 유명합니다.
268 ☐☐	**paradox** [pǽrədɑ̀ks]	It's a paradox that in such a rich country there can be so much poverty. 그런 부유한 나라에 이렇게 큰 가난이 있다는 것은 역설이다. It is a paradox that the French eat so much rich food and yet have a relatively low rate of heart disease. 프랑스인들이 기름진 음식을 그렇게 많이 먹으면서도 상대적으로 심장병 발병률이 낮다는 것은 역설이다 .
269 ☐☐	**partial** [pɑ́:rʃəl]	He suffered a stroke and partial paralysis. 그는 뇌일혈로 쓰러져 부분 마비가 왔다. His views are partial. 그의 견해는 편파적이다
270 ☐☐	**perpetual** [pərpétʃuəl]	They heard the perpetual noises of the machines. 그들은 기계의 끊임없는 소음을 들었다. I'm tired of your perpetual complaints. 나는 너의 끊임없는 불평에 지쳤다.
271 ☐☐	**pertinent** [pə́:rtənənt]	The point is not pertinent to the matter in hand. 그 점은 당면 문제와는 관련이 없다. The chapters which are pertinent to the post-war period are essential reading. 전후시대와 관련있는 장(章)들은 꼭 읽을 필요가 있다.
272 ☐☐	**phlegmatic** [flegmǽtik]	He's a very phlegmatic character. 그는 매우 침착한 성격이다. I certainly share Ms. Applebaum's admiration for the phlegmatic and sensible British disposition. 영국인들의 침착하고 분별력 있는 성격에 대한 Ms. Applebaum의 칭찬은 나도 확실히 공감한다.

☐ lout _____ ☐ luster _____ ☐ mandate _____ ☐ manifest _____

Definition	Meaning/Relation
무시해도 좋은; 사소한	ⓐ not significant or important enough to be worth considering; trifling **a negligible amount** (무시해도 좋을 만큼의) 얼마되지 않는 양[액수], 소량 **a negligible quantity** 적은 양, 소량
악명높은	ⓐ known widely and usually unfavorably **notorious as** …로서 악명 높은 **notorious for** …로 악명 높은
역설	ⓝ a seemingly contradictory statement that may nonetheless be true
부분적인; 편파적인	ⓐ of, relating to, being, or affecting only a part; favoring one person or side over another or others **partial to** …을 몹시 좋아하는
끊임없는, 영원한	ⓐ continuing or lasting for a long time lasting for eternity **a perpetual calendar** 만세력 **perpetual check** 비김수, 영구 장군 **a perpetual frown** 늘상 찡그린 얼굴
관련있는	ⓐ having logical, precise relevance to the matter at hand
침착한	ⓐ having or suggesting a calm **a phlegmatic temperament** 냉정한 기질

PART 1 / PART 2 / PART 3 / PART 4 / PART 5 / PART 6

☐ maxim _____ ☐ mentor _____ ☐ myriad _____

NO.	Entry Word	Example Sentence
273 □□	**pious** [páiəs]	Charles I was a generous and pious prince. 찰스 1세는 너그럽고 신앙심이 두터운 왕자였다. She is a pious follower of the faith, never missing her prayers. 그녀는 신앙심이 깊은 신도여서 기도를 거르는 적이 없다.
274 □□	**plausible** [plɔ́ːzəbəl]	His explanation sounds fairly plausible to me. 그의 설명은 내게는 아주 그럴 듯하게 들린다. People tend to believe Fred because he seems plausible, but we know he speaks with a forked tongue. 프레드는 그럴듯하게 보여 모두 그를 믿기 쉬운데, 우리들은 그가 거짓말장이라는 것을 알고 있다.
275 □□	**pliable** [plái əbəl]	Cane is pliable when wet. 등나무는 젖으면 유연해진다. What he calls his pliable outlook on life seems to me simply a lack of any firm moral standards. 그의 말대로 그의 유연한 인생관이란 내가 보기엔 단지 확고한 도덕적 기준의 결핍인 것 같다.
276 □□	**potent** [póutənt]	The nation has a potent new weapons system. 그 나라는 강력한 새 무기 체제를 갖추고 있다. Violence on TV may turned out to be a potent influence on some young people. TV에 나오는 폭력이 어떤 젊은이들에게는 강력한 영향을 주는 것으로 밝혀졌다.
277 □□	**preclude** [priklúːd]	The temporary cease-fire agreement does not preclude possible retaliatory attacks later. 일시적인 휴전 협정 때문에 나중에 있을 수 있는 보복 공격을 막을 수는 없다. That precluded him from escaping. 그것 때문에 그는 도망칠 수 없게 되었다.
278 □□	**precocious** [prikóuʃəs]	Her precocious mathematical ability astounded her parents. 그녀의 조숙한 수학 능력은 그녀의 부모를 깜짝 놀라게 하였다. By her rather adult manner of discussing serious topics, the child demonstrated that she was precocious. 진지한 화제를 성인다운 태도로 토론함으로써 그 어린이는 조숙함을 나타내 보였다.
279 □□	**precursor** [priːkə́ːrsər]	German World War Two rocket weapons were the precursors of modern space rockets. 2차 대전 시 독일의 로켓 무기는 현대 우주 로켓의 선구자였다. Experience has shown that an increase in housing construction is the precursor of a general economic upturn. 주택건설의 증가는 일반적인 경제 호전의 전조임을 경험적으로 알았다.

□ negligible _____   □ notorious _____   □ paradox _____   □ partial _____

Definition	Meaning/Relation
신앙심이 깊은	ⓐ having or exhibiting religious reverence **a pious hope** 실현성 없는 희망
그럴듯한	ⓐ seemingly or apparently valid, likely, or acceptable
유연한	ⓐ receptive to change **the pliable minds of children** 아이들의 유연한 마음
강력한	ⓐ possessing inner or physical strength **a potent[stiff, strong] drink** 독한 술 **a potent[powerful, strong] drug** 독한 약 **(a) potent[strong] medication** 약효가 강한(독한) 약
불가능하게 하다, 막다	ⓥ to make impossible, as by action taken in advance **preclude from** …하지 못하게 방해하다 **preclude *sb*. from doing *sth*.** …하지 못하도록 …을 방해하다
조숙한	ⓐ manifesting or characterized by unusually early development or maturity, especially in mental aptitude **a precocious child** 조숙한 아이
선구자; 전조	ⓝ one that precedes and indicates, suggests, or announces someone or something to come; one that precedes another **a precursor of[to]** …의 선구자

☐ perpetual _____ ☐ pertinent _____ ☐ phlegmatic _____

NO.	Entry Word	Example Sentence
280 ☐☐	**premise** [prémis]	The illogical proof was based on a faulty premise. 그 비논리적 논증은 그릇된 전제를 바탕으로 했다. The premise of the festival is always to discover new directors. 영화제의 전제 조건은 언제나 신인 감독을 발굴하는 것이다.
281 ☐☐	**prestige** [prestí:dʒ]	The school has immense prestige. 그 학교는 엄청난 명성을 지니고 있다. The mayor's prestige is known throughout the country. 그 시장의 명성은 전국에 걸쳐 알려져 있다.
282 ☐☐	**pristine** [prísti:n]	The car was in pristine condition. 그 자동차는 새 것과 같은 상태였다. Within three months, our speech was pristine and pure. 3개월 내에 우리의 말투는 순박해지고 순수했다.
283 ☐☐	**probe** [proub]	Scientists say they will continue to probe the teenage brain. 과학자들은 앞으로도 계속 10대의 뇌를 정밀 조사할 것이라고 말합니다. Police officials' indifference is hampering investigators who probe into the black market. 경찰관들이 무관심으로 조사반원들의 암시장 정밀 조사가 저지되고 있다.
284 ☐☐	**proliferate** [proulífərèit]	At Christmastime biographies of the famous proliferate in the bookshops. 크리스마스 때가 되면 유명인의 전기들이 서점에 급격히 증가한다. During the 1980s, computer companies proliferated. 1980년 대에 컴퓨터 회사의 수가 급격히 증가했다.
285 ☐☐	**prolific** [proulífik]	He was probably the most prolific song-writer of his generation. 그는 아마 그 세대에 가장 작품을 많이 쓴 작곡가였을 것이다. Mr. Graces was a prolific writer, publishing an average of two books a year. Graces 씨는 활발한 저술가로서 해마다 평균 2권의 책을 내놓았습니다.
286 ☐☐	**prosaic** [prouzéiik(əl)]	I do not like this author because he is so unimaginative and prosaic. 매우 상상력이 부족하고 평범하기 때문에 나는 이 작가를 싫어한다. He's too prosaic to think of sending me flowers. 그는 너무 평범해서 나에게 꽃을 보낼 생각을 하지 않는다.

☐ pious _____   ☐ plausible _____   ☐ pliable _____   ☐ potent _____

Definition	Meaning/Relation
전제	ⓝ a proposition upon which an argument is based or from which a conclusion is drawn 　the major premise 대전제
명성	ⓝ the level of respect at which one is regarded by others 　enjoy[have] prestige 신망이 있다, 신망을 누리다 　gain prestige 신망을 얻다
초기의; 순박한	ⓐ of, realting to, or typical of the earliest time or condition; remaining in a pure state
정밀 조사하다	ⓥ to investigate 　probe thoroughly [deeply] 철저하게 조사하다 　probe about[on] …에 대해 조사하다
급격히 증가하다	ⓥ to grow or multiply by rapidly producing new tissue, parts, cells, or offspring 　cancer cells proliferating 증식하는 암세포
다작의	ⓐ producing abundant works or results 　a prolific author 다작 작가 　a prolific contributor 기고를 많이 하는 사람 　a prolific writer (책을 많이 쓰는) 다산(多産) 작가
평범한	ⓐ lacking in imagination and spirit

280_286　97

PART 1

PART 2

PART 3

PART 4

PART 5

PART 6

☐ preclude _____　☐ precocious _____　☐ precursor _____

NO.	Entry Word	Example Sentence
287 ☐☐	**provincial** [prəvínʃəl]	The Guangdong provincial government also came up with some assessment. 광둥성 지방 정부도 자체적으로 조사를 실시했습니다.
		The KHC estimated that about 230,000 vehicles returned to Seoul from provincial areas yesterday. 한국도로공사측은 어제 23만대의 차량이 지방에서 서울로 돌아온 것으로 추산했다.
288 ☐☐	**proximity** [prɑksíməti]	The restaurant benefits from its proximity to several cinemas. 그 식당은 몇몇 영화관에 근접한 덕을 보고 있다.
		We would appreciate your sending us samples of the closest proximity to the enclosed patterns. 동봉한 모형과 아주 가까운 견본을 몇 개 보내주시면 감사하겠습니다.
289 ☐☐	**pseudonym** [súːdənim]	Mark Twain was the pseudonym of Samuel Langhorne Clemens. Mark Twain은 Samuel Langhorne Clemen의 필명이었다.
		She also writes under the pseudonym of Barbara Vine. 그녀는 Barbara Vine이라는 필명으로 글을 쓴다.
290 ☐☐	**quaint** [kweint]	"What a quaint idea!" she said, laughing at him. "정말 기묘한 생각이야!"라고 그녀는 그를 비웃으며 말했다.
		Some of the quaint customs still exist in this part of the country. 그 기묘한 풍습들의 일부는 이 지방에 아직도 남아 있다.
291 ☐☐	**quell** [kwel]	The general quelled a rebellion. 그 장군은 반란을 진압했다.
		The government's reassurances have done nothing to quell the doubts of the public. 정부의 재보증은 대중의 의심을 잠재우지 못했다.
292 ☐☐	**quizzical** [kwízikəl]	She showed a quizzical expression on his face. 그녀는 어리둥절한 표정을 지었다.
		His expression was quizzical. 그의 표정은 어리둥절 해보였다.
293 ☐☐	**rancor** [rǽŋkər]	I have deep-rooted rancor against him. 나는 그에 대한 원한이 뼈에 사무쳤다.
		We have no rancor (at heart) against them. 우리는 그들에게 원한이 없다.

☐ premise _____ ☐ prestige _____ ☐ pristine _____ ☐ probe _____

Definition	Meaning/Relation
지방의	ⓐ of or relating to a province the provincial[municipal, city] assembly 도〔시〕 의회, 지방 의회 a provincial capital 도청소재지 a provincial city 지방 도시 (a) provincial government 지방 정부 a provincial parliament 지방 의회 a provincial[jerkwater, one-horse, sleepy, small] town 작은〔시골〕 마을
근접	ⓝ the state, quality, sense, or fact of being near or next close proximity 인접, 아주 가까움 proximity to …에 가까움 in proximity to …에 근접하여 in the proximity of …의 부근에
필명	ⓝ a fictitious name assumed by an author adopt a pseudonym 필명을 채택하다 use a pseudonym 필명을 사용하다 under a pseudonym 필명으로
기묘한	ⓐ odd, especially in an old-fashioned way a quaint custom 기이한 풍습
진압하다	ⓥ to put down forcibly quell[break up] a demonstration 데모를 진압하다 quell[put down] a disturbance 소동을 가라앉히다〔진압하다〕 quell[crush, put down, suppress] an insurrection 반란을 진압하다 quell[put down, crush] a mutiny 폭동을 진압하다 quell[put down] a protest 항의 집회를 진압하다 quell[crush, put down, quash, smash, stifle] a revolt 반란을 진압하다 quell[crush, put down] a riot 폭동을 진압하다
어리둥절한	ⓐ suggesting puzzlement a quizzical expression 어리둥절한〔의아한〕 표정 a quizzical glance 의아해하는 시선 a quizzical[puzzled, bemused] look 어리둥절해하는 표정
원한	ⓝ bitter, long-lasting resentment stir up rancor 원한을 갖게 하다 express rancor 원한을 드러내다

287_293 99

PART 1

PART 2

PART 3

PART 4

PART 5

PART 6

☐ proliferate _____ ☐ prolific _____ ☐ prosaic _____

NO.	Entry Word	Example Sentence	
294 ☐☐	**ratify** [rǽtəfài]	The National Assembly is expected to ratify the treaty during this session. 국회는 이번 회기 중에 그 조약을 비준할 예정이다. Congress ratified this bill, so it will become effective from the first of the next month. 이 법안은 의회의 승인을 받았으므로, 다음 달 1일부터 발효될 것이다.	
295 ☐☐	**realm** [relm]	Such a thing is not within the realms of possibility. 이러한 것은 가능한 영역 안에 있지 않다. Spiritual heroes usually have their spiritual realms. 정신적인 영웅들은 보통 그들의 정신적인 영역를 가지고 있다.	
296 ☐☐	**reconcile** [rékənsàil]	It's difficult to reconcile different points of view. 다른 견해를 조정하기란 어렵다. The U.N. Commission tried, in vain, to reconcile the opposing parties. 유엔위원회는 적대적인 당사자들을 화해시키려고 노력했으나 허사였다.	
297 ☐☐	**recrimination** [rikrímənéiʃən]	Loud and angry recriminations were her answer to his accusations. 큰소리의 화난 비난이 그의 비난에 대한 그녀의 응수였다. It's the story of a lovelorn girl whose suicide provokes bitter recriminations. 그것은 애인에게 버림받은 여자의 이야기로서 그녀의 자살이 심한 비난을 불러 일으킨다.	
298 ☐☐	**redundant** [ridʌ́ndənt]	The report was cluttered with redundant detail. 그 보고서는 불필요한 설명으로 뒤죽박죽이었다. In the sentence 'She is a single unmarried woman', the word 'unmarried' is redundant. '그녀는 독신의 결혼하지 않은 여성이다'라는 문장에서 '결혼하지 않은'은 불필요한 말이다.	
299 ☐☐	**relinquish** [rilíŋkwiʃ]	He relinquished all his riches for poor people. 그는 가난한 사람들을 위해 그의 전 재산을 포기했다. He was preparing to relinquish his presidency and step out of the military and government career that occupied two thirds of his life. 그는 대통령직을 그만두고 그의 인생의 2/3를 몸담아 온 군과 정부에서 물러날 준비를 하고 있었다.	
300 ☐☐	**reprehensible** [rèprihénsəbəl]	Your conduct is most reprehensible. 네 행동은 대단히 비난받을 만하다. I don't know which was more reprehensible - making improper use of the money or lying about it later. 나는 돈을 잘못 쓰는 것과 뒤에 가서 그것에 관해 거짓말을 하는 것 중 어느 쪽이 더 비난을 받을 일이었는지 모르겠다.	

☐ provincial _____ ☐ proximity _____ ☐ pseudonym _____

Definition	Meaning/Relation
비준하다, 승인하다	ⓥ to approve and give formal sanction to **ratify an amendment** 수정안을 비준〔재가〕하다 **ratify a constitution** 헌법을 비준하다 **ratify a contract** 계약을 승인하다 **ratify[confirm] a treaty** 조약을 비준하다
영역	ⓝ a field, sphere, or province **in a realm** 영역〔부문〕에
화해시키다; 조정하다	ⓥ to reestablish a close relationship between; to bring two parties into agreements **reconcile to** …을 감수하다 **reconcile with** …와 화해〔일치〕시키다
맞비난	ⓝ the act of recriminating
불필요한	ⓐ exceeding what is necessary or natural
포기하다; 사임하다	ⓥ give up or abandon; to retire from
비난 받아야 할	ⓐ deserving rebuke or censure

294_300 101

PART 1

PART 2

PART 3

PART 4

PART 5

PART 6

☐ quaint _____   ☐ quell _____   ☐ quizzical _____   ☐ rancor _____

NO.	Entry Word	Example Sentence
301 ☐☐	**reprimand** [réprəmænd]	The lifeguard is reprimanding one of the tourists. 인명구조원은 관광객 중의 한 명을 꾸짖고 있다. Have you ever had to reprimand an employee before? 직원을 꾸짖어 본 적 있습니까?
302 ☐☐	**resilient** [rizíljənt]	Steel is highly resilient and therefore is used in the manufacture of springs. 강철은 탄력이 너무도 좋아서 용수철의 재료로 사용된다. This rubber ball is very resilient and immediately springs back into shape after you've squashed it. 이 고무공은 매우 탄력성이 좋아서 뭉그러뜨린 후에도 곧 제 모양으로 되돌아온다.
303 ☐☐	**resolve** [rizálv]	I resolved to go on a stricter diet. 나는 좀 더 엄격한 다이어트 하기로 결심했다. The House resolved to take up the bill. 의회는 그 법안의 채택을 결의했다.
304 ☐☐	**rudimentary** [rù:dəméntəri]	Her knowledge is still only rudimentary. 그녀의 지식은 여전히 초보적일 뿐이다. He lacks even a rudimentary knowledge of English grammar. 그는 영문법에 있어서는 초보 지식도 없다.
305 ☐☐	**scoff** [skɔ:f]	They scoff at the plan as utopian. 그들은 그 계획을 공상적이라고 비웃다. Old people scoff at the recent fad. 나이 든 사람들은 최근의 유행을 조소한다.
306 ☐☐	**solace** [sáləs]	Her mother seeks solace in religion. 그녀의 어머니는 종교에서 위안을 구한다. I know it isn't much solace, but several people did worse in the exam than you. 이게 별로 위안이 되지 않는다는 것을 알지만 몇몇 사람들은 너보다 더 시험을 못 봤어.
307 ☐☐	**specious** [spíːʃəs]	Let us not be misled by such specious arguments. 그런 허울좋은 주장에 속지 말자. We are mostly likely to fall victim to specious reasoning when we have an emotional desire to believe what we are being told. 우리가 듣고 있는 말을 감정적으로 믿고 싶을 때는 그럴듯한 논리에 희생되기가 매우 쉽다.

☐ ratify _____   ☐ realm _____   ☐ reconcile _____   ☐ recrimination _____

Definition	Meaning/Relation
꾸짖다	ⓥ to reprove severely, especially in a formal or official way **reprimand for** ···때문에 질책하다
탄력성이 좋은	ⓐ capable of returning to an original shape or position, as after having been compressed
결정[결심]하다	ⓥ to make a firm decision about **resolve against** ···을 하지 않기로 결정하다 **resolve on[upon]** ···을 하겠다고 결정(결심)하다
초보의	ⓐ being in the earliest stages of development
비웃다	ⓥ to mock at or treat with derision **scoff at** ···을 비웃다(조소하다)
위안	ⓝ comfort in sorrow, misfortune, or distress; consolation **find solace in** ···에서 위안을 찾다(얻다) **derive[get] solace from** ···에서 위안을 구하다
허울좋은, 그럴듯한	ⓐ having the ring of truth or plausibility but actually fallacious **a specious[spurious] argument** 그럴듯한 주장 **a specious claim** 그럴듯한 요구 **specious[false, spurious] logic** 그럴듯한(진짜 같은) 논리

□ redundant _____ □ relinquish _____ □ reprehensible _____

NO.	Entry Word	Example Sentence	
308 ☐☐	**squander** [skwɑ́ndər]	He squandered a fortune on bad investments. 그는 잘못된 투자에 거금을 낭비했다. The prodigal son squandered his inheritance. 방탕한 아들은 자기의 유산을 낭비했다.	
309 ☐☐	**subjective** [səbdʒéktiv]	Every assessment of loyalty involves a subjective element. 충성심 평가에는 으레 주관적 요소가 내포된다. More specific and less subjective criteria should be used in selecting people for promotion. 승진할 사람들을 선발하는 데에는 좀 더 구체적이고 좀 덜 주관적인 기준을 사용해야 한다.	
310 ☐☐	**substantiate** [səbstǽnʃièit]	I intend to substantiate my statement by producing a witness. 나는 증거를 제시함으로써 나의 주장을 입증하려고 한다. We have evidence to substantiate allegations that corruption took place. 우리는 부정이 있었다는 주장을 입증할 수 있는 증거를 갖고 있다.	
311 ☐☐	**surfeit** [sə́ːrfit]	A surfeit of food makes us sick. 과식하면 병난다. It's wrong that some people have a surfeit of food, while others don't have any. 어떤 사람들은 먹을 것이 전혀 없는 반면 어떤 사람들은 먹을 것이 넘쳐 난다는 것은 잘못된 일이다.	
312 ☐☐	**surreptitious** [sə̀ːrəptíʃəs]	News of their surreptitious meeting gradually leaked out. 그들의 비밀 회담에 대한 소식은 점차적으로 누설되었다. He started making surreptitious visits to the pub on his way home. 그는 집으로 가는 길에 남몰래 그 술집에 드나들기 시작했다.	
313 ☐☐	**susceptible** [səséptəbl]	This passage is susceptible to another interpretation. 이 귀절은 또 다른 해석의 여지가 있다. Some people are more susceptible to alcohol than others. 어떤 사람들은 다른 사람들보다 알코올에 더 영향을 받기 쉽다.	
314 ☐☐	**tangential** [tændʒénʃəl]	I agree it's an important subject, but it's tangential to the problem under discussion. 그것이 중요한 문제라는 데에는 나도 동의하지만, 지금 토의 중인 문제와는 별 관계가 없다. Overseas conflicts have at most a tangential relationship to U.S. security. 다른 나라와의 갈등은 기껏해야 미국의 안보와 거의 관련이 없다.	

☐ reprimand _____   ☐ resilient _____   ☐ resolve _____

308_314 105

PART 1

PART 2

PART 3

PART 4

PART 5

PART 6

Definition	Meaning/Relation
낭비하다	ⓥ to spend wastefully or extravagantly **squander on** …에 낭비하다
주관적인	ⓐ proceeding from or taking place within a person's mind such as to be unaffected by the external world **a subjective analysis** 주관적인 분석 **subjective reasoning** 주관적 추리〔추론〕
입증하다	ⓥ to support or verify with proof or evidence **substantiate an allegation** 혐의를 입증하다 **substantiate[prove] a charge** 혐의를 입증하다 **substantiate[back up, establish, press, authenticate] a claim** 주장〔권리〕을 입증하다
과다	ⓝ an excessive amount
비밀의; 은밀한	ⓐ acting with or marked by stealth; sneaky **a surreptitious[stolen] glance** 훔쳐봄
(…의) 여지가 있는; ~에 영향을 받기 쉬운	ⓐ able to admit it; easily influenced or affected **susceptible to** …에 걸리기 쉬운
거의 관계가 없는	ⓐ merely touching or slightly connected **tangential to** …에 거의 관계가 없는

☐ rudimentary _____   ☐ scoff _____   ☐ solace _____   ☐ specious _____

NO.	Entry Word	Example Sentence	
315 ☐☐	**tangible** [tǽndʒəbəl]	It's like a tangible reward. 확실한 보상이다. A chair is a tangible object. 의자는 만질 수 있는(유형의) 물체이다.	
316 ☐☐	**temperament** [témpərəmənt]	He has a nervous temperament. 그는 신경질적인 기질을 가졌다. He has a changeable temperament. 그는 변하기 쉬운 기질을 가지고 있다.	
317 ☐☐	**temperate** [témpərit]	She spoke in a temperate manner. 그녀는 온건한 태도로 말을 했다. He is a sensible and temperate man who managed to negotiate an agreement between the two sides. 그는 쌍방의 동의를 합의를 이끌어 낸 현명하고 온건한 사람이다.	
318 ☐☐	**tenacious** [tinéiʃəs]	They were confronted with a tenacious foe. 그들은 완강한 적과 직면했다. The conservation group was tenacious in its opposition to the new airport. 환경보존 집단은 새로운 공항건설에 대해 완강하게 반대의 입장을 취했다.	
319 ☐☐	**toxic** [táksik]	Fumes from an automobile are toxic. 자동차 배기가스는 유독하다. Our research has been unable to prove the chemicals have any toxic effects. 우리가 조사한 바로는 그 화공약품들이 유독성이 있다는 것을 입증할 수가 없었다.	
320 ☐☐	**transient** [trǽnʃənt]	How transient all happiness is in this world! 이 세상 행복이란 것이 모두 다 얼마나 덧없는가! A glass of whisky has only a transient warming effect. 위스키 한 잔은 일시적으로 몸을 따뜻하게 하는 효과가 있을 뿐이다.	
321 ☐☐	**utopia** [juːtóupiə]	He has some wild-eyed scheme to build a Utopia in the twenty-first century. 그는 21세기에 이상향을 건설하겠다는 엉뚱한 계획을 갖고 있다. She left home and travelled across the sea in search of utopia, but she never found it. 그녀는 집을 떠나 이상향을 찾아 바다를 건너 돌아다녔지만, 이상향을 결코 찾지 못했다.	

☐ squander _____ ☐ subjective _____ ☐ substantiate _____

Definition	Meaning/Relation
만져서 알수있는; 유형의	ⓐ discernible by the touch; real or concrete **a tangible benefit** 유형의 이익 **a tangible[positive] gain** 확실한〔실제〕이익
기질	ⓝ the manner of thinking, behaving, or reacting characteristic of a specific person
온건한	ⓐ exercising moderation and self-restraint **temperate in** …에 있어 절제하는
완강한	ⓐ holding or tending to hold persistently to something, such as a point of view
유독한	ⓐ of, relating to, or caused by a toxin or other poison **a toxic agent** 유독 물질 **a toxic[dangerous] drug** 위험한〔유독한〕 약물 **toxic[noxious] fumes** 유독 가스
덧없는; 일시적인	ⓐ passing with time; transitory **a transient population** 일시적인〔단기 체류〕 인구
이상향	ⓝ an ideally perfect place, especially in its social, political, and moral aspects

☐ surfeit _____   ☐ surreptitious _____   ☐ susceptible _____   ☐ tangential _____

322 □□	**veneer** [vəníər]	Beneath that veneer of respectability there lurked a cunning and unscrupulous criminal. 겉으로는 존경할 만한 모습을 가지고 있지만 교활하고 사악한 범죄 의도가 숨어 있었다. Both sides will work hard to maintain the veneer of friendship this year, but mutual suspicions remain. 양측은 올해에도 겉으로는 친분을 유지하려고 노력을 할 것이지만 상호간의 의심은 여전하다.
323 □□	**venerate** [vénərèit]	He venerates the gods of his ancestors. 그는 조상 신들을 숭배하고 있다. Robert Burns is perhaps Scotland's most venerated poet. Robert Burns는 아마 스코틀랜드의 가장 존경받는 시인일 것이다
324 □□	**vicarious** [vaikɛ́əriəs]	There's a certain vicarious pleasure in reading books about travel. 여행에 관한 책을 읽으면 어떤 대리 만족을 맛보게 된다. He got a vicarious thrill out of watching his son score the winning goal. 그는 아들이 승리를 결정짓는 골을 넣는 것을 보고 마치 자신이 넣은 것처럼 전율을 느꼈다.
325 □□	**vindictive** [vindíktiv]	The prevailing opinion is that the move is a vindictive attack on press freedom. 다수의 견해는 그러한 움직임은 언론의 자유에 대해 보복성이 있는 공격이라는 것이다. She can be extremely vindictive. 그녀는 극도로 앙심을 품을 수 있는 사람이다.
326 □□	**visionary** [víʒənèri]	She was given to visionary schemes which never materialized. 그녀는 실현될 수 없는 공상적인 계획을 부여받았다. President Reagan is depicted as a visionary and a stubborn chief executive in the memoirs of his secretary of state. 레이건 대통령은 그의 재임 때 국무장관의 회고록에서 공상가이며 고집 센 대통령으로 묘사되고 있다.
327 □□	**wistful** [wístfəl]	She looked with wistful eyes at the dolls in the window. 그녀는 쇼윈도의 인형을 바라는 듯이 처다보았다. With a wistful expression on his face, the prisoner looked through the window of his cell at the blue patch of sky. 얼굴에 무엇을 바라는 듯한 표정을 하고 그 죄수는 감방의 창을 통해 파란 하늘을 바라보았다.
328 □□	**wrath** [ræθ]	A soft answer turns away wrath. 유순한 대답은 분노를 쉬게 하리라. That won't be enough to mollify the public's wrath. 그 정도로는 국민의 분노를 달래기에 충분치 않다

□ tangible _____   □ temperament _____   □ temperate _____

Definition	Meaning/Relation
겉치레	ⓝ a deceptive external appearance **a polished veneer** 광택이 나는 화장판 **a superficial[thin] veneer** 허울뿐인 겉치레
숭배하다; 존경하다	ⓥ to regard with respect; to revere with awe **venerate as** …로서 존경하다
대리의	ⓐ felt or undergone as if one were taking part in the experience or feelings of another **a vicarious pleasure** 대리 만족
보복적인; 앙심깊은	ⓐ disposed to seek revenge; showing spite **a vindictive action** 보복적인 행위 **a vindictive person** 복수심이 강한 사람
공상적인; 공상가	ⓐ not practicable or realizable ⓝ a utopian **a visionary dream** 비현실적인 꿈
바라는 듯한	ⓐ full of wishful yearning **a wistful gaze** 동경하는 눈길 **a wistful glance** 애석해하는 눈빛
분노	ⓝ forceful, often vindictive anger **arouse *sb's* wrath** …을 격노하게 하다 **incur *sb's* wrath** …의 화를 돋우다

322_328 109

PART 1

PART 2

PART 3

PART 4

PART 5

PART 6

□ tenacious _____ □ toxic _____ □ transient _____ □ utopia _____

필수 영단어
★★

Ranking **4**

NO.	Entry Word	Example Sentence
329 □□	**admonish** [ædmániʃ]	He was frequently admonished by his teachers for being late. 그는 지각한다고 선생님한테서 자주 꾸중을 들었다. The dean admonished the members of the team for neglecting their homework assignments. 학장이 팀 멤버들에게 숙제를 게을리했다고 꾸중을 했다.
330 □□	**adversary** [ǽdvərsèri]	He defeated his old adversary. 그는 자신의 오랜 적수를 물리쳤다. The lawyer was disconcerted by the evidence produced by her adversary. 그 변호사는 상대방이 내놓은 증거에 당황했다.
331 □□	**agnostic** [ægnάstik]	He is an agnostic. 그는 불가지론자이다. Although he was born a Catholic, he was an agnostic for most of his adult life. 그는 카톨릭 교도로 태어났지만, 성인이 된 후에는 대부분 불가지론자로 지냈다.
332 □□	**agrarian** [əgrɛ́əriən]	Agrarian production in the region has increased in recent years. 그 지역의 농업 생산은 최근 몇 년 동안 증가했다. She is an agrarian reformer. 그녀는 농지 개혁자이다.
333 □□	**allege** [əlédʒ]	This man alleges that his watch has been stolen. 이 사람은 자기 시계를 도난당했다고 주장한다. The two men allege that the police forced them to make false confessions. 그 두 남자는 경찰이 강제로 거짓 자백을 하게 강요했다고 주장한다.
334 □□	**amass** [əmǽs]	He would later amass a fortune from the small investment. 그는 그 작은 투자로 인해 후에 부를 모으게 될 것이다. He has amassed a lot of money by doing a casual business. 그는 뜨내기장사로 많은 돈을 모았다.
335 □□	**amorphous** [əmɔ́ːrfəs]	She was frightened by the amorphous mass which had floated in from the sea. 그녀는 바다에서 떠내려 온 무형의 덩어리를 보고 놀랐다. The musical composition, with no melodic pattern and no well-defined structure of development, seemed amorphous to my ear. 멜로디 형식이나 선명한 전개과정이 없는 이 곡은 내 귀에는 형식이 없는 것으로 들린다.

□ veneer _____   □ venerate _____   □ vicarious _____   □ vindictive _____

Definition	Meaning/Relation
꾸중을 하다	ⓥ to reprove gently but earnestly **admonish for** …에 대해 나무라다 **admonish** *sb.* **to do** *sth.* …에게 …하도록 권고하다
적수; 상대방	ⓝ enemy; an opponent
불가지[회의]론자	ⓝ one who believes that there can be no proof of the existence of god but does not deny the possibility that god exists
농업의, 농지의	ⓐ relating to or concerning the land and its ownership, cultivation, and tenure **(an) agrarian[land] reform** 농지 개혁
주장하다	ⓥ to state (a plea or excuse, for example) in support or denial of a claim or accusation
모으다	ⓥ to gather together for oneself, as for one's pleasure or profit **amass[accumulate, make] a fortune** 축재(蓄財)하다, 재산을 모으다 **amass riches** 부(재산)를 축적하다 **amass[accumulate, acquire, attain] wealth** 재산을 축적하다
무형의; 형식이 없는	ⓐ shapeless; lacking definite form **an amorphous mass of cells** 무정형의 세포 덩어리 **an amorphous organization** 무정형의 조직

329_335 113

PART 1

PART 2

PART 3

PART 4

PART 5

PART 6

□ visionary _____ □ wistful _____ □ wrath _____

NO.	Entry Word	Example Sentence	
336 ☐☐	**ample** [æmpl]	Ample opportunities were given. 기회가 충분히 주어졌다. There is ample room for another car. 차가 한 대 더 들어갈 공간은 충분히 있다.	
337 ☐☐	**amplify** [ǽmpləfài]	The technology exists to complement and amplify the human mind. 기술의 존재 이유는 인간의 두뇌를 보완하고 증폭시키는 것이다. A funeral can amplify the feelings of regret and loss for the relatives. 장례식은 친척들에게 후회와 상실의 감정을 증폭시킬 수 있다.	
338 ☐☐	**appall** [əpɔ́ːl]	It appalled me to see such sloppy work. 그처럼 조잡하게 일처리하는 것을 보고 나는 놀랐다. He was appalled by the multiplicity of details he had to complete before setting out on his mission. 임무를 수행하기 앞서 완성시켜야 했던 갖가지 세세한 것들에 그는 소름이 오싹했다.	
339 ☐☐	**arcane** [ɑːrkéin]	What was arcane to us was clear to the psychologist. 우리에게는 난해한 것들이 심리학자에게는 명백한 것들이었다. Many are still mired in local traditions, arcane regulations and rampant corruption. 많은 사람들이 아직 그 지방 특유의 전통과 난해한 규정들, 그리고 만연하는 부패의 늪에 빠져 있다.	
340 ☐☐	**artifice** [ɑ́ːrtəfis]	He used every artifice to win the game. 그는 게임에 이기기 위해 모든 속임수를 사용했다. His remorse is just an artifice to gain sympathy. 그의 후회는 동정을 얻기 위한 속임수일 뿐이다.	
341 ☐☐	**ascetic** [əsétik]	An ascetic monk meditates in front of a clay figure of the Buddha. 한 금욕적인 수도승이 진흙으로 만들어진 부처님 상 앞에서 명상을 한다. Her sister is extrovert and fun-loving, while she is ascetic and strict. 그녀가 금욕적이고 엄격한 반면, 그녀의 언니는 외향적이고 장난기가 있다.	
342 ☐☐	**assiduous** [əsídʒuəs]	The government has been assiduous in the fight against inflation. 정부는 인플레이션을 잡기 위해 지속적인 노력을 기울여 왔다. In the present, Koreans are well known to be extremely diligent, assiduous, and hardworking. 현재 한국 사람들은 매우 부지런하고 근면하며 열심히 일하는 것으로 알려져 있다.	

☐ admonish _____ ☐ adversary _____ ☐ agnostic _____

336_342 115

PART 1

PART 2

PART 3

PART 4

PART 5

PART 6

Definition	Meaning/Relation
충분한	ⓐ of large or great size, amount, extent, or capacity an ample[considerable, enormous, huge, large, tremendous] amount 막대한〔충분한, 엄청난〕양〔액수〕 an ample bosom 풍만한 가슴 ample facilities 충분한 설비| ample grounds 충분한 근거 ample opportunity 충분한 기회
증폭시키다	ⓥ to make larger or more powerful amplify the volume 음량을 증폭시키다
오싹하게 하다	ⓥ to fill with consternation or dismay
난해한	ⓐ known or understood by only a few
속임수	ⓝ an artful or crafty expedient; a stratagem employ[resort to] artifice 술책을 쓰다
금욕적인	ⓐ leading a life of self-discipline and self-denial, especially for spiritual improvement an ascetic[austere] life 금욕적〔엄격한〕 생활 the ascetic existence of monks and hermits 수도승과 은둔자의 금욕적 생활
지속적인; 근면한	ⓐ constant in application or attention; diligent

☐ agrarian _____ ☐ allege _____ ☐ amass _____ ☐ amorphous _____

NO.	Entry Word	Example Sentence
343 ☐☐	**asylum** [əsáiləm]	It supports the U.K.'s new global asylum and immigration strategy. 그것은 영국의 새로운 세계적인 보호시설과 이민 전략을 지지한다. Hundreds of African refugees, Israeli and foreign activists protested today calling for asylum. 수 백명의 아프리카 난민과 이스라엘과 해외 활동가들은 오늘 보호시설을 요구하면서 항의 시위를 했다.
344 ☐☐	**attest** [ətést]	The child's good health attests his mother's care. 그 아이가 건강한 것은 어머니가 잘 돌보고 있다는 것을 증명해준다. The Indian lore that's found in the Grand Canyon region attests to the Canyon's importance in human history. 그랜드 캐년 지역에서 전해 내려오는 인디안들의 이야기는 인류 역사에서 그랜드 캐년이 가지는 중요성을 증명해 준다.
345 ☐☐	**auspicious** [ɔːspíʃəs]	With favorable weather conditions, it was an auspicious moment to set sail. 기상 조건이 좋아서 항해하기 좋은 시간이었다. We felt that the campaign to elect Ellen captain was off to an auspicious beginning. Ellen을 회장에 당선시키려는 운동은 길조의 시작이라고 느꼈다.
346 ☐☐	**aversion** [əvə́ːrʒən]	I have an aversion to falsehood in any form. 어떤 거짓말이든 거짓말은 싫어한다. She has a deep aversion to getting up in the morning. 그녀는 아침에 일어나는 것에 대해 깊은 혐오감을 지니고 있다.
347 ☐☐	**avid** [ǽvid]	The dictator had an avid desire for power. 그 독재자는 권력에 대한 불타는 욕망을 가지고 있었다. She was an avid proponent of equal rights for immigrants. 그녀는 이민자의 동등한 권리를 열광적인 지지자이다.
348 ☐☐	**belittle** [bilítl]	Don't belittle yourself. 너 자신을 과소평가 하지 말아라. She felt belittled by her husband's arrogant behaviour. 그녀는 남편의 거만한 행동 때문에 부끄러워졌다.
349 ☐☐	**benefactor** [bénəfæ̀ktər]	He is looked up to as their benefactor. 그는 그들의 은인으로서 앙모를 받고 있다 An anonymous benefactor donated 2 million dollars. 한 익명의 은인이 2백만 달러를 기증했다.

☐ ample _____   ☐ amplify _____   ☐ appall _____   ☐ arcane _____

Definition	Meaning/Relation
보호시설	ⓝ an institution for the care of people, especially those with physical or mental impairments, who require organized supervision or assistance give[grant] asylum to ··· 에게 망명을 허용하다 ask for[seek] asylum 망명을 요청하다 receive asylum 망명을 허용받다 deny[refuse] *sb* asylum ···의 망명을 거절하다 political asylum 정치적 망명
증명하다	ⓥ to affirm to be correct, true, or genuine attest to ···을 입증하다
좋은; 길조의	ⓐ attended by favorable and propitious circumstances; promising future success an auspicious[promising] beginning 전조가 좋은 시작 an auspicious event 상서로운 사건 an auspicious[opportune] moment 상서로운 순간
싫음, 혐오	ⓝ a fixed, intense dislike and repugnance feel[have] an aversion to ···을 혐오하다 take an aversion to ···을 혐오하게 되다 a deep[deep-rooted, distinct, marked] aversion 뿌리깊은 혐오감 a natural aversion 당연한 반감 a pet aversion 가장 싫은 것〔사람〕 an aversion to ···을 싫어함
몹시 탐내는; 열광적인	ⓐ having an ardent desire or unbounded craving; marked by keen interest and enthusiasm avid for ···을 갈망하여
과소 평가하다	ⓥ to represent or speak of as contemptibly small or unimportant
은인	ⓝ one that gives aid, especially financial aid

□ artifice _____ □ ascetic _____ □ assiduous _____

NO.	Entry Word	Example Sentence	
350 ☐☐	**benevolent** [bənévələnt]	He was a benevolent old man; he wouldn't hurt a fly. 그는 인정 많은 노인이여서 파리 한 마리 해치려 하지 않았다. A benevolent fund is an amount of money used to help particular people in need. 자선기금이란 특히 곤궁에 처한 사람들을 돕는 데에 쓰이는 돈을 말한다.	
351 ☐☐	**bland** [blænd]	He said so with his face expanding in a bland smile. 얼굴에 부드러운 미소를 띄우며 그가 그렇게 말했다. The principal made a few bland comments about the value of education. 교장은 교육의 가치에 관해 몇 마디 부드러운 논평을 했다.	
352 ☐☐	**blatant** [bléitənt]	It is difficult to think of a more blatant example of unlawful sex discrimination. 불법적 성차별의 예로 이보다 너 노골직인 것을 생각하기 힘들다. A blatant example of the EU's warped foreign policy was with Algeria in 1992. EU의 왜곡된 외교정책 노골적인 예는 1992년 알제리와의 일이였다.	
353 ☐☐	**boon** [buːn]	They are entitled to enjoy such a boon. 그들은 그런 혜택을 누릴 자격이 있다. The airport construction will provide thousands of jobs for local workers, and will be a boon to our economy. 공항 공사는 수천 명의 지역 노동자들에게 직업을 제공해주고 우리 경제에는 커다란 이익을 가져다줄 것입니다.	
354 ☐☐	**brook** [bruk]	I cannot brook interference. 나는 간섭을 받으면 못 참는다. This problem doesn't brook a moment's delay. 이것은 분초를 다투는 문제이다.	
355 ☐☐	**cacophony** [kækáfəni]	As we entered the farmyard, we were met with a cacophony of animal sound. 농가 마당에 들어서자 동물들이 내는 불협화음이 우리를 맞았다. Some people seem to enjoy the cacophony of an orchestra that is tuning up. 일부 사람들은 연주 중에 나오는 불협화음을 즐기는 것처럼 보인다.	
356 ☐☐	**castigate** [kǽstəgèit]	The report castigates the general failure to make football grounds safe. 그 보도는 전반적으로 축구장을 안전하게 만들지 못한 것을 혹평하고 있다. In Gulliver's Travels and other books, Jonathan Swift castigated the human race for its follies and wickedness. Gulliver 여행기와 다른 책들에서 Jonathan Swift는 인간의 어리석음과 사악함에 대해서 인간을 혹평했다.	

☐ asylum _____ ☐ attest _____ ☐ auspicious _____

Definition	Meaning/Relation
인정 많은; 자선적인	ⓐ characterized by or suggestive of doing good; organized for the benefit of charity **benevolent towards** …에게 자애로운
부드러운	ⓐ characterized by a moderate, unperturbed, or tranquil quality **a bland diet** 담백한 음식 **a bland disposition** 붙임성이 좋은 성격
노골적인	ⓐ totally or offensively conspicuous or obtrusive **a blatant attempt** 노골적인 시도 **blatant discrimination** 노골적인 차별 **blatant disobedience** 노골적인 반항 (a) blatant[callous, complete, flagrant, total] disregard 완전 무시, 노골적인 무시 blatant[abysmal, appalling, complete, crass, profound, total] ignorance 완전 무지 (a) blatant[gross, rank] injustice 심한 부정 a blatant[bald-faced, barefaced, brazen] lie 뻔뻔스러운 거짓말
혜택, 이익	ⓝ a benefit bestowed, especially one bestowed in response to a request **a boon to** …에 대단히 유용한 것
참다	ⓥ to put up with **brook an insult** 모욕을 참다
불협화음	ⓝ jarring, discordant sound
혹평하다	ⓥ to criticize severely

☐ aversion _____ ☐ avid _____ ☐ belittle _____ ☐ benefactor _____

350_356 119

PART 1 PART 2 PART 3 PART 4 PART 5 PART 6

NO.	Entry Word	Example Sentence	
357 ☐☐	**cataclysm** [kǽtəklìzəm]	Only a cataclysm such as a flood or earthquake would stop this football match. 홍수나 지진같은 격변이 일어나야만 이 축구경기가 멈출 것이다. A cataclysm such as the French Revolution affects all countries. 프랑스혁명과 같은 대격변은 모든 나라에 영향을 미친다.	
358 ☐☐	**cipher** [sáifər]	As a former intelligent expert, he had information about enemy cipher. 전직 정보전문가로서 그는 적 암호에 관한 정보를 가지고 있었다. The science of breaking codes and ciphers without a key is called cryptanalysis. 아무런 실마리 없이 암호나 부호를 해독하는 기술은 암호 해독법이라고 불린다.	
359 ☐☐	**circumlocution** [sə̀ːrkəmloʊkjúːʃən]	Politicians are experts in circumlocution. 정치가들은 완곡한 표현의 전문가들이다. 'Economical with truth' is a circumlocution for 'lying.' '진실을 아낀다'는 말은 '거짓말한다'를 완곡하게 표현한 것이다.	
360 ☐☐	**compelling** [kəmpéliŋ]	I have no compelling reasons to refuse. 나는 거절할 강한 이유가 없다. Children said they went there by a compelling curiosity. 어린이들은 어쩔수없는 호기심에 이끌려 그곳에 갔다고 말했다.	
361 ☐☐	**concede** [kənsíːd]	We must concede that this is right. 우리는 이것이 옳다고 인정해야 한다. He finally conceded the election to his opponent. 그는 결국 상대 후보의 당선을 인정했다.	
362 ☐☐	**condone** [kəndóun]	If the government is seen to condone violence, the bloodshed will never stop. 만약 정부가 폭력을 용인하는 것으로 비친다면 유혈 참사는 결코 멈추지 않을 것이다. Corrupt politicians who condone the activities of the gamblers are equally culpable. 도박 행위를 눈감아 주는 타락한 정치인들도 똑같이 비난받아 마땅하다.	
363 ☐☐	**conflagration** [kɑ̀nfləgréiʃən]	Seven workers were killed and three others were injured in the conflagration. 그 화재에서 7명의 노동자가 사망하고 다른 3명이 부상을 당했다. In the conflagration that followed the 1906 earthquake, much of San Francisco was destroyed. 1906년의 지진에 따른 대화재에서 샌프란스시코의 상당 부분이 파괴되었다.	

☐ benevolent ＿＿＿＿＿＿ ☐ bland ＿＿＿＿＿＿ ☐ blatant ＿＿＿＿＿＿

Definition	Meaning/Relation
(정치적 · 사회적) 대격변	ⓝ a violent upheaval that causes great destruction or brings about a fundamental change
암호	ⓝ a cryptographic system in which units of plain text of regular length, usually letters, are arbitrarily transposed or substituted according to a predetermined code **break[solve] a cipher** 암호를 해독하다 **in cipher** 암호로
완곡한 표현	ⓝ a roundabout expression
강제적인, 저항할 수 없는	ⓐ drivingly forceful **a compelling argument** 저항할 수 없는 주장 **compelling circumstances** 부득이한 사정 **compelling[clear, cogent, convincing] evidence** 설득력이 있는(분명한) 증거
(마지못해) 인정하다	ⓥ to acknowledge, often reluctantly, as being true, just, or proper
용인하다	ⓥ to overlook, forgive, or disregard (an offense) without protest or censure
큰 화재	ⓝ a large, destructive fire **a major conflagration** 대화재

□ boon _____ □ brook _____ □ cacophony _____ □ castigate _____

NO.	Entry Word	Example Sentence	
364 ☐☐	**conjecture** [kəndʒéktʃər]	I will end all your conjectures. 나는 당신의 모든 추측을 종식시키고자 한다. It was based on a mere conjecture. 그것은 단순히 추측에 근거한 것이다.	
365 ☐☐	**contrive** [kəntràiv]	The company contrived a new kind of engine. 그 회사는 신형 엔진을 고안했다. She somehow contrived to arrange a meeting. 그녀는 이리저리 하여 간신히 모임을 주선했다.	
366 ☐☐	**convert** [kənvə́ːrt]	To convert dried peas and beans into an edible food they must first be soaked. 마른 완두콩과 일반 콩을 먹을 수 있는 식품으로 바꾸려면 우선 물에 푹 담가야 한다. The missionary went to Africa to convert people to Christianity. 그 선교사는 사람들을 기독교로 개종시키기 위해 아프리카로 갔다.	
367 ☐☐	**cordial** [kɔ́ːrdʒəl]	Relations between the two leaders are said to be cordial. 두 지도자 사이의 관계는 진심에서 우러나온 관계라고들 한다. Our hosts greeted us at the airport with a cordial welcome and a hearty hug. 마중 나온 사람들은 공항에서 진심에서 우러나오는 환영과 포옹으로 우리에게 인사했다.	
368 ☐☐	**corrosive** [kəróusiv]	This acid is highly corrosive so be careful with it. 이 산은 매우 부식성이 높으므로 다룰 때 조심하시오. The new compound's resistance to corrosive chemicals is only fair. 새 화합물의 부식물에 대한 저항력도 보통 수준이다.	
369 ☐☐	**crass** [kræs]	It was crass of him to ask how much you earn. 그가 너에게 얼마나 버느냐고 묻다니 참 아둔한 짓이었다. The philosophers deplored the crass commercialism. 그 철학자들은 아둔한 상업주의를 비난했다.	
370 ☐☐	**cryptic** [kríptik]	I found a scrap of paper with a cryptic message saying 'The time has come.' '그 시간이 왔다'라는 내용의 비밀 같은 메시지를 담은 종이 쪽지를 나는 발견했다. I can't understand the problem because the message is too vague or cryptic. 나는 메시지가 너무 모호하거나 비밀스러워서 문제를 이해할 수 없습니다.	

☐ cataclysm _____   ☐ cipher _____   ☐ circumlocution _____

Definition	Meaning/Relation
추측	ⓝ inference or judgment based on inconclusive or incomplete evidence **hazard a conjecture** 어림짐작하다 **pure conjecture** 순전한 추측
고안하다; 간신히 …하다	ⓥ to plan with cleverness or ingenuity; to manage **a contrived plot** 부자연스러운〔무리해서 쓴〕 줄거리
바꾸다; 개종하다	ⓥ to change (something) into another form, substance, state, or product; transform; to persuade or induce to adopt a particular religion, faith, or belief **convert from** ···에서 개종하다 **convert to** ···으로 개종하다 **gain a convert** 개종자를 만들다 **a convert to** ···로의 개종자
진심에서 우러나오는	ⓐ warm and sincere **a cordial welcome** 따뜻한 환영
부식하는	ⓐ having the capability or tendency to cause corrosion **corrosive acid** 부식성의 산
아둔한	ⓐ so crude and unrefined as to be lacking in discrimination and sensibility
비밀스런	ⓐ having hidden and mystifying meaning **a cryptic comment** 애매한 발언 **a cryptic[secret] message** 비밀 메시지 **a cryptic[puzzling] remark** 수수께끼 같은〔알쏭달쏭한〕 말

☐ compelling _____ ☐ concede _____ ☐ condone _____ ☐ conflagration _____

NO.	Entry Word	Example Sentence	
371 ☐☐	**curtail** [kə:rtéil]	We must try to curtail our spending. 우리는 지출을 줄이도록 해야 한다. Do you think it will be necessary to curtail production? 생산량을 줄이는 것이 필요하다고 생각하세요?	
372 ☐☐	**deference** [défərəns]	You must always show deference to older people. 어른들께 항상 존경을 표해야 한다. He treats his mother with as much deference as if she were the Queen. 그는 자기 어머니를 마치 여왕인 것처럼 최대의 존경을 다해 대했다.	
373 ☐☐	**deft** [deft]	She is deft at dealing with administrators. 그녀는 행정 관리들을 다루는 데 능숙하다. He's very deft at handling awkward situations. 그는 거북한 상황을 다루는 데 아주 능숙하다.	
374 ☐☐	**deleterious** [dèlətíəriəs]	Workers in nuclear research must avoid the deleterious effects of radioactive substances. 핵연구소에서 일하는 사람들은 방사능 물질이 끼칠 수 있는 유해한 영향을 피해야만 한다. These drugs have a proven deleterious effect on the nervous system. 이 약들은 신경계에 증명된 유해 효과를 가진다.	
375 ☐☐	**depose** [dipóuz]	The king was deposed in a military coup. 그 왕은 군사 쿠데타로 퇴위했다. The army attempted to depose the king and set up a military government. 군대는 왕을 퇴위시키고 군사정부를 세우려고 했다.	
376 ☐☐	**didactic** [daidǽktik]	The didactic qualities of his poetry overshadow its literary qualities. 시의 교훈적 내용 때문에 문학적 우수성의 빛이 바랬다. I don't like her didactic way of explaining everything. 나는 그녀가 모든 것을 설명하는 가르치려 하는 방식이 싫다.	
377 ☐☐	**dire** [daiər]	He responded to the parliamentary pressure with vague threats of unspecified dire action. 그는 의회의 압력에 대해 구체적으로 밝히지 않은 무서운 행동을 취하겠다는 막연한 협박으로 응수했다. It was stressed that drastic measures were needed to cope with the dire financial situation. 극심한 재정난에 대처하기 위해서는 긴급한 조치가 필요하다는 점이 강조되었다.	

☐ conjecture _____   ☐ contrive _____   ☐ convert _____

Definition	Meaning/Relation
줄이다	ⓥ to cut short curtail[end, terminate] discussions 회담을 끝내다 curtail[curb, cut down (on), reduce] expenditures 경비를 절감하다 curtail[curb, cut down (on), reduce] expenses 비용을 줄이다
존경	ⓝ courteous respect show deference to …에게 경의를 표하다 blind deference 맹종
능숙한	ⓐ quick and skillful deft at …에 능숙한〔능란한〕
유해한	ⓐ having a harmful effect deleterious to …에 유해한
퇴위시키다	ⓥ to remove from office or power depose from …에서 물러나게 하다〔퇴위시키다〕
교훈적인; 가르치려 하는	ⓐ intended to instruct; inclined to teach or moralize excessively
무서운; 긴박한	ⓐ warning of or having dreadful or terrible consequences; urgent a dire[crushing, grave, great] calamity 대참사 dire [disastrous] consequences 비참한 결과 an dire[absolute] necessity 절대적인 필수품

□ cordial _____ □ corrosive _____ □ crass _____ □ cryptic _____

371_377 125

PART 1

PART 2

PART 3

PART 4

PART 5

PART 6

NO.	Entry Word	Example Sentence
378 ☐☐	**disclaim** [diskléim]	We disclaim all responsibility for this disaster. 우리는 이 재난에 대한 모든 책임을 부인한다. If I grant you this privilege, will you disclaim all other rights? 내가 당신에게 이 특권을 주면 당신은 모든 권리를 포기할 것인가?
379 ☐☐	**disclose** [disklóuz]	GM did not disclose details of the agreement. GM은 계약에 관한 세부사항을 공개하지 않았다. He opened the box, disclosing its contents to the audience. 그가 상자를 열어 관중들에게 내용물을 공개했다.
380 ☐☐	**discomfit** [diskʌmfit]	This ruse will discomfit the enemy. 이 계략은 적을 당황케 할 것이다. She was not in the least discomfited by the large number of press photographers. 그녀는 많은 신문기자들 앞에서도 전혀 당황하지 않았다.
381 ☐☐	**disconcert** [dìskənsə́ːrt]	It disconcerted us to learn that they had refused our offer. 그들이 우리 제의를 거절했다는 것을 알고 우리는 걱정했다. He was disconcerted to find the other guests formally dressed. 그는 다른 손님들이 정장을 입은 것을 알고 걱정했다.
382 ☐☐	**disinterested** [disíntəristid]	The umpire makes disinterested decisions. 그 심판은 사심 없는 판정을 내린다. I am confident that you will give me a disinterested opinion. 너라면 사심 없는 의견을 말해줄 것이라고 나는 확신한다.
383 ☐☐	**dissent** [disént]	In the recent Supreme Court decision, Justice Marshall dissented from the majority opinion. 최근 최고 재판소 판결에서 마르셀 판사는 대다수 의견과 다른 의견을 냈다. Nobody can express dissent on the prosecution's decision to enhance protection of the rights of suspects. 피의자의 인권보호를 강화하려는 검찰의 결정에 대해 아무도 이의를 제기할 수는 없다.
384 ☐☐	**dissipate** [dísəpèit]	This aroma may dissipate after a short period of time. 이 냄새는 시간이 좀 지나면 없어질 것입니다. The young man quickly dissipated his inheritance and was soon broke. 그 청년은 그의 유산을 낭비하여 곧 파산했다.

☐ curtail _____   ☐ deference _____   ☐ deft _____

PART 1

PART 2

PART 3

PART 4

PART 5

PART 6

Definition	Meaning/Relation
부인하다; 포기하다	ⓥ to deny or renounce any claim to or connection with; to give one's right disclaim[abdicate, abandon, dodge, evade, shirk] (a) responsibility 책임을 회피하다
공개하다	ⓥ to expose to view, as by removing a cover
당황하게 하다	ⓥ to make uneasy or perplexed
걱정하게 하다	ⓥ to make feel doubt and anxiety
사심 없는	ⓐ free of bias and self-interest a disinterested party (이해관계가 없는) 제3자
의견이 다르다; 의견의 차이	ⓥ to differ in opinion from ⓝ diflerence of opinion or feeling express dissent 이의를 제기하다
없어지다; 낭비하다	ⓥ to drive away; to spend or expend intemperately or wastefully dissipate *sb's* energy ⋯의 정력을 낭비하다 dissipate[run through, spend, squander] a fortune 재산을 낭비하다 dissipate[squander] wealth 재산을 낭비하다

☐ deleterious _____ ☐ depose _____ ☐ didactic _____ ☐ dire _____

NO.	Entry Word	Example Sentence
385 ☐☐	**dormant** [dɔ́ːrmənt]	The long-dormant volcano has recently shown signs of life. 그 장기 휴면 화산이 최근에 활동하고 있다는 신호를 보여 주었다. So long as the local government lacks the necessary funds, this worthwhile project will have to remain dormant. 지방 정부가 필요한 기금이 없는 한 이 훌륭한 계획은 휴면상태로 남아 있어야 할 것이다.
386 ☐☐	**ebullient** [ibúljənt]	Our ebullient host couldn't stop laughing and talking. 우리의 활기찬 사회자는 웃고 말하는 것을 멈출 수 없었다. The president has been in an ebullient mood since he took the oath of office in February. 대통령은 2월에 취임한 이래 활기에 넘치고 있다.
387 ☐☐	**elicit** [ilísit]	The questionnaire was intended to elicit information on eating habits. 그 설문지는 식습관에 대한 정보를 끌어내려는 의도였다. Ms. Mizote is so accomplished a teacher that she can elicit some degree of interest and attention from even the most withdrawn children. Mizote여사는 매우 훌륭한 교사이기 때문에 가장 수줍어하는 학생들에게서도 어느 정도의 흥미와 주의를 끌어낼 수 있다.
388 ☐☐	**embellish** [imbéliʃ]	His writing was embellished with flourishes. 그의 글은 미사 여구들로 꾸며졌다. He admits that he embellished the account of events originally given to him. 그는 원래 자신에게 주어진 사건 설명을 꾸몄음을 인정하고 있다.
389 ☐☐	**eminent** [émənənt]	He produced eminent achievements. 그는 뛰어난 업적을 쌓았다. He is an eminent philosopher and mathematician. 그는 뛰어난 철학자이자 수학자이다.
390 ☐☐	**enmity** [énməti]	He has enmity against me. 그는 나에게 원한을 품고 있다. There is bitter enmity between them. 그들은 견원지간이다.
391 ☐☐	**ephemeral** [ifémərəl]	Fame in the world of rock and pop is largely ephemeral. 록과 팝 음악계의 명성은 대체로 덧없는 것이다. But how, given the kaleidoscopic nature of contemporary world affairs, are we to distinguish the important from the ephemeral? 그러나 만화경처럼 변화무쌍한 현 세계 정세에서 덧없는 것과 중요한 것을 어떻게 구별할 것인가?

☐ disclaim _____   ☐ disclose _____   ☐ discomfit _____   ☐ disconcert _____

Definition	Meaning/Relation
휴면 상태의	ⓐ inactive lie[remain, stay] dormant 동면 중이다, 정지하고 있다, 휴면 상태이다
활기찬	ⓐ zestfully enthusiastic an ebullient mood 열광적인 분위기
끌어내다	ⓥ to bring or draw out (something latent) elicit from …에서 이끌어내다
(문장을) 꾸미다	ⓥ to make a story embellish with …으로 꾸미다[윤색하다]
뛰어난	ⓐ towering or standing out above others eminent as …로서 명망있는 eminent in …에 있어서 명망이 있는
원한, 증오	ⓝ deep-seated, often mutual hatred stir up enmity 증오심을 자극하다 have[harbor, cherish] enmity against *sb.* …에게 적의를 품다 incur *sb's* enmity …의 증오를 초래하다 (a) bitter enmity 심한 증오 (a) longstanding enmity 오랜 증오[반목] enmity against[towards] …에 대한 적의 enmity between[among] …사이의 반목
덧없는	ⓐ lasting for a markedly brief time

☐ disinterested _____ ☐ dissent _____ ☐ dissipate _____

385_391 129

PART 1

PART 2

PART 3

PART 4

PART 5

PART 6

NO.	Entry Word	Example Sentence
392 ☐☐	**esoteric** [èsətérik]	She has a rather esoteric taste in clothes. 그녀는 다소 난해한 의상 취향을 가지고 있다. Vallee summarized this esoteric hypothesis by stating: It could enlist the resources of leading corporations. Vallee는 그것은 선도 기업의 자원을 기재할 수 있다라고 말함으로써 이 난해한 가설을 요약했다.
393 ☐☐	**evanescent** [èvənésənt]	Life is as evanescent as morning dew. 인생은 초로와 같이 무상하다. The evanescent post-war economic boom was quickly followed by a deep recession. 점점 사라져가는 경제 호황 뒤에 깊은 경기 침체가 빠르게 이어졌다.
394 ☐☐	**exalt** [igzɔ́ːlt]	The poor will be exalted. 가난한 사람들은 신분이 높아질 것이다. He was exalted as a pillar of the community. 그는 지역사회의 기둥이라고 칭송받았다.
395 ☐☐	**exhort** [igzɔ́ːrt]	The teacher kept exhorting us to work harder. 선생님은 우리들에게 더 열심히 공부하라고 계속 타일렀다. The chairman exhorted the party workers to action. 의장이 당 노동자들에게 행동하도록 촉구했다.
396 ☐☐	**exonerate** [igzɑ́nərèit]	We exonerated him from[of] an accusation. 우리는 그의 혐의를 벗겼다. A commission of inquiry exonerated him. 조사위원회가 (그 사건에 대한 모든 책임에 대해) 그의 혐의를 벗겨 주었다.
397 ☐☐	**extant** [ekstǽnt]	Medieval customs are extant in some parts of Europe. 중세의 관습이 유럽 일부 지역에 남아 있다. Although the authorities suppressed the book; many copies are extant and may be purchased at exorbitant prices. 당국은 그 책의 발행을 금지시켰지만 많은 복사판이 남아 있어서 매우 비싼 가격에 구입이 가능할지 모른다.
398 ☐☐	**exult** [igzʌ́lt]	The nation exulted at the team's success. 그 팀의 성공에 전 국민이 크게 기뻐했다. Crowds exulted when victory was announced. 승리가 발표되자 군중이 크게 기뻐했다.

☐ dormant _____ ☐ ebullient _____ ☐ elicit _____ ☐ embellish _____

392_398 131

PART 1

PART 2

PART 3

PART 4

PART 5

PART 6

Definition	Meaning/Relation
난해한	ⓐ intended for or understood by only a particular group
무상한, 사라져가는	ⓐ vanishing or likely to vanish like vapor
(지위 · 명예 등을) 높이다; 칭송하다	ⓥ to raise or elevate in rank, character, or status; to praise
타이르다; 촉구하다	ⓥ to urge by strong, often stirring argument, admonition, advice, or appeal **exhort to** …하도록 타이르다
혐의를 벗기다	ⓥ to free from blame or criminal charge **exonerate from** …에서 해방하다, …을 면제하다
남아 있는	ⓐ still in existence
크게 기뻐하다	ⓥ to rejoice greatly **exult at[in, over]** …에 크게 기뻐하다

☐ eminent _____ ☐ enmity _____ ☐ ephemeral _____

NO.	Entry Word	Example Sentence	
399 ☐☐	**fabricate** [fǽbrikèit]	Stop fabricating a story. 빗대지 마라 Belgian scouts fabricated eco-paper during the International Scout Camp "Kanderjam." 벨기에 스타우트들은 국제 스카우트 캠프 "Kandrjam" 기간 동안 환경보고서를 작성했다.	
400 ☐☐	**feign** [fein]	He feigned himself (to be) mad. 그는 미친 체했다. However much I asked, he persisted in feigning ignorance. 아무리 물어봐도 그는 모른다고 잡아뗐다.	
401 ☐☐	**finesse** [finés]	It was a disappointing performance which lacked finesse. 그것은 섬세한 기교가 떨어지는 실망스러운 공연이었다. Though being young, he showed finesse in dealing with people. 어린 나이에도 불구하고 그는 사람을 다루는 데 뛰어난 솜씨를 보여 주었다.	
402 ☐☐	**forgo** [fɔːrgóu]	The workers agreed to forgo a pay increase for the sake of greater job security. 그 노동자들은 더 큰 직업 안정을 위해 임금 인상을 포기하기로 동의했다. At noon he got tired but decided to forgo his nap. 오후에 그는 피곤하였지만 낮잠을 포기하기로 했다.	
403 ☐☐	**garner** [gáːrnər]	Fire Balls garnered an unexpected following. Fire Balls은 뜻밖의 지지자들을 얻었다. The Socialist party won no seats as none of their candidates garnered more than 5% of the vote. 사회당은 후보자 중 단 한 명도 5% 이상 표를 얻지 못했기 때문에 한 석도 획득하지 못했다.	
404 ☐☐	**gratuitous** [grətjúːətəs]	A lot of viewers complained that there was too much gratuitous sex and violence in the film. 많은 관객들이 그 영화에는 불필요한 섹스와 폭력 장면이 지나치게 많이 나온다고 불평했다. Since you've never seen me play tennis, your assumption that you can beat me is quite gratuitous. 내가 테니스 하는 것을 본 적이 없으니까 당신이 나를 이기리라는 생각은 전혀 근거가 없다.	
405 ☐☐	**hamper** [hǽmpər]	Our progress was hampered by the bad weather. 우리의 진행은 나쁜 날씨로 방해를 받았다. He's hampered by a lack of tools. 그는 연장 부족으로 일에 지장을 받고 있다.	

☐ esoteric _____ ☐ evanescent _____ ☐ exalt _____

Definition	Meaning/Relation
꾸며내다; 만들다	ⓥ to forge; to make **fabricate[concoct , cook up, trump up] a charge** 혐의를 날조하다 **a fabricated[baseless, false, trumped-up] charge** 무고, 근거없는 혐의 **fabricate [falsify, trump up] evidence** 증거를 조작하다
…인체하다	ⓥ to give a false appearance of **feign death** 죽은 체하다 **feign[affect] indifference** 무관심한 척하다
기교, 솜씨	ⓝ refinement and delicacy of performance, execution, or artisanship
포기하다	ⓥ to sacrifice something **forgo a pleasure** 유희를 삼가다
얻다, 획득하다	ⓥ to gather and store in or as if in a granary
불필요한; 근거없는	ⓐ unnecessary or unwarranted; unjustified **a gratuitous insult** 이유없는 모욕
방해하다	ⓥ to prevent the free movement, action, or progress of **hamper in** …을 저지하다

□ exhort _____   □ exonerate _____   □ extant _____   □ exult _____

NO.	Entry Word	Example Sentence	
406 ☐☐	**humane** [hju:méin]	The humane treatment of prisoners is claimed. 죄수의 인도적인 대우가 요구되고 있다. The new prison governor is much more humane than his predecessor. 새로운 간수장은 전임자보다 훨씬 더 인도적이다.	
407 ☐☐	**humid** [hjú:mid]	New York is very hot and humid in the summer. 뉴욕은 여름에 매우 덥고 습하다. The air felt humid and oppressive, saturated with heat and moisture. 열과 습기로 가득한 공기는 습하고 숨이 막힐 듯했다.	
408 ☐☐	**immutable** [immjú:təbəl]	Scientists are constantly seeking to discover the immutable laws of nature. 과학자들은 불변의 자연 법칙을 발견하려고 계속 노력하고 있다. Some people regard grammar as an immutable set of rules that must be obeyed. 어떤 사람들은 문법을 반드시 지켜야 할 불변의 규칙으로 여긴다.	
409 ☐☐	**impeccable** [impékəbəl]	Although French is her native language, she speaks with an impeccable English accent. 그녀의 모국어는 프랑스어이지만 영어 억양이 완벽하다. Each dish is surprising and delightful, the wine's impeccable. 음식 하나하나가 다 놀라울 정도로 맛있으며, 와인 역시 나무랄 데가 없습니다.	
410 ☐☐	**impending** [impéndiŋ]	Let's discuss the impending matter first. 우선 시급한 문제부터 협의합시다. The entire country was saddened by the news of his impending death. 전국은 그의 임박한 임종 소식으로 슬픔에 빠졌다.	
411 ☐☐	**impenetrable** [impénətrəbəl]	The fortifications of the castle were massive and impenetrable. 성의 방어가 굳세어 도저히 꿰뚫을 수 없었다. To Watson, the mystery was impenetrable. Watson에게 그 미스터리는 이해가 되지 않았다.	
412 ☐☐	**impetuous** [impétʃuəs]	Don't be so impetuous! 그렇게 성급하게 굴지 마라! We tried to curb his impetuous behavior because we felt that in his haste he might offend some people. 성급해서 몇몇 사람들을 화나게 만들 수 있다고 생각했기 때문에 우리는 그의 성급한 행동을 자제시키려 했다.	

☐ fabricate _____   ☐ feign _____   ☐ finesse _____   ☐ forgo _____

Definition	Meaning/Relation
인도적인	ⓐ characterized by kindness, mercy, or compassion
습한	ⓐ containing or characterized by a high amount of water or water vapor **humid air** 눅눅한 공기 **a humid climate** 습한 기후 **humid[muggy] weather** 푹푹 찌는(후텁지근한) 날씨
불변의	ⓐ not subject or susceptible to change
완벽한, 나무랄 데 없는	ⓐ having no flaws **an impeccable[irreproachable, stainless, unblemished] character** 나무랄(흠잡을) 데가 없는 성격 **impeccable[excellent, sound] credentials** 우수한 자격 **a impeccable[clean, spotless, unblemished] record** 깨끗한 경력 **an impeccable[enviable, excellent, fine, good, spotless, unblemished, unsullied, untainted, untarnished] reputation** 훌륭한(좋은) 평판
시급한, 임박한	ⓐ (usually of something unpleasant) about to happen **an impending crisis** 절박한 위기 **(an) impending[imminent, immediate] danger** 바로 눈 앞에 닥친 위험 **an impending disaster** 임박한 재난 **impending doom** 임박한 종말 **impending hostilities** 임박한(곧 있을) 교전
꿰뚫을 수 없는; 이해할 수 없는	ⓐ impossible to penetrate or enter; not capable of being understood **an impenetrable[airtight, adequate] defense** 적절한(완벽한) 방어(수비) **an impenetrable forest** 앞이 안보이게 울창한 숲 **an impenetrable[impregnable, strong] fortress** 난공불락의 요새
성급한	ⓐ characterized by sudden and forceful energy or emotion

□ garner _____   □ gratuitous _____   □ hamper _____

413 ☐☐	**incidental** [ìnsədéntl]	Try not to be distracted by trivial incidental details. 사소한 부수적 세부사항에 주의를 뺏기지 않도록 하시오. His success was not incidental. 그의 성공은 우연이 아니었다.
414 ☐☐	**incisive** [insáisiv]	His novels are somehow incisive. 그의 소설은 어딘가 예리한 데가 있다. In the Lincoln-Douglas debates, Lincoln asked a few incisive questions. Lincoln과 Douglas의 토론에서 Lincoln은 몇 가지 예리한 질문을 했다.
415 ☐☐	**incongruous** [inkáŋgruəs]	Such traditional methods seem incongruous in this modern technical age. 그러한 전통적인 방법은 이러한 현대의 과학적인 시대에는 어울리지 않는 것처럼 보인다. The modern building looked incongruous in that quaint old village. 그 현대적인 건물은 흉칙스럽고 오랜 마을에서 어울리지 않았다.
416 ☐☐	**incontrovertible** [ìnkɑntrəvɔ́ːrtəbəl]	It is incontrovertible that they have made a mistake. 그들이 실수를 했다는 것에는 논의할 여지가 없다. We must yield to the incontrovertible evidence which you have presented and free your client. 당신이 제시한 명백한 증거를 받아들여서 당신의 변호 의뢰인을 풀어주고자 한다.
417 ☐☐	**incredulous** [inkrédʒələs]	The incredulous judge refused to accept the statement of the defendant. 의심 많은 판사는 피고의 진술을 받아들이지 않았다. The scientists were incredulous when they heard that research funding was to stop. 과학자들은 연구 자금 조달이 중단될 거라는 얘기를 들었을 때 쉽사리 믿지 않았다.
418 ☐☐	**incumbent** [inkΛmbənt]	It is incumbent on you to do it. 그것을 하는 것은 당신의 책임이다. The incumbent president faces problems which begun many years before he took office. 현직 대통령은 그가 취임하기 여러 해 전 시작된 문제에 직면해 있다.
419 ☐☐	**indigenous** [indídʒənəs]	The indigenous medical traditions in the area make extensive use of plants. 그 지역의 토착 전통 의학은 식물을 다방면에 걸쳐 이용한다. Tobacco is one of the indigenous plants which the early explorers found in this country. 담배는 초기 탐험가들이 이 나라에서 발견한 고유한 토착 식물 중의 하나다.

☐ humane _____   ☐ humid _____   ☐ immutable _____   ☐ impeccable _____

Definition	Meaning/Relation
(…에) 부수하여 일어나는; 우연히	ⓐ of a minor, casual, or subordinate nature; occurring or likely to occur as an unpredictable or minor accompaniment **incidental to** …에 부수적인
예리한	ⓐ penetrating, clear, and sharp, as in operation or expression
어울리지 않는	ⓐ lacking in harmony **incongruous with** …와 어울리지 않는
논의할 여지없는; 명백한	ⓐ impossible to dispute; unquestionable a **incontrovertible**[cold, dry, hard, incontestable, indisputable, irrefutable, proven, undeniable, unquestionable] fact 엄연한(명백한) 사실 **incontrovertible logic** 명백한 논리
의심 많은	ⓐ skeptical
책임인; 현직의	ⓐ imposed as an obligation or a duty; currently holding a specified office **incumbent on**[upon] …에게 의무로 지워지는 **unseat an incumbent** 현직에서 내쫓다(낙선시키다)
토착의	ⓐ originating and growing or living in an area or environment **indigenous to** …에 있어서 고유한

PART 1
PART 2
PART 3
PART 4
PART 5
PART 6

☐ impending _____ ☐ impenetrable _____ ☐ impetuous _____

NO.	Entry Word	Example Sentence	
420 ☐☐	**indulgent** [indʌ́ldʒənt]	He is indulgent toward others. 그는 남에게 관대하다. His indulgent mother was willing to let him do anything. 그의 관대한 어머니는 그가 어떤 일이든지 하도록 기꺼이 허락했다.	
421 ☐☐	**ineffable** [inéfəbəl]	Such ineffable joy must be experienced; it cannot be described. 그런 형언할 수 없는 기쁨은 직접 경험해 봐야 한다. 그것은 말로써 설명될 수 없다. Visiting Aceh, the area severely damaged by the Tsunami, gave me ineffable grief and concern. 쓰나미 때문에 피해가 심했던 Aceh를 방문했을 때 나는 말로 설명할 수 없는 슬픔과 우려를 느꼈다.	
422 ☐☐	**innocuous** [inάkjuːəs]	Some mushrooms look innocuous but are in fact poisonous. 어떤 버섯들은 해가 없어 보이지만 실제로는 독성이 있다. I made a perfectly innocuous remark and he got most upset. 나는 말을 불쾌감을 주지 않는 말을 했지만 그는 화가 많이 났다	
423 ☐☐	**insidious** [insídiəs]	You'd be better careful of his insidious character. 당신은 그의 교활한 성격을 조심하는 것이 좋을 것이다. The fifth column is insidious because it works secretly within our territory for our defeat. 반역자들은 우리의 패배를 위해 우리의 영역 내에서 은밀히 일하기 때문에 교활하다.	
424 ☐☐	**insipid** [insípid]	I am bored by your insipid talk. 나는 당신의 지루한 이야기에 싫증을 느낀다. Why anyone buys music with such insipid lyrics is a mystery. 왜 사람들이 그런 지루한 가사가 담긴 음악을 사는지가 수수께끼이다.	
425 ☐☐	**instigate** [ínstəgèit]	They instigated a rebellion. 그들은 반란을 유발시켰다. I'm afraid that this statement will instigate a revolt. 나는 이러한 진술이 반역을 조장할까봐 두렵다.	
426 ☐☐	**insular** [ínsələr]	Japan is an insular country. 일본은 섬나라입니다. Theirs is a very insular culture, protected as it is from outside influences. 그들의 문화는 외부의 영향으로부터 보호받아 온 편협한 문화였다.	

☐ incidental _____ ☐ incisive _____ ☐ incongruous _____ ☐ incontrovertible _____

PART 1
PART 2
PART 3
PART 4
PART 5
PART 6

Definition	Meaning/Relation
관대한	ⓐ characterized by, being favorable **indulgent to[towards]** …에 관대한, …을 눈감아 주는
형언할 수 없는, 말로 설명할 수 없는	ⓝ incapable of being expressed
해(독)이 없는; 불쾌감을 주지않는	ⓐ having no adverse effect; not likely to offend or provoke to strong emotion
교활한	ⓥ unpleasant or dangerous and develops gradually without being noticed **an insidious[avowed, bitter, deadly, implacable, arch, irreconcilable, mortal, relentless, sworn, vicious] enemy** 불구대천의 원수
지루한	ⓐ lacking flavor, zest, excitement, stimulation, or interest
유발시키다; 조장하다	ⓥ to urge on; to stir up **instigate *sb.* to do *sth.*** …을 선동하여 …하게 하다
섬의; 편협한	ⓐ of, relating to, or constituting an island; circumscribed and detached in outlook and experience

☐ incredulous _____　☐ incumbent _____　☐ indigenous _____

NO.	Entry Word	Example Sentence	
427 ☐☐	**intrinsic** [intrínsik]	The job is of little intrinsic interest. 그 일은 본질적인 흥미 요소가 거의 없다. It is immoral to treat animals as if they had no intrinsic value. 동물들을 아무런 고유의 가치가 없는 것처럼 다루는 것은 부도덕한 일이다.	
428 ☐☐	**intrude** [intrú:d]	Don't intrude yourself on her privacy. 그녀의 사생활에 끼어들지 마시오. Newspapers should not intrude on people's private grief. 신문 보도가 사람들의 사적인 슬픔을 침해해서는 안 된다.	
429 ☐☐	**invoke** [invóuk]	Invoking morality on this occasion would not be appropriate. 이 상황에서 도덕성에 호소하는 것은 적절치 않을 것이다. She invoked her advisor's aid in filling out her financial aid forms. 그녀는 자신의 지도 교수에게 자신의 재정 보조 양식을 작성하는데 도와 달라고 호소했다.	
430 ☐☐	**laborious** [ləbɔ́:riəs]	Writing books is a laborious task. 책쓰기는 힘든 일이다. Checking the entire report for mistakes was a laborious business. 실수를 찾아내기 위해 전체 보고서를 다 검토하는 것은 힘든 일이었다.	
431 ☐☐	**loath** [louθ]	He is loath to go in there. 그는 그곳에 가기를 싫어한다. She'd be loath to admit it but she doesn't really want to go away for the weekend. 자신은 인정하기 싫겠지만, 그녀는 주말에 집을 떠나 있고 싶은 마음이 별로 없었다.	
432 ☐☐	**luminous** [lú:mənəs]	The east grows faintly luminous. 동쪽이 빤하게 트였다. You should always wear luminous clothing when riding a bicycle at night. 밤에 자전거를 탈 때에는 언제나 야광옷을 입어야 한다.	
433 ☐☐	**marshal** [mɑ́:rʃəl]	Many marshals did not get any regular pay. 많은 보안관들은 정규적인 봉급을 받지 않았다. Marshal Red Lucas, who lived to be the oldest marshal in Oklahoma, made 3,600 arrests and never had to kill a single outlaw. 오클라호마에서 가장 오랫동안 보안관으로 살았던 레드 루카스 보안관은 3,600명을 체포를 했고 한 명의 무법자도 결코 죽인 일이 없다.	

☐ indulgent _____   ☐ ineffable _____   ☐ innocuous _____

Definition	Meaning/Relation
고유한	ⓐ of or relating to the essential nature of a thing **intrinsic in[to]** …에 내재된
(남의 일에) 끼어들다; 침입하다	ⓥ to come in rudely or inappropriately **intrude into** …을 침입하다 **intrude on[upon]** …을 침해하다
호소하다	ⓥ to appeal to or cite in support or justification **invoke authority** 권한을 내세우다 **invoke[impose] cloture** 토론 종결 절차를 강행(발동)하다 **invoke [plead, take] the Fifth** 묵비권을 행사하다
힘든	ⓐ hard-working and industrious **diligent[laborious, painstaking] research** 공들인 연구(조사)
싫어하는	ⓐ unwilling or reluctant
빛을 내는, 야광의	ⓐ glowing in the dark emitting light, especially emitting self-generated light
(연방) 보안관	ⓝ a U.S. federal officer of a judicial district who carries out court orders and discharges duties similar to those of a sheriff **an air marshal** 공군 원수 **a field marshal** 육군 원수

□ insidious _____ □ insipid _____ □ instigate _____ □ insular _____

NO.	Entry Word	Example Sentence	
434 ☐☐	**meager** [mí:gər]	She was a small, meager woman. 그녀는 작고 마른 여자였다. The refugees, clutching their meager possessions, wait some more to find out if they will be allowed to partake of the American Dream. 난민들은 보잘것없는 소지품을 부둥켜 안고, 자신들을 아메리칸 드림에 동참하게 해 줄 것인지를 알아보기 위해 좀 더 기다리고 있다.	
435 ☐☐	**mediate** [mí:dièit]	Let us mediate our differences rather than engage in a costly strike. 희생이 심한 파업을 하기보다 서로간의 차이를 조정해 보자. The teachers and parents couldn't agree and she had to mediate between them. 교사들과 부모들이 의견의 일치를 볼 수 없었기에 그녀가 그들 사이를 중재해야만 했다.	
436 ☐☐	**nefarious** [nifέəriəs]	Could resale price maintenance deals be used for nefarious purposes? 재판매 가격 유지 거래가 사악한 목적으로 사용될 수 있습니까? It's the most serious, most nefarious chapter in the short history of the Palestinian Authority. 그것은 팔레스타인 자치 정부의 역사에서 가장 심각하고 극악한 사건이다.	
437 ☐☐	**negligence** [néglidʒəns]	His negligence lost him his job. 그는 태만해서 직장을 잃었다. The official was sharply reprimanded for his negligence. 그 공무원은 직무 태만으로 엄한 견책을 받았다	
438 ☐☐	**nihilism** [náiəlìzəm]	Nihilism holds that existence has no meaning. 허무주의는 존재하는 것은 아무런 의미가 없다고 주장한다. Their blanket rejection of the standards and values on which our society is founded seems to be little short of nihilism. 우리 사회가 바탕을 두고 있는 기준과 가치를 전적으로 거부하는 것은 거의 무정부주의로 보인다.	
439 ☐☐	**nullify** [nʌ́ləfài]	An unhealthy diet will nullify the effects of training. 건강에 해로운 식이요법은 훈련의 효과를 무효화 시킬 것이다. Thailand's top court has nullified the country's April second parliamentary elections and ordered a new vote. 태국의 헌법재판소는 지난 4월 2일에 실시됐던 총선을 무효로 하고 새로운 총선을 실시할 것을 명령했다.	
440 ☐☐	**nurture** [nə́:rtʃər]	The Smiths nurture their children in a loving environment. 스미스 부부는 자녀들을 사랑의 환경에서 양육한다. The United Nations health agency found that all children are similar in how they develop if they are adequately nurtured. UN 산하 보건기구는 만약 적절히 양육되면 모든 아동은 유사한 성장과정을 거친다는 것을 발견했습니다.	

☐ intrinsic _____   ☐ intrude _____   ☐ invoke _____   ☐ laborious _____

Definition	Meaning/Relation
마른; 빈약한	ⓐ having little flesh; deficient in quantity, fullness, or extent **a meager repast** 불충분한 식사 **meager reserves** 제한된〔빈약한〕 매장량 **meager resources** 제한된〔빈약한〕 자원
조정하다, 중재하다	ⓥ to resolve or settle (differences) by working with all the conflicting parties **mediate between** …사이를 중재하다
사악한, 극악한	ⓐ infamous by way of being extremely wicked **a nefarious scheme** 사악한 계획
태만	ⓝ the state or quality of being negligent **contributory negligence** 기여 과실 **criminal negligence** 형사상의 과실
허무주의; 무정부주의	ⓝ an extreme form of skepticism that denies all existence; the belief that destruction of existing political or social institutions is necessary for future improvement
무효로 하다	ⓥ to make null **nullify the effect** 효과를 무색하게 만들다 **nullify a gain** 이익을 무가치하게 만들다 **nullify a goal** 득점을 무효로 하다
양육하다	ⓥ to nourish

☐ loath _____   ☐ luminous _____   ☐ marshal _____

NO.	Entry Word	Example Sentence
441 □□	**obstinate** [ábstənit]	His mother is as obstinate as himself. 그의 어머니는 그처럼 고집이 세다. He is the most obstinate fellow I have ever seen. 저렇게 고집이 센 사람은 일찍이 본 일이 없다.
442 □□	**onerous** [ánərəs]	He asked for an assistant becasue his work load was too onerous. 그는 그의 일이 너무 성가셔 조력자를 요구했다. He achieved the rather onerous honor after 56 percent of respondents voted against him. 응답자의 56%가 반대한 이후로 그는 다소 부담이 되는 명예를 얻었다.
443 □□	**opaque** [oʊpéik]	The water is so charged with mud and sand that it is opaque. 그곳 물은 진흙과 모래가 많이 섞여 불투명했다. Natural diamonds vary from colorless to black, and may be opaque, translucent, or transparent. 천연 다이아몬드는 무색으로부터 검정색에 이르기까지 다양해서 색깔이 불투명하거나 반투명하거나 투명할 수 있다.
444 □□	**opportune** [àpərtjúːn]	Your arrival was most opportune. 당신의 도착은 아주 시의 적절했다. If you are going to wait for an occasion that seems opportune in every respect, then in all probability you will have to wait forever. 모든 면에서 적절하다고 보여지는 기회를 기다린다면 아마 영원히 기다려야 할 것이다.
445 □□	**ostensible** [asténsəbəl]	This ostensible children's play has turned out to be more appealing to grown-ups. 표면상으로는 어린이 연극은 성인들이 더 재밌어 했다. The ostensible purpose of this expedition is to discover new lands. 이 원정의 표면상의 목적은 새로운 땅을 발견하는 것이다.
446 □□	**palatable** [pǽlətəbəl]	The truth is not always very palatable. 진실이 항상 마음에 드는 것은 아니다. The material is palatable even for the layperson of business. 이 책은 비즈니스에 문외한인 사람도 읽으면 기분을 좋게 한다.
447 □□	**pathetic** [pəθétik]	It was pathetic to watch her condition deteriorate day by day. 그녀의 병세가 나날이 악화되어 가는 것을 보고 애처로왔다. He was often cast as a pathetic little man because he looked the part. 그는 애처롭고 작은 남자 배역을 맡는 경우가 많았는데 정말로 그 역이 잘 어울렸기 때문이었다.

□ meager _____ □ mediate _____ □ nefarious _____

Definition	Meaning/Relation
고집이 센	ⓐ stubbornly adhering to an attitude, an opinion, or a course of action **obstinate about** …에 대해 완고한 **obstinate in** …에 있어서 고집센
성가신; 부담이 되는	ⓐ troublesome or oppressive; burdensome **a onerous[crushing, heavy] burden** 힘든 일, 무거운 짐 **an onerous task** 귀찮은(부담이 따르는) 일
불투명한	ⓐ impenetrable by light, neither transparent nor translucent **an opaque projector** 반사식 투서기
적절한	ⓐ suited or right for a particular purpose **an opportune[auspicious] moment** 상서로운 순간
표면상의	ⓐ represented or appearing as such
기분좋은	ⓐ acceptable or agreeable to the mind or sensibilities
애처로운	ⓐ arousing or capable of arousing sympathetic sadness and compassion

☐ negligence _____ ☐ nihilism _____ ☐ nullify _____ ☐ nurture _____

NO.	Entry Word	Example Sentence
448 ☐☐	**pedestrian** [pədéstriən]	His car skidded on the icy road and hit a pedestrian. 그의 차는 빙판길에서 미끄러져 보행자를 치었다. In fact, about 40 percent of all people who died from car accidents were pedestrians. 실제로 교통 사고로 사망한 사람들 중의 약 40%가 보행자들이었다.
449 ☐☐	**penchant** [péntʃənt]	He shows a penchant for jazz music. 그는 재즈 음악을 좋아한다. This is another example of the Japanese penchant for trying to keep outsiders ignorant of their nation's sins. 이것은 제3국이 자기 나라의 죄를 모르도록 하기 위한 일본이 잘쓰는 경향의 한 예이다.
450 ☐☐	**penitent** [pénətənt]	The penitent boy promised not to cheat again. 참회하는 그 소년은 다시는 속이지 않겠다고 약속했다. Rodion is not yet truly penitent for the murder. Rodion은 범죄행위에 대해 아직 진심으로 참회하고 있지 않다.
451 ☐☐	**perennial** [pəréniəl]	The film White Christmas is a perennial favorite. 영화 White Chrismas는 지속적으로 대중의 사랑을 받는 영화다. Jim Boren is representative of another kind of perennial presidential candidate. Jim Boren은 만년 대통령 후보 중 또 다른 종류의 대표적 인물이라고 할 수 있다.
452 ☐☐	**permeate** [pə́ːrmièit]	Soon the gas permeated the entire area. 곧 가스가 전 지역에 퍼졌다. Water permeated through the racks in the wall. 물이 벽에 갈라진 틈을 통해 퍼졌다.
453 ☐☐	**posthumous** [pástʃuməs]	The posthumous publication of the actor's memoirs aroused a lot of interest. 그 배우의 사후에 출판된 회고록은 많은 흥미를 불러 일으켰다. It was only after the posthumous publication of his last novel that they recognized his great talent. 그들이 그의 뛰어난 재능을 안 것은 그의 마지막 소설이 사후 출판된 이후였다.
454 ☐☐	**postulate** [pástʃəlèit]	She postulates that a cure will be found by the year 2000. 그녀는 2000년이 되면 치료법이 발견될 것으로 가정하고 있다. Even if we postulate that she had a motive for the murder, that still doesn't mean that she did it. 그녀가 살해할 동기가 있다고 가정한다 하더라도, 그것이 그녀가 살인을 했다는 것을 의미하지 않는다.

☐ obstinate _____ ☐ onerous _____ ☐ opaque _____ ☐ opportune _____

Definition	Meaning/Relation
보행자	ⓝ a person traveling on foot
기호; 경향	ⓝ a definite liking; a strong inclination **a penchant for** …에 대한 기호
참회하는	ⓐ feeling or expressing remorse for one's misdeeds or sins **penitent for** …을 회개하는
지속하는	ⓐ lasting or active through the year or through many years **a hardy perennial** 내한성(耐寒性) 다년생 식물
퍼지다	ⓥ to spread or flow throughout
사후의	ⓐ occurring or continuing after one's death **a posthumous award** 사후(死後)에 수여하는 상
가정하다	ⓥ to assume or assert the truth, reality, or necessity of, especially as a basis of an argument

□ ostensible _____ □ palatable _____ □ pathetic _____

NO.	Entry Word	Example Sentence	
455 ☐☐	**precarious** [prikɛ́əriəs]	Soldiers on the battlefield lead a precarious life. 전장의 병사들은 불안정한 삶을 영위한다. This stock is a precarious investment and I advise against its purchase. 이 주식에 대한 투자는 불안정하므로 나는 그것을 사지 말 것을 충고한다.	
456 ☐☐	**precedent** [présədənt]	There is no precedent for it. 그것에 대한 전례가 없다. This course of action is quite without precedent. 이런 행동 방침은 전례가 없다.	
457 ☐☐	**precipitate** [prisípotèit]	An invasion would certainly precipitate a political crisis. 침입은 확실히 정치적 위기를 촉진시킬 것이다. Fears about solvency oh the banks precipitated the great economic crash. 은행의 유동성 부족에 대한 두려움이 커다란 경제적 혼란을 촉진시켰다.	
458 ☐☐	**preeminent** [priémənənt]	The visiting athletes were preeminent in the high jump. 원정 중인 선수들은 높이뛰기에 기량이 탁월했다. He enjoyed a preeminent position among the writers of his day. 그는 자기 시대의 작가들 중에서 탁월한 위치를 누렸다.	
459 ☐☐	**privation** [praivéiʃən]	She didn't find the lack of a car a great privation. 그녀는 차가 없는 것이 크게 궁핍하다고 생각하지 않았다. The survivors suffered many privations before they were rescued. 생존자들은 구출되기 전에 많은 궁핍을 겪었다.	
460 ☐☐	**profusion** [prəfjúːʒən]	She'd never seen flowers so beautiful and in such profusion. 그녀는 그렇게 아름답고 많은 꽃을 본 적이 없다. Every year from June to October a profusion of mugunghwa blossoms graces the entire country. 해마다 6월에서 10월까지 많은 무궁화가 전국을 뒤덮습니다.	
461 ☐☐	**proponent** [prəpóunənt]	She was an avid proponent of equal rights for immigrants. 그녀는 이민자의 동등한 권리를 열렬히 지지하는 사람이었다. He entered politics as a proponent of the free market. 그는 자유시장경제의 지지자로 정치에 입문했다.	

☐ pedestrian _____ ☐ penchant _____ ☐ penitent _____ ☐ perennial _____

PART 1

PART 2

PART 3

PART 4

PART 5

PART 6

Definition	Meaning/Relation
불안정한	ⓐ dangerously lacking in security or stability **a precarious existence** 위태로운 생활 **a precarious foothold** 불안한 발판
전례	ⓝ an act or instance that may be used as an example in dealing with subsequent similar instances **create[establish, set] a precedent** 선례를 만들다 **cite a precedent** 선례를 인용하다
촉진시키다	ⓥ to make happen sooner **precipitate into** …로 빠지게 하다
탁월한	ⓐ superior to or notable above all others **preeminent in** …에 있어 우수한[탁월한]
궁핍	ⓝ lack of the basic necessities or comforts of life **a life of privation and misery** 궁핍하고 비참한 생활
다량, 다수	ⓝ the state of being abundant **in profusion** 풍부하게
지지자	ⓝ one who argues in support of something

☐ permeate _____ ☐ posthumous _____ ☐ postulate _____

NO.	Entry Word	Example Sentence	
462 ☐☐	**querulous** [kwérjələs]	Men become querulous with age. 나이를 먹으면 넋두리도 나오는 법이다. "Georgia, I'm tired of waiting", complained Grandfather in a querulous voice. "Georgia, 나는 기다리는데 지쳤어", 라고 할아버지께서 불평하는 목소리로 말씀하셨다.	
463 ☐☐	**reactionary** [riːǽkʃənèri]	Byron would have become a reactionary bourgeois had he lived longer. 만약 Byron이 더 오래 살았더라면 그는 반항적인 부르주아가 되었을 것이다. He has proved one of the most reactionary conservatives of modern times. 그는 현대에 가장 반동적인 보수주의 중의 하나라는 것이 증명되었다.	
464 ☐☐	**rebuff** [ribʌ́f]	He rebuffed my attempts to help. 그는 내가 도우려고 한 것을 거절했다. She rebuffed his invitation so smoothly that he did not realize he had been snubbed. 그녀는 그의 초대를 너무도 부드럽게 거절하였기 때문에 그는 자기가 퇴짜 맞은 것을 알지 못했다.	
465 ☐☐	**redolent** [rédələnt]	The air was redolent with the smell of exotic spices. 공기 중에 이국적인 향신료 냄새가 났다. The cottage was redolent of lavender and furniture polish. 그 전원주택에는 라벤더향과 가구광택제 냄새가 났다.	
466 ☐☐	**regimen** [rédʒəmən]	After his heart attack, the doctor put him on a strict regimen. 그가 심장 발작을 겪자 의사는 그에게 엄격한 식이요법을 처방했다. A home monitor allows patients to chart their progress, a strong incentive to stay with a treatment regimen. 가정용 측정계는 환자들이 자신들의 (병의) 진전 상황을 차트로 만들 수 있게 해 치료 요법을 계속하는데 강한 동기를 부여해 줍니다.	
467 ☐☐	**relish** [réliʃ]	Food has no relish when one is ill. 아플 때는 음식 맛을 모른다. He drank up the wine with relish. 그는 맛있게 포도주를 마셨다.	
468 ☐☐	**replicate** [répləkèit]	These tissue cells replicate themselves. 이러한 조직 세포는 스스로 복제한다. The results of the experiment could not be replicated. 그 실험의 결과는 복제가 불가능했다.	

☐ precarious _____   ☐ precedent _____   ☐ precipitate _____

PART 1

PART 2

PART 3

PART 4

PART 5

PART 6

Definition	Meaning/Relation
불만이 많은	ⓐ given to complaining **a querulous tone** 불평하는 어조
반동적인	ⓐ characterized by reaction, especially opposition to progress or liberalism
거절하다	ⓥ to reject and snub bluntly, often disdainfully
향이나는	ⓐ having or emitting fragrance **redolent with[of]** …냄새가 나는
(식사 · 운동) 요법	ⓝ a regulated system, as of diet, therapy, or exercise, intended to promote health or achieve another beneficial effect **put** *sb*. **on a regimen** …을 양생법에 따르게 하다 **follow a regimen** 양생법을 따르다 **a daily regimen** 매일의 양생법 **a strict regimen** 엄격한 양생법
맛; 기색	ⓝ an appetite for something; a strong appreciation or liking **show relish for** …에 흥미를 보이다 **with relish** 맛있게
복제하다	ⓥ to duplicate, copy, reproduce, or repeat **replicate an experiment (on)** (…에 관한) 실험을 되풀이하다

□ preeminent _____ □ privation _____ □ profusion _____ □ proponent _____

NO.	Entry Word	Example Sentence	
469	**reproach** [ripróutʃ]	His conscience reproached him for the deed. 그는 그 행위로 인해 양심의 가책을 받았다. Do not reproach him with laziness, he has done his utmost. 게으르다고 나무라지 마세요, 그는 최선을 다했어요.	
470	**repudiate** [ripjúːdièit]	He used his position to repudiate the policies of the leadership. 그는 수뇌부의 정책을 거부하기 위해 자신의 지위를 이용했다. To limit the free expression of unpopular ideas is to repudiate the basic spirit of the Bill of Rights. 인기 없는 사상의 자유로운 표현을 제한하는 것은 권리장전의 기본정신을 부인하는 것이다.	
471	**resignation** [rèzignéiʃən]	His resignation made a vacancy. 그의 사임으로 결원이 생겼다. The president's resignation was really unusual. 대통령의 사임은 정말 이례적이었다.	
472	**rhapsodize** [rǽpsədàiz]	You rhapsodize about beauty and my eyes glazed. 당신이 아름다움에 대해 이야기 하자 나의 눈은 흐려졌다. People tend to rhapsodize, quality is more important than quantity. 사람은 양보다는 질이 더 중요하다고 말하는 경향이 있다.	
473	**ruthless** [rúːθlis]	She is ruthless in pursuing her goals. 그녀는 자신의 목적을 추구함에 있어 냉혹하다. The country is ruled by a ruthless dictator. 그 나라는 무자비한 독재자의 통치를 받는다.	
474	**sanctimonious** [sæ̀ŋktəmóuniəs]	It's the government's sanctimonious attitude that really sticks in my throat. 내가 정말 받아들이기 힘든 것은 정부가 경건한 체하는 태도이다. You do not have to be so sanctimonious to prove that you are devout. 당신이 독실하다는 것을 보이기 위해 그렇게 경건한 체할 필요는 없다.	
475	**savor** [séivər]	This soup has a savor of onion. 이 수프는 양파 맛이 난다. If the salt have lost its savor, wherewith shall it be salted? 만일 소금이 그 짠맛을 잃으면 무엇으로 다시 짜게 만들겠느냐?	

☐ querulous _____ ☐ reactionary _____ ☐ rebuff _____

Definition	Meaning/Relation
비난하다	ⓥ to express disapproval of, criticism of, or disappointment in (someone) **reproach bitterly** 심하게 비난〔질책〕하다 **reproach for** ⋯을 비난〔질책〕하다
거부하다, 부인하다	ⓥ to reject the validity or authority of **repudiate a charge** 혐의를 부인하다 **repudiate a confession** 자백을 부인하다 **repudiate[abrogate, cancel] a contract** 계약을 파기하다 **repudiate a debt** 채무의 이행을 거부하다 **repudiate one's heritage** 유산상속을 거부하다 **repudiate[break, renege on] a promise** 약속을 어기다 **repudiate[recant, retract] (one's) testimony** 증언을 취소하다
사임	ⓝ the act or an instance of resigning **hand in[offer, submit, tender] one's resignation** 사표를 내다 **withdraw one's resignation** 사표를 철회하다 **reject sb's resignation** ⋯의 사표를 받아들이지 않다 **a resignation from** ⋯에서의 사직〔사임〕
(열광적으로) 이야기하다	ⓥ to express oneself in an immoderately enthusiastic manner **rhapsodize over** ⋯에 대해 열정적으로 말하다
냉혹한, 무자비한	ⓐ having no compassion or pity; merciless **ruthless in** ⋯에 있어서 무자비한〔가차없는〕
경건한 체하는	ⓐ feigning piety or righteousness
맛, 풍미	ⓝ the taste or smell of something

☐ redolent _____ ☐ regimen _____ ☐ relish _____ ☐ replicate _____

NO.	Entry Word	Example Sentence	
476 ☐☐	**scrupulous** [skrú:pjələs]	She was scrupulous in avoiding references to her opponent. 그녀는 신중을 기하여 상대를 들먹이지 않으려고 애썼다. A scrupulous politician would not lie about her business interests. 양심적인 정치인이라면 자신의 사업적 이해관계에 대해 거짓말을 하지 않을 것이다.	
477 ☐☐	**scrutinize** [skrú:tənàiz]	She scruntinized through her spectacles. 그녀는 안경을 쓰고 사람의 얼굴을 자세히 보았다. He scrutinized minutely all the documents relating to the trial. 그는 그 재판에 관련된 모든 서류를 세밀히 조사했다.	
478 ☐☐	**shun** [ʃʌn]	I've been shunned by my class. 나는 반에서 따돌림을 당했다. Because he switched from one party to another, his former friends shunned him as an apostate. 그가 다른 당으로 옮겼기 때문에 그의 이전 친구들은 그를 변절자라고 따돌렸다.	
479 ☐☐	**spate** [speit]	There's been a spate of accidents on this stretch of road recently. 최근에 이 도로에서 사고가 갑작스럽게 증가해 왔다. The religious leaders got together to express their distress at the on going spate of abductions. 종교 지도자들은 낙태가 현재 범람하고 있는 것에 우려를 표명하기 위해 모였다.	
480 ☐☐	**steadfast** [stédfæst]	He was a steadfast servant of his country. 그는 자기 조국의 확고부동한 종복이었다. She commended the steadfast courage of families caring for handicapped children. 그녀는 장애 아동을 돌보는 가정들의 확고한 용기를 칭찬했다.	
481 ☐☐	**stem** [stem]	The stem of ivy is thick. 담쟁이 덩굴의 줄기는 굵다. This flower has a long stem. 이 꽃의 줄기는 길다.	
482 ☐☐	**stoic** [stóuik]	My father is a stoic by nature and found it hard to express his grief when my mother died. 우리 아버지는 천성적인 금욕주의자로 우리 어머니가 돌아가셨을 때도 당신의 슬픔을 나타내는 것을 힘들어하셨다. Donna felt angry at being portrayed as a stoic who cared little for the institution of marriage. Donna는 결혼 제도에 거의 신경쓰지 않는 금욕주의자로 묘사되고 있는 것에 화가 났다.	

☐ reproach _____   ☐ repudiate _____   ☐ resignation _____

476_482 155

PART 1

PART 2

PART 3

PART 4

PART 5

PART 6

Definition	Meaning/Relation
신중한; 양심적인	ⓐ wise or careful in condnct; conscientious and exact **scrupulous in** …에 신중한 **with scrupulous care** 꼼꼼히 주의하여
자세히 조사하다	ⓥ to examine or observe with great care **scrutinize closely[intently, thoroughly]** 면밀히〔철저하게〕조사하다
따돌리다	ⓥ to avoid deliberately **shun[avoid] publicity** 사람들의 눈을 피하다
갑자기 쏟아져 나옴	ⓝ a sudden, rush, or increased quantity **in full spate** 《영》홍수가 져서; 활기〔힘〕가 넘쳐, 열을 올려 **in spate** 홍수가 져서, 범람하여
확고한	ⓐ fixed or unchanging **(an) steadfast[enduring, abiding] faith** 불변의〔영속적인〕신념 **steadfast[deep-rooted,strong,unquestioned, unshakable, unswerving] loyalty** 강한〔확고한〕충성심
줄기	ⓝ the main ascending axis of a plant
금욕주의자	ⓝ one who is seemingly indifferent to or unaffected by joy, grief, pleasure, or pain

☐ rhapsodize _____   ☐ ruthless _____   ☐ sanctimonious _____   ☐ savor _____

483 ☐☐	**subversive** [səbvə́ːrsiv]	We must destroy such subversive publications. 우리는 그 같은 체제 전복적인 출판물을 없애야만 한다. The government is trying to ban this magazine because it prints subversive ideas. 정부는 이 잡지가 체제 전복적인 사상을 출판하고 있기 때문에 출판을 금지시키려고 노력하고 있다.	
484 ☐☐	**timorous** [tímərəs]	His timorous manner betrayed the fear he felt at the moment. 그의 우려하는 태도가 그 당시 그가 느끼던 공포를 나타내주었다. Koreans seem to think that to observe such rules is to be timorous. 한국 사람들은 이러한 규칙을 지키는 것은 겁쟁이가 되는 것으로 생각하는 듯하다.	
485 ☐☐	**transcend** [trænsénd]	The grandeur of the scenery transcends description. 그 경치의 웅장함은 필설을 뛰어넘는다. The best films are those which transcend national or cultural barriers. 가장 뛰어난 영화는 민족적, 문화적 장벽을 뛰어넘는 영화들이다.	
486 ☐☐	**travesty** [trǽvəsti]	The ridiculous decision the jury has arrived at is a travesty of justice. 배심원이 내린 어리석은 결정은 재판을 우스꽝스럽게 만들고 있다. Since she knew in advance whom she would choose for each role, the so-called "try-outs" for the play were no more than a travesty. 각각의 역에 누구를 뽑을지 그녀가 미리 알고 있었기 때문에 그 연극의 소위 "시험연기"는 희화에 불과했다.	
487 ☐☐	**tumult** [tjúːmʌlt]	The shout of "Fire!" caused a tumult. "불이야!" 하는 외침에 소동이 일어났다. You couldn't hear her speak over the tumult from the screaming fans. 날카롭게 소리를 내지르는 팬들의 소란 때문에 당신은 그녀가 하는 말을 들을 수 없을 겁니다.	
488 ☐☐	**turmoil** [tə́ːrmɔil]	The town was in turmoil. 그 마을은 혼란에 빠졌다. The political turmoil in India is at an end as a new Prime Minister is nominated. 신임 총리가 지명됨에 따라 인도의 정치 혼란은 일단락되었습니다.	
489 ☐☐	**unassuming** [ʌ̀nəsjúːmiŋ]	He's such an unassuming guest, one scarcely knows he's there. 그는 겸손한 손님이어서 와 있어도 아무도 알아채지 못할 정도다. He is so unassuming that some people fail to realize how great a man he really is. 그는 너무나 겸손해서 몇몇 사람들은 그가 실제로 얼마나 위대한지 깨닫지 못한다.	

☐ scrupulous _____   ☐ scrutinize _____   ☐ shun _____

Definition	Meaning/Relation
체제 전복적인	ⓐ intended or serving to subvert, especially intended to overthrow or undermine an established government **subversive activity** 파괴(사회전복) 활동 **subversive agitation** 체제전복적인 선동 **a subversive character** 체제 전복적 성격
우려하는; 겁많은	ⓐ full of apprehensiveness; timid
(범위·한계점을) 뛰어넘다	ⓥ to pass beyond the limits of
희화화(한 작품)	ⓝ an exaggerated or grotesque imitation, such as a parody of a literary work
소동, 소란	ⓝ a disorderly commotion or disturbance **cause tumult** 소동을 일으키다 **in tumult over** …으로 동요하여
혼란	ⓝ state of extreme confusion or agitation **complete turmoil** 진짜 혼란 **in (a) turmoil** 혼란 상태인
겸손한	ⓐ exhibiting no pretensions, boastfulness, or ostentation

□ spate _____ □ steadfast _____ □ stem _____ □ stoic _____

NO.	Entry Word	Example Sentence	
490 ☐☐	**urbane** [ə́ːrbéin]	John Herschel was an urbane, kindly and generous man. John Herschel은 세련되고 친절하며 너그러운 사람이었다. He was an erudite icon with his silver hair, urbane style. 그는 은색 머리결과 세련된 스타일을 가진 학구적인 아이콘이다.	
491 ☐☐	**usurp** [juːsə́rp]	The powers of local councils are being usurped by central government. 지방의회의 힘이 중앙정부에 의해 빼앗기고 있다. Streets intended for pedestrians are being usurped by motorists. 보행자들을 위해 만들어진 거리가 운전자들에게 빼앗기고 있다.	
492 ☐☐	**vacillate** [væ̀səléit]	She vacillated between hope and fear. 그녀는 마음이 희망과 두려움사이에서 흔들렸다. He vacillated for too long and the opportunity to accept was lost. 그는 너무 오랫동안 머뭇거렸고 받아들일 기회를 잃었다.	
493 ☐☐	**vapid** [væpid]	The vapid conversation bored her. 맥 빠진 대화에 그녀는 지루했다. She delivered an uninspired and vapid address. 그녀는 생기없고 지루한 연설을 했다.	
494 ☐☐	**vestige** [véstidʒ]	There was no vestige of the castle. 그 성은 흔적조차 없었다. He has promised to eradicate the last vestiges of military rule. 그는 군사 통치의 잔재를 완전히 제거하겠다고 약속했다.	
495 ☐☐	**virtuoso** [və̀ːrtʃuóusou]	I lacked virtuoso talent and I hated to practice. 나는 연주가로 대성할 자질도 없었고 연습하는 것도 싫었다. Famous mainly for his wonderful voice, Cole was also a virtuoso on the piano. Cole은 주로 멋진 목소리로 유명했지만, 또한 피아노의 거장이기도 했다.	
496 ☐☐	**viscous** [vískəs]	The oil in its thick and viscous form can kill birds and animals by poisoning them. 되직하고 끈끈한 형태의 그 기름은 새와 동물들을 중독시켜 죽일 수 있다. Bitumen is a heavy viscous crude oil that contains high amounts of sulfur. 역청은 고유황이 있는 무게가 나가는 끈적끈적한 기름이다.	

☐ subversive _____   ☐ timorous _____   ☐ transcend _____

Definition	Meaning/Relation
세련된	ⓐ polite, refined, and often elegant in manner
빼앗다	ⓥ to seize and hold (the power or rights of another, for example) by force and without legal authority **usurp authority** 권한을 침해하다 **usurp a throne** 왕위를 빼앗다
흔들리다; 주저하다	ⓥ to swing indecisively from one course of action or opinion to another; to waver **vacillate between** …사이에서 마음이 흔들리다 **vacillate in** …에 마음이 흔들리다, …을 결정하기 어렵다
지루한	ⓐ lacking liveliness, animation, or interest
흔적; 잔재	ⓝ a visible trace, evidence, or sign of something that once existed but exists or appears no more; a surviving trace
(특히 음악 분야) 거장	ⓝ a person with masterly skill or technique in the arts
끈적끈적한	ⓐ having relatively high resistance to flow

☐ travesty _____ ☐ tumult _____ ☐ turmoil _____ ☐ unassuming _____

NO.	Entry Word	Example Sentence	
497 ☐☐	**vitiate** [víʃièit]	Carbonic acid gas vitiates the air of the room. 탄산 가스는 방의 공기를 오염시킨다. The moral strength of his argument was vitiated by its impracticality. 도덕이 중요하다는 그의 주장은 비현실적이어서 가치가 떨어졌다.	
498 ☐☐	**vivacious** [vivéiʃəs]	I remember her as vivacious. 나는 그녀가 활기가 넘쳤던 것으로 기억하고 있다. The vivacious and colorful street life of Bangkok was tourist attraction in itself. 방콕의 활기 넘치고 다채로운 거리 생활은 그 자체로 관광 명소였다.	

☐ urbane _____   ☐ usurp _____   ☐ vacillate _____   ☐ vapid _____

Definition	Meaning/Relation
가치를 떨어뜨리다, 더럽히다	ⓥ to reduce the value or impair the quality of
활기가 넘치는	ⓐ full of animation and spirit

☐ vestige _____   ☐ virtuoso _____   ☐ viscous _____

기본 영단어

★

Let's go!

Ranking 5

NO.	Entry Word	Example Sentence
499 ☐☐	**abash** [əbǽʃ]	He looked rather abashed at her criticisms. 그는 그녀의 비판에 다소 당황한 듯 보였다. He was not at all abashed by her open admiration. 그는 그녀의 공개적 칭찬에도 전혀 당황해 하지 않았다.
500 ☐☐	**abate** [əbéit]	The recession is not expected to abate until year's end. 불경기의 기세가 연말까지는 누그러지지 않을 것으로 보인다. This trend is showing no sign of abating. 이런 추세가 누그러질 기미가 보이지 않는다.
501 ☐☐	**abbreviate** [əbríːvièit]	"United Nations" is commonly abbreviated to "UN." United Nations는 보통 UN으로 줄여 쓴다. He persuaded his son to abbreviate his first name to Bob. 그는 그의 아들에게 이름을 Bob으로 줄여 쓰도록 설득했다.
502 ☐☐	**aberration** [æbəréiʃən]	Bob and Susan are not an aberration. Bob과 Susan은 별난 사람들이 아니다. He said that the decline in the company's sales last month was just a temporary aberration. 그는 지난 달 회사의 판매 부진은 일시적 이상 현상이라고 말했다.
503 ☐☐	**aboriginal** [æbərídʒənəl]	She studied the variations of aboriginal practices throughout the world. 그녀는 전세계에 있는 원주민의 생활습관들에 대한 다양성에 관해서 연구하였다. His studies of the primitive art forms of the aboriginal Indians were widely reported in the scientific journals. 그의 인디안 원주민의 초기 예술 형태에 대한 연구는 과학저널들에서 널리 인용되었다.
504 ☐☐	**absolve** [əvzɑ́lv]	The father confessor absolved him of his sins. 고해 신부는 그의 죄를 사면해 주었다. The jury may have found him not guilty, but the court of public opinion will never absolve him of responsibility for the crime. 배심원은 그가 죄가 없다고 판단했을지 모르지만, 소위 여론 재판이 그 범죄에 대한 그의 책임을 사면해 주지 않을 것이다.
505 ☐☐	**accost** [əkɔ́ːst]	She was accosted in the street by a complete stranger. 그녀는 길거리에서 전혀 낯선 사람의 접근을 받았다. As the tourist entered the square, the inevitable beggars accosted them, imploring arms. 관광객들이 광장에 들어서자 의례히 거기 있는 거지들이 접근해서 동냥을 청했다.

☐ vitiate _____   ☐ vivacious _____

Definition	Meaning/Relation
당황하게 하다	ⓥ to make ashamed or uneasy **be[feel] abashed** 겸연쩍어하다, 당황하다
누그러지다	ⓥ to reduce in amount, degree, or intensity **abate a nuisance** (불법) 방해를 제거하다
줄여 쓰다	ⓥ to reduce (a word) to a short form forming intended to represent the full form
정도에서 벗어남, 이상	ⓝ a deviation from the proper or expected course **a mental aberration** 정신 이상 **a sexual aberration** 성적 일탈
원주민의	ⓐ having existed in a region from the beginning **aboriginal tribes/inhabitants** 원주민 **aboriginal art/culture** 원주민의 예술/문화
사면하다	to pronounce clear of guilt or blame
접근하다	ⓥ to approach and speak to in an aggressive, hostile, or sexually suggestive manner

PART 1
PART 2
PART 3
PART 4
PART 5
PART 6

NO.	Entry Word	Example Sentence
506 ☐☐	**acrimonious** [ækrəmóuniəs]	His tendency to utter acrimonious remarks alienated his audience. 그는 신랄한 발언을 하는 경향이 있기 때문에 청중은 그를 싫어했다. It took 15 months of acrimonious negotiations to achieve the peace treaty. 평화 협정에 이르는 데 15개월에 걸친 격렬한 협상이 있었다.
507 ☐☐	**adorn** [ədɔ́ːrn]	Graffiti adorned the empty train. 낙서가 텅 빈 기차를 장식했다. Her hair was adorned with flowers. 그녀의 머리는 꽃으로 장식되었다.
508 ☐☐	**adverse** [ædvə́ːrs]	Adverse winds hinder planes. 역풍이 항공기들의 진로를 방해한다. The decision was adverse to our interests. 그 결정은 우리의 관심과 정반대였다.
509 ☐☐	**adversity** [ædvə́ːrsəti]	His family fell into adversity. 그의 가족은 역경에 처했다. She was always cheerful in adversity. 그녀는 역경 속에서도 항상 유쾌했다.
510 ☐☐	**affable** [ǽfəbəl]	She is affable to everybody. 그녀는 누구에게나 상냥하다. Although he held a position of responsibility, he was an affable individual and could be reached by anyone with a complaint. 비록 그는 책임자의 자리에 있었지만 상냥한 사람이었으므로 누구나 불평 있는 사람은 그를 만날 수 있었다.
511 ☐☐	**affront** [əfrʌ́nt]	His speech was an affront to all decent members of the community. 그의 연설은 그 지역의 모든 점잖은 구성원들에게 모욕이었다. The boy next door offered an affront to the town people. 동네 주민들에게 그 소년은 무례한 짓을 했다.
512 ☐☐	**aghast** [əgǽst]	She was aghast at the extent of the damage to her car. 그녀는 자기 차의 손상 정도를 보고 깜짝 놀랐다. He was aghast at the nerve of the speaker who had insulted his host. 그는 그의 주인을 모욕한 연사의 무례함에 깜짝 놀랐다.

☐ abash _____   ☐ abate _____   ☐ abbreviate _____   ☐ aberration _____

PART 1

PART 2

PART 3

PART 4

PART 5

PART 6

Definition	Meaning/Relation
신랄한; 격렬한	ⓐ bitter and sharp in language or tone; rancorous **an acrimonious[bitter, heated, sharp, stormy] debate** 격론
장식하다	ⓥ to lend beauty to **adorn with** …으로 꾸미다
반대의	ⓐ acting or serving to oppose **adverse to** …에 반대의〔불리한〕 **adverse comment [criticism]** 불리한 논평〔악평〕 **under adverse circumstances** 역경에 처하여
역경	ⓝ a state of hardship or affliction **face (up to) adversity** 역경에 맞서다 **overcome adversity** 역경을 극복하다 **companions in adversity** 불운한 처지일 때의 동료 **in (the face of) adversity** 역경에 처하여
상냥한	ⓐ ready to listen and help
모욕, 무례	ⓥ an open or intentional offense, slight, or insult **(격식) suffer an affront** 모욕을 받다〔당하다〕 **a personal affront** 개인적인 모욕 **an affront to** …에 대한 모욕
깜짝 놀란	ⓐ struck by shock, terror, or amazement **aghast at** …에 기겁을 한

☐ aboriginal _____ ☐ absolve _____ ☐ accost _____

513 ☐☐	**alleviate** [əlíːvièit]	Heat often alleviates pain. 열은 흔히 고통을 완화해 준다. The drugs did nothing to alleviate her pain. 그 약들은 그녀의 통증을 완화시키는 데 아무 효과가 없었다.
514 ☐☐	**allusion** [əlúːʒən]	Her novels are packed with literary allusions. 그녀의 소설은 문학적 암시로 가득 차 있다. His erudite writing was difficult to read because of the many allusions which were unfamiliar to most readers. 그의 박식한 글은 대부분의 독자들에게 생소한 암시들이 많아 읽기가 어렵다.
515 ☐☐	**aloof** [əlúːf]	He keeps aloof [or far] from society. 그는 사회로부터 떨어져 있다. Some of them wanted to be close to you but they felt you were aloof. 당신과 친해지고 싶었던 몇몇에게도 당신은 거리를 뒀다.
516 ☐☐	**amorous** [ǽmərəs]	The film centers around the amorous adventures of its handsome hero, Mike Mather. 그 영화는 잘생긴 주인공 Mike Mather의 호색적인 모험을 중심으로 한다. She refused his amorous advances. 그녀는 그의 사랑의 시도를 거절했다.
517 ☐☐	**anachronism** [ənǽkrənìzəm]	His ideas are nothing but an anachronism. 그의 착상은 시대 착오에 지나지 않는다 For some people, marriage is an anachronism from the days when women needed to be protected. 어떤 사람들은 결혼이 여성들이 보호받아야 했던 시절로부터 전해진 시대착오적인 것이라고 생각한다.
518 ☐☐	**anarchy** [ǽnərki]	The concept of anarchy is decidedly outmoded. 무정부의 개념은 분명히 시대에 뒤떨어진 생각이다. What we are witnessing is the country's slow slide into anarchy. 그 나라는 서서히 무정부 상태가 되어 가고 있다.
519 ☐☐	**anguish** [ǽŋgwiʃ]	His brows gathered in anguish. 그는 고통으로 얼굴을 찌푸렸다. His heart was torn with anguish. 그의 마음은 괴로워서 찢어질 것만 같았다.

☐ acrimonious _____ ☐ adorn _____ ☐ adverse _____ ☐ adversity _____

Definition	Meaning/Relation
완화하다	ⓥ to make (pain, for example) more bearable **alleviate[ease, relieve] one's anxiety** 걱정을〔불안감을〕덜어주다 **alleviate [lift, lighten, relieve] a burden** 짐을 덜다 **alleviate discomfort** 불편을 덜다. **alleviate[ease] distress** 고통을 완화시키다〔덜다〕 **alleviate the heat** 열을 내리다 ((격식)) **alleviate[ally, appease] one's hunger** 시장기를 달래다 **alleviate[relieve] (the) itching** 가려움을 누그러뜨리다〔완화하다〕
암시	ⓝ the act of alluding; indirect reference **make an allusion to** …을 암시하다〔내비치다〕 **a vague allusion** 넌지시 내비침 **in allusion to** 암암리에 …을 가리켜
떨어져(있는), 거리를 두는	ⓐ distant physically or emotionally **hold oneself [keep, remain, stand] aloof** (사람들과)거리를 두다〔가까이 어울리지 않다〕 **aloof from** …와 거리를 두는
호색적인, 사랑의	ⓐ strongly attracted or disposed to love, especially sexual love
시대 착오적인 것[일]	ⓝ representation of someone as existing or something as happening in other than the chronological, proper, or historical order
무정부 상태	ⓝ absence of any form of political authority **complete[total, utter] anarchy** 완전한 무정부 상태 **anarchy reigns** 무정부 상태가 지배하다
(심신의 심한) 고통	ⓝ agonizing physical or mental pain **cause anguish** 고통을 주다 **acute anguish** 모진 고통

☐ affable _____ ☐ affront _____ ☐ aghast _____

NO.	Entry Word	Example Sentence	
520 ☐☐	**animosity** [ænəmásəti]	I could sense the animosity between them. 나는 그들 사이에서 증오를 느낄 수 있었다. The animosity between the rival candidates was obvious to the voters. 경쟁 후보 사이의 적개심이 유권자들의 눈에도 명백히 보였다.	
521 ☐☐	**antithesis** [æntíθəsis]	Slavery is the antithesis of freedom. 예속은 자유의 정반대이다. Their solution to the problem was in complete antithesis to mine. 그 문제에 대한 그들의 해결책과 나의 해결책은 완전한 대립을 이루었다.	
522 ☐☐	**apathy** [ǽpəθi]	The citizens' apathy to local affairs resulted in poor government. 지역 일에 대한 시민들의 무관심으로 형편없는 정부가 생겨났다. We lost the election because of the apathy of our supporters. 우리는 지지자들의 무관심 때문에 선거에서 졌다.	
523 ☐☐	**appellation** [æpəléiʃən]	He was amazed when the witches hailed him with his correct appellation. 그는 마녀가 그의 정확한 명칭을 부르며 환영할 때 깜짝 놀랐다. The Sauternes appellation is allowed to include Barsac. 발삭 포도주도 소테른 포도주의 명칭에 포함되는 것이 허용되었다.	
524 ☐☐	**appraise** [əpréiz]	I had an expert appraise the house beforehand. 미리 전문가에게 그 집을 평가하게 했다. It is difficult to appraise the value of old paintings. 오래된 그림의 가치를 평가하는 것은 어렵다.	
525 ☐☐	**aptitude** [ǽptitùːd]	He has an aptitude for drawing and painting. 그는 그림에 재능이 있다. We will take your personal aptitudes and abilities into account. 우리는 당신의 개인적 적성과 능력을 참작할 것입니다.	
526 ☐☐	**arduous** [áːrdʒuəs]	He enjoys an arduous workout in the gymnasium. 그는 체육관에서 힘든 운동하기를 즐긴다. The trail to the North of Scotland may be arduous but once you're here, it can become luxurious. 스코틀랜드의 북부로 가는 길은 험준할지는 몰라도 일단 이곳에 도착하고 나면 호화로움을 만끽할 수 있습니다.	

☐ alleviate _____   ☐ allusion _____   ☐ aloof _____   ☐ amorous _____

Definition	Meaning/Relation
증오; 적의	ⓝ bitter hostility or open enmity; active hatred **arouse the animosity of** …의 적개심〔증오심, 적의〕을 유발하다 **feel[harbor] animosity** 적개심을 느끼다〔품다〕 **bitter[burning, deep, seething] animosity** 심한 적의, 끓어오르는 증오심 **personal animosity** 개인적 증오 **racial animosity** 인종간의 적의 **animosity against[to, towards]** …에 대한 적의 **animosity between** …사이의 반목〔대립〕
반대; 대립	ⓝ direct contrast; opposition **the direct[very] antithesis** 정반대, 현저한 대조 **an antithesis between** …사이의 대조
무관심	ⓝ lack of interest or concern, especially regarding matters of general importance or appeal; indifference **feel apathy towards** …에 냉담하다 **show apathy towards** …에 대해 무관심하다
명칭, 이름	ⓝ a name, title, or designation
평가하다	ⓥ to evaluate, especially in an official capacity **appraise at** …이라 평가하다, …이라 견적하다
재능; 적합(성)	ⓝ an inherent ability, as for learning; appropriateness **display [demonstrate, show] (an) aptitude** 소질을 발휘하다〔나타내다〕 **great[outstanding] aptitude** 뛰어난 소질 **inborn[innate, natural] aptitude** 타고난〔천부적인〕 소질 **special aptitude** 특별한 소질 **mechanical aptitude** 기계에 대한 소질 **scholastic aptitude** 학자적인 소질 **an aptitude for[in]** …의 소질
몹시 힘든; 험한	ⓐ demanding great effort or labor; steep **an arduous [difficult, hard] climb** 힘든 길 **an arduous journey** 힘든 여행 **an arduous task** 힘든 일 **arduous [backbreaking, unremitting] toil** 힘든〔고된〕 일

☐ anachronism _____　　☐ anarchy _____　　☐ anguish _____

520_526　171

PART 1　PART 2　PART 3　PART 4　PART 5　PART 6

527 □□	**ascribe** [əskráib]	He ascribed his failure to bad luck. 그는 자기의 실패를 불운 탓으로 돌렸다. This play is usually ascribed to Shakespeare. 이 연극은 통상 셰익스피어 작품이라고 일컬어지고 있다.
528 □□	**aspersion** [əspə́ːrʒən]	It is unfair to cast aspersions on his performance at university. 그의 대학 성적을 비방하는 것은 적절하지 못하다. By casting aspersions on the ability and character of others, you reveal the misgivings you have about yourself. 다른 사람들의 능력과 인격을 비방함으로서 당신은 자신에 대해서 갖고 있는 불안을 드러내고 있다.
529 □□	**assent** [əsént]	Jane nodded her assent to my proposal. 제인은 고개를 끄덕여 내 제안에 동의의 뜻을 내보였다. It gives me great pleasure to assent to your request. 당신의 요구를 받아들일 수 있어 매우 기쁘다.
530 □□	**austere** [ɔːstíər]	The monks led an austere life in the mountains. 수도승은 산 속에서 금욕적인 삶을 살았다. She was an austere elegance in her plain grey and black clothes. 그녀는 수수한 회색과 검은색 옷을 입은 엄숙한 우아함 그 자체였다.
531 □□	**avarice** [ǽvəris]	What unbelievable avarice; he wants all the money! 정말 터무니없는 탐욕이군. 그가 그 돈 모두를 원한다니! She earned wealth beyond the dreams of avarice from her business empire. 그녀는 자신의 기업 제국에서 탐욕이 꿈꿀 수 있는 한도 이상으로 부를 벌어들였다.
532 □□	**balk** [bɔːk]	Though he had a generous nature, he balked at picking up the check yet again. 그 사람은 후한 심성을 가졌지만, 이번에도 계산을 해야 하는 것에는 망설였다. Hungry North Koreans have balked at borrowing expensive grain from the South. 식량난으로 굶주린 북한 주민들도 남한으로부터의 값비싼 곡물 차용을 주저해왔다.
533 □□	**banal** [bənǽl]	He just sat there making banal remarks all evening. 그는 거기 앉아 저녁 내내 진부한 이야기를 늘어 놓았다. His frequent use of cliches made his essay seem banal. 상투어의 빈번한 사용으로 그의 에세이는 진부하게 보인다.

□ animosity _____ □ antithesis _____ □ apathy _____ □ appellation _____

Definition	Meaning/Relation
…의 탓으로 돌리다, 간주하다	ⓥ to attribute to a specified cause, source, or origin **ascribe to** …의 결과라고 간주하다
비방	ⓝ an unfavorable or damaging remark **cast aspersions on** …을 비방(중상)하다
동의하다, 받아들이다	ⓥ to agree, as to a proposal **assent to** …에 대해 동의(찬성)하다
금욕적인, 엄숙한	ⓐ severe or stern in disposition or appearance **an austere[ascetic] life** 금욕적 생활 **austere surroundings** 검소한 환경
탐욕	ⓝ immoderate desire for wealth
망설이다, 주저하다	ⓥ to stop short and refuse to go on **balk at** …에 망설이다
진부한	ⓐ drearily commonplace and often predictable; trite

□ appraise _____ □ aptitude _____ □ arduous _____

NO.	Entry Word	Example Sentence	
534 ☐☐	**barrage** [bərɑ́ːdʒ]	The company was forced to retreat through the barrage of heavy cannons. 중대는 중포들의 집중사격을 뚫고 후퇴를 해야만 했다. When the speaker asked for opinions from the audience, he was greeted with a barrage of critical remarks and angry questions. 연사가 청중들에게 의견을 물었을 때 비판적인 말과 화난 질문이 빗발쳐 나왔다.	
535 ☐☐	**belabor** [biléibər]	He chose not to belabor the argument. 그는 그 주장을 공격하지 않기로 했다. The debate coach warned her student not to bore the audience by belaboring his point. 그 토론 지도자는 자기 학생에게 자신의 의도를 장황하게 말해서 청중을 따분하게 만들지 말도록 일렀다.	
536 ☐☐	**belie** [bilái]	Her behavior belied her story. 그녀의 행동은 말과 모순되었다. His avuncular image belies his steely determination. 굳은 결심은 부드러운 그의 이미지와는 모순된다.	
537 ☐☐	**benighted** [bináitid]	Some of the early explorers thought of the local people as benighted savages who could be exploited. 초창기 탐험가 중 몇 사람은 현지인을 이용해도 되는 미개한 야만인이라고 생각했다. Rich white nations imposed their rule on benighted people of color around the world. 부유한 백인 국가들은 전 세계에 미개한 유색 인종에게 그들의 통치를 강요했다.	
538 ☐☐	**benign** [bináin]	On a warm sunny day the river seems placid and benign. 따뜻하고 햇빛 나는 날에는 그 강은 평온하고 온화해 보인다. The old man was well liked because of his benign attitude toward friend and stranger alike. 노인은 친구를 대하는 태도와 똑같이 낯선 사람에게도 온화하여 모두 그를 좋아했다.	
539 ☐☐	**beset** [bisét]	The enemies beset the village. 적은 그 마을을 포위했다. The police beset every road to the town. 경찰은 마을로 통하는 모든 길을 봉쇄했다.	
540 ☐☐	**bestow** [bistóu]	He wished to bestow great honors upon the hero. 그는 영웅들에게 커다란 영광을 주기를 원했다. Several gifts were bestowed on the foreign visitors. 여러 개의 선물이 외국인 방문객들에게 주어졌다.	

☐ ascribe _____   ☐ aspersion _____   ☐ assent _____

Definition	Meaning/Relation
집중사격; 빗발침	ⓝ a heavy curtain of artillery fire directed in front of friendly troops to screen and protect them; an overwhelming, concentrated outpouring, as of words **lay down a barrage** 탄막 포화를〔일제 엄호사격을〕 퍼붓다 **lift a barrage** 탄막의 사정거리를 넓히다 **an artillery barrage** 연속 포격 **a roll- ing barrage** 이동 탄막 사격 **an advertising barrage** 광고 공세 **a propaganda barrage** (주의·신념의) 선전 공세 **a barrage of questions** 질문 공세
공격하다; 장황하게 말하다	ⓥ to attack with blows; to discuss repeatedly or at length **belabor a point** …의 문제에 대해 장황하게 말하다
모순되다	ⓥ to show to be false
미개한	ⓐ overtaken by night or darkness
온화한	ⓐ of a kind and gentle disposition **a benign[non-cancerous, non- malignant] growth** 양성〔암이 아닌, 비악성〕 종양 **benign neglect** (외교·경제 관계에서) 은근한 무시 **a benign polyp** 양성 폴립 **a benign tumor** 양성종양
포위하다; 봉쇄하다	ⓥ to attack from all sides; to surround on every side **beset by[with]** …으로 괴로움을 당하는
주다, 수여하다	**bestow on [upon]** …에게 헌정하다

534_540 175

PART 1

PART 2

PART 3

PART 4

PART 5

PART 6

☐ austere _____ ☐ avarice _____ ☐ balk _____ ☐ banal _____

541 ☐☐	**bombast** [bámbæst]	His speech was full of bombast. 그의 연설은 호언장담으로 가득했다. He might have mentioned the bombast of Toyotomi Hideyoshi (1536-98), invading Korea to conquer the Ming China. 그는 명나라를 정복하기 위해 조선을 침략하면서 도요토미 히데요시의 호언장담을 언급했을지도 모른다.
542 ☐☐	**bourgeois** [buərʒwá:]	They cried him down as a bourgeois. 그들은 그를 자본가로 매도했다. Born in Istanbul in 1952, he grew up in a wealthy yet declining bourgeois family. 1952년 Istanbul에서 태어난 그는 부유하지만 쇠퇴해 가는 중산층 가정에서 자랐다.
543 ☐☐	**bravado** [brəvá:dou]	Their behavior was just sheer bravado. 그들의 행동은 그저 순전한 허세였다. The passengers had to suffer the consequences of their bravadoes. 승객들은 과시의 결과에서 오는 고통을 겪어야 했다.
544 ☐☐	**burgeoning** [bə́:rdʒəniŋ]	Korea's burgeoning auto industry will threaten the foreign carmakers. 한국의 급성장하는 자동차산업은 외국 자동차 제조회사들에 위협이 될 것이다. This remarkable growth has fueled a burgeoning market for software. 이 괄목할 만한 증가는 소프트웨어 시장의 성장을 더욱 가속화시켰습니다.
545 ☐☐	**cajole** [kədʒóul]	She was cajoled into accepting a part in the play. 그녀는 감언이설에 넘어가서 그 연극에서 역을 맡았다. The confession had to be cajoled out of him. 그를 구슬려서 자백을 받아 내어야 했다.
546 ☐☐	**calamity** [kəlǽməti]	A miserable calamity befell him. 처참한 불행이 그에게 닥쳤다. The report contains numerous portentous references to a future environmental calamity. 그 보고서에는 미래의 환경 재난을 예고하는 수많은 언급이 담겨있다.
547 ☐☐	**calumny** [kǽləmni]	She has been the victim of a series of completely unjustified calumnies. 그녀는 전혀 정당화될 수 없는 연속된 비방의 희생자였다. All the eulogies of his friends could not remove the sting of the calumny heaped upon him by his enemies. 그의 친구들이 보낸 어떤 찬사도 그의 적들이 그에게 퍼부은 비방의 고통을 씻어낼 수는 없었다.

☐ barrage _____   ☐ belabor _____   ☐ belie _____

Definition	Meaning/Relation
호언 장담	ⓝ grandiloquent, pompous speech or writing
자본가; 중산층	ⓝ a member of the property-owning class; a person belonging to the middle class
허세; 과시	ⓝ a false show of bravery; defiant or swaggering behavior **sheer bravado** 순전한 허세 **an act of bravado** 허세에 찬 행동
급성장하는	ⓐ growing and flourishing quickly
감언으로 꾀다, 구슬리다	ⓥ to urge with gentle and repeated appeals, teasing, or flattery **cajole from** …을 구슬려서 …을 뜯어내다 **cajole into** …을 구슬려서 …하게 하다
불행; 재난	ⓝ an event that brings terrible loss, lasting distress; a catastrophe, disaster **avert[ward off] a calamity** 참사를 피하다(막다) **survive a calamity** 재난을 면하다(이기고 살아남다) **a calamity befalls sb.** …에게 재난이 닥치다 **a crushing[dire, grave, great] calamity** 대참사 **a national calamity** 국가적인 재난 **a natural[unavoidable] calamity** 천재(天災) **a calamity for** …에게 닥 친 재난(재해)
비방	ⓝ a false statement maliciously made to injure another's reputation **heap calumny on** …에게 비방을 퍼붓다

□ benighted _____ □ benign _____ □ beset _____ □ bestow _____

PART 1 PART 2 PART 3 PART 4 PART 5 PART 6

NO.	Entry Word	Example Sentence	
548 ☐☐	**candor** [kǽndər]	His candor at the meeting was praiseworthy. 회의 석상에서 보여준 그의 솔직함은 칭찬할 만했다. We really don't know what to do about it, she said with surprising candor. 정말 이 일을 어떻게 해야 할지 모르겠다고 그녀는 놀라우리만치 솔직하게 말했다.	
549 ☐☐	**capacious** [kəpéiʃəs]	There was a rather fat man wearing a capacious stripy suit. 다소 뚱뚱한 남자가 크기가 넓은 줄무늬 정장을 입고 있었다. In the capacious areas of the railroad terminal, thousands of travelers lingered while waiting for their train. 널찍한 철도 터미널에서 수천 명의 여행객들이 열차를 기다리며 시간을 보냈다.	
550 ☐☐	**catastrophe** [kətǽstrəfi]	He survived a catastrophe to a miracle. 그는 대참사에서 기적적으로 살아남았다. The flood was a major catastrophe, causing heavy loss of life. 이번 홍수는 많은 인명 피해를 입힌 큰 재앙이었다.	
551 ☐☐	**categorical** [kæ̀təgɔ́ːrikəl]	The government has issued a categorical denial of this rumor. 정부는 이러한 루머에 대해 단정적인 부인을 했었다. After exhaustive research I believe we have a categorical understanding of the issue at hand. 철저한 연구 후에 나는 우리가 금방 이 이슈에 대한 절대적인 이해를 하였다고 믿는다.	
552 ☐☐	**catharsis** [kəθáːrsis]	Aristole maintained that tragedy created a catharsis by pouring the soul of base concepts. 아리스토텔레스는 비극이 기본 개념으로서의 영혼을 정화함으로써 카타르시스를 만들어 낸다고 주장했다. Public enterprises should not be misused as a subject of catharsis for the government to pacify people's discontent. 공기업은 정부가 대중들의 불만을 진정시키기 위한 카타르시스의 원인으로 악용되어서는 안된다.	
553 ☐☐	**catholic** [kǽθəlik]	He is a man of catholic tastes. 그는 폭넓은 취미를 가진 사람이다. What was of catholic rather than national interest? 국익보다 오히려 보편적인 것은 무엇인가?	
554 ☐☐	**caustic** [kɔ́ːstik]	John's always making caustic comments about your work. John는 항상 너의 작품에 대해 신랄한 논평을 한다. The caustic yet perceptive actor-comedian died Saturday, 10 December 2005. 신랄하지만 지각이 있는 배우이자 코메디언은 2005년 12월 10일 토요일에 사망했다.	

☐ bombast _____   ☐ bourgeois _____   ☐ bravado _____

솔직

ⓝ frankness or sincerity of expression

complete candor 허심탄회함
disarming candor 상대방을 무장 해체시키는[상대방이 마음을 열게 만드는]
with candor 허심탄회하게

넓은

ⓐ spacious or roomy

대참사, 큰 재난

ⓝ a great, often sudden calamity

suffer a catastrophe 큰 재앙을 입다
avert a catastrophe 큰 재해를 피하다

단정적인; 절대적인

ⓐ being without exception or qualification; absolute

categorical[complete, unconditional] assurance 무조건적인 보증
A categorical[emphatic] denial 단호한 부인
a categorical grant ((美)) 무상[무조건적인] 보조금

카타르시스 (감정의 정화작용)

ⓝ a purifying or figurative cleansing of the emotions, especially pity and fear, described by aristotle as an effect of tragic drama on its audience.

폭넓은; 보편적인

ⓐ of broad or liberal scope; comprehensive

a catholic[broad-minded, magnanimous] person 포용력이 큰 사람

신랄한

ⓐ corrosive and bitingly trenchant

a caustic[critical, derogatory, sarcastic, scathing, unfavorable] comment 신랄한 발언

☐ burgeon _____ ☐ cajole _____ ☐ calamity _____ ☐ calumny _____

555 □□	**cavalier** [kӕvəlíər]	He displayed a cavalier attitude towards the feelings of others. 그는 다른 사람들의 감정을 등한시하는 거만한 태도를 보였다. He always treats people in a cavalier manner. 그는 항상 사람들을 거만한 태도로 대한다.	
556 □□	**chronicle** [kránikl]	He knows the writer of this chronicle. 그는 이 연대기의 저자를 알고 있다. We heard the sad chronicle of his accidents. 우리는 그가 당한 사고의 슬픈 이야기를 들었다.	
557 □□	**circuitous** [sə:rkjú:itəs]	He took a circuitous road by his car. 그는 우회도로로 갔다. Because of the traffic congestion on the main highways, she took a circuitous route. 주요 간선도로에서 교통이 혼잡하여 그녀는 우회해서 갔다.	
558 □□	**circumspect** [sə́:rkəmspèkt]	It was a very circumspect action. 그것은 매우 신중한 행동이었다. Forty years of twists and turns in politics have taught them to remain circumspect. 그들은 40년의 정치적 우여곡절 끝에 신중을 배웠다.	
559 □□	**circumvent** [sə̀:rkəmvént]	She was circumvented with villains. 그녀는 악당들에게 둘러싸였다. Ships were registered abroad to circumvent employment and safty regulations. 고용수칙 및 안전수칙을 회피하기 위해 배들은 외국에서 등록했다.	
560 □□	**citadel** [sítədl]	The town has a 14th century citadel overlooking the river. 그 마을에는 강을 내려다 보는 14세기에 지어진 요새가 있다. Bam with its 2,000-year-old historic citadel was a major Iranian tourist attraction. 2천년 역사를 자랑하는 고성(古城)이 있는 밤 시(市)는 이란의 대표적인 관광 명소였다.	
561 □□	**clandestine** [klӕndéstin]	Federal police launched a massive operation shutting down clandestine sawmills. 연방 경찰은 비밀 제재소를 폐쇄하기 위한 대규모 작전을 시행했다. The article says that he authorized a clandestine unit to use 'rough tactics' including physical coercion. 기사에 따르면 비밀 부대가 신체적 압박을 포함하는'잔혹한 방식'을 쓸 수 있도록 그가 승인했다고 한다.	

□ candor _____ □ capacious _____ □ catastrophe _____

Definition	Meaning/Relation
거만한	ⓐ showing arrogant or offhand disregard **a cavalier attitude** 오만한 태도 **an cavalier[arrogant, imperious, overbearing] manner** 거만한 태도
연대기; 이야기	ⓝ an extended account in prose or verse of historical events, sometimes including legendary material, presented in chronological order and without authorial interpretation or comment; detailed narrative record or report **keep a chronicle** 기록을 하다 **a chronicle of the war** 전기(戰記)
우회하는	ⓐ being or taking a roundabout, lengthy course **a circuitous route** 돌아서 가는 길, 우회로
신중한	ⓐ heedful of circumstances and potential consequences **circumspect about** …에 관해 신중한[주의깊은] **circumspect in** …에 있어 신중한[용의주도한]
둘러싸이다; 회피하다	ⓥ to surround(an enemy, for example); to avoid having to obey the rule or restriction in a clever and perphaps dishonest way **circumvent the real issues** 실질적인 문제를 회피하다
요새, 성채	ⓝ a fortress in a commanding position in or near a city
비밀의	ⓐ kept or done in secret, often in order to conceal an illicit or improper purpose **a clandestine[secret] affair** 은밀한 정사 **a clandestine[secret] meeting** 비밀회의

☐ categorical _____ ☐ catharsis _____ ☐ catholic _____ ☐ caustic _____

562 □□	**clique** [kli:k]	The club is dominated by a small clique of intellectuals. 그 클럽은 소규모의 지식인 일당에 의해 지배되고 있다. The government blamed on the Dalai Lama clique to undermine the Olympic Games in Beijing in August. 정부는 8월 베이징 올림픽을 음해하는 달라이 라마 일당에 대해 비난했다.
563 □□	**coalesce** [kòuəlés]	The views of party leaders coalesced to form a coherent policy. 정당 지도자들의 견해는 일관된 정책을 형성하기 위해 연합했다. I'm willing to coalesce with anyone and will talk to all forces and rivals. 나는 기꺼이 모든 사람들과 융합할 것이고 모든 세력과 경쟁자들과 대화할 것이다.
564 □□	**coerce** [kouə́:rs]	The friends coerced her into drinking. 친구들은 그녀에게 강제로 술을 먹였다. We were coerced into signing the contract. 우리는 강제로 그 계약서에 서명해야 했다.
565 □□	**cogent** [kóudʒənt]	She presented cogent arguments to the jury. 그녀는 배심원에게 설득력 있는 주장들을 제시했다. He produced cogent reasons for the change of policy. 그는 정책 변화에 대해 설득력 있는 이유를 내놓았다.
566 □□	**cognitive** [kágnətiv]	The accident has significantly impaired several of her cognitive functions. 그 사고는 그녀의 몇몇 인지 기능을 중대하게 손상했다. The theory of infantile amnesia suggests that we have no cognitive memory before the age of three. 유아기의 기억상실증에 대한 이론에선 3세 이전에는 인식 기억이 없다고 주장한다.
567 □□	**cohesion** [kouhí:ʒən]	Wet sand has more cohesion than dry sand. 젖은 모래가 마른 모래보다 응집력이 있다. The lack of cohesion within the party lost them votes at election time. 당 내부의 응집력 부족 때문에 그들은 선거 때 표를 얻지 못했다.
568 □□	**colloquial** [kəlóukwiəl]	It was a colloquial expression. 그것은 구어체 표현이었다. "He's off his head!" is a colloquial way of saying "His behavior is not reasonable." "He's off his head!"라는 말은"그의 행동은 이성적이지 않다"를 구어로 표현한 것이다.

□ cavalier _____   □ chronicle _____   □ circuitous _____

562_568 183

PART 1

PART 2

PART 3

PART 4

PART 5

PART 6

Definition	Meaning/Relation
일당	ⓝ a small, exclusive group of friends or associates **a military clique** 군벌 **a ruling clique** 집권층, 집권세력
연합하다; 융합하다	ⓥ to come together so as to form one whole **coalesce into** …으로 합동〔연합〕하다
강제로 …하게 하다	ⓥ to force to act or think in a certain way by use of pressure, threats, or intimidation **coerce into** …하도록 강요하다 **coerce *sb.* into doing *sth.*** …에게 …하도록 강요하다
설득력 있는	ⓐ appealing to the intellect or powers of reasoning **a cogent argument** 정곡을 찌르는 주장 **cogent[clear, compelling, convincing] evidence** 설득력이 있는〔분명한〕 증거 **a cogent[compelling] reason** 납득할 만한 이유
인지의, 인식의	ⓐ relationg to the mental process involved in knowing, learning, and understanding things **cognitive learning** 인지 학습 **cognitive psychology** 인지 심리학 **cognitive power** 인식력
응집력	ⓝ the act, process, or condition of cohering **cohesion among[between]** …사이의 결속〔단결〕
구어의	ⓐ characteristic of or appropriate to the spoken language or to writing that seeks the effect of speech **colloquial English** 구어체 영어 **a colloquial flavor** 구어의 특성 **a colloquial form** 구어체

☐ circumspect _____ ☐ circumvent _____ ☐ citadel _____ ☐ clandestine _____

569 ☐☐	**collusion** [kəlúːʒən]	The swindlers were found guilty of collusion. 사기꾼들의 공모죄가 밝혀졌다. They discovered a spy acting in collusion with their competitors. 그들은 한 스파이가 자신들의 경쟁자들과 공모하여 행동하고 있다는 것을 발견했다.	
570 ☐☐	**compact** [kəmpǽkt]	The space was in a compact mass with restaurants. 그 공간은 식당으로 밀집하여 있었다. The signers of the Mayflower Compact were establishing a form of government. 메이플라워호 협정에 서명한 사람들은 일종의 정부 형태를 설립하고 있었다.	
571 ☐☐	**complicity** [kəmplísəti]	You cannot keep your complicity in this affair secret very long. 너는 이 일의 공모를 오랫동안 비밀로 할 수는 없을 것이다. He was suspected of complicity in her murder. 그는 그녀의 살인에 공모 혐의를 받았다.	
572 ☐☐	**compress** [kəmprés]	She compressed the package under her feet. 그녀는 발아래에 짐을 밀어 넣었다. Poor posture compresses the body's organs. 자세가 나쁘면 내장기관이 압박을 받는다.	
573 ☐☐	**confidant** [kɑ̀nfidǽnt]	He was perhaps Mike's closest confidant. 그는 아마도 Mike의 가장 가까이에 있는 절친한 친구였다. Madame Chiang became her husband's interperter, confidant and propagandist. Madame Chiang은 그녀 남편의 통역자이고 절친한 친구이자 선교자가 되었다.	
574 ☐☐	**congeal** [kəndʒíːl]	The soup had congealed by the time we returned. 우리가 돌아갔을 때 스프는 이미 굳어 있었다. Use hot water to rinse the congealed fat off the dinner plates. 식기에 굳은 기름기를 씻어내려면 뜨거운 물을 사용해라.	
575 ☐☐	**congenial** [kəndʒíːnjəl]	He was congenial to company. 그는 일행과 마음이 맞았다. A good politician must be able to appear congenial even when he cannot do what people want him to do. 훌륭한 정치가는 국민들이 원하는 것을 할 수 없을 때도 즐거워보일 수 있어야 한다.	

☐ clique _____ · ☐ coalesce _____ ☐ coerce _____ ☐ cogent _____

Definition	Meaning/Relation
공모	ⓝ a secret agreement between two or more parties for a fraudulent, illegal, or deceitful purpose **collusion between** …사이의 공모 **in collusion with** …와 공모하여
밀집한; 협정	ⓐ closely and firmly united or packed together ⓝ a contract or agreement **make a compact with** …와 협정을 맺다 **compact between** …사이의 협정
공모	ⓝ involvement as an accomplice in a questionable act or a crime. **complicity between** …사이의 공모 **complicity in (a crime)** (범죄)에 공모
누르다; 압박하다	ⓥ to press together; to make more compact by or as if by pressing **apply a compress to** …에 압박 붕대〔습포〕를 대다 **compress into** …으로 압축하다
절친한 친구	ⓝ one to whom secrets or private matters are disclosed
굳다, 응고시키다	ⓥ to solidify by or as if by freezing; to coagulate
마음이 맞는; 즐거운	ⓐ suited to one's needs or nature; agreeable **a congenial [convivial] atmosphere** 유쾌한 분위기 **a congenial[gracious] host** (초대한 집의) 상냥한 주인

569_575 185

PART 1

PART 2

PART 3

PART 4

PART 5

PART 6

□ cognitive _____   □ cohesion _____   □ colloquial _____

NO.	Entry Word	Example Sentence	
576 ☐☐	**connoisseur** [kɑ̀nəsə́ːr]	She had developed into a connoisseur of fine china. 그녀는 예술 도자기의 감정가로 발전했다. I'm no connoisseur but I know a good champagne when I taste one. 나는 전문가는 아니지만 좋은 샴페인은 마셔 보면 알 수 있다.	
577 ☐☐	**consecrate** [kɑ́nsikrèit]	We shall consecrate our lives to this noble purpose. 우리는 이 숭고한 목적에 우리의 삶을 바칠 것이다. She has consecrated one's life to the service of God and to the relief of suffering 그녀는 자신의 삶을 신에게 봉사하고 고통을 줄이는 데 바쳤다.	
578 ☐☐	**console** [kənsóul]	Nothing could console her grief. 아무것도 그녀의 슬픔을 달랠 수는 없었다. When her father died, Marius did his best to console Cosette. 그녀의 아버지가 죽었을 때 마리우스는 코셋을 위로하는데 최선을 다했다.	
579 ☐☐	**consort** [kɑ́nsɔːrt]	Do not consort with criminals. 범죄자들과 어울리지 마라. This idea does not consort with our company's goals. 이러한 생각은 우리 회사의 목표와 일치하지 않는다.	
580 ☐☐	**contrite** [kəntráit]	Gloria looked contrite, even distressed. Gloria는 회개하는 듯, 심지어 비통해 하는 듯 보였다. Her contrite tears did not influence the judge when he imposed sentence. 그녀가 보인 참회의 눈물은 판사가 형을 부과했을 때 아무런 영향도 미치지 못했다.	
581 ☐☐	**conundrum** [kənʌ́ndrəm]	Ms. Brandy is caught in a vicious conundrum of fame acquired young. Brandy는 나이 어린 가수로서의 명성 뒤에 따르는 난제에 빠져 있다. He resolved what for too long has looked like an insoluble conundrum. 그는 오랫 동안 해결할 수 없는 것 같이 보였던 난제를 해결했다.	
582 ☐☐	**convene** [kənvíːn]	General manager plans to convene his employees to review security procedures. 총감독은 보안 절차를 재조사하기 위해 직원들을 소집할 계획입니다. The program began when community leaders were convened to discuss topics for education seminars. 프로그램이 시작된 계기는 마을 지도자들이 모여서 교육 세미나 주제를 논의하면서였다.	

☐ collusion _____   ☐ compact _____   ☐ complicity _____

Definition	Meaning/Relation
감정가; 전문가	ⓝ a person with expert knowledge or training, especially in the fine arts; a person of informed and discriminating taste
바치다	ⓥ to dedicate solemnly to a service or goal **consecrate as** …로 성직에 임명하다
달래다, 위로하다	ⓥ to allay the sorrow or grief of **console on** …에 대해 위로하다
어울리다; 일치하다	ⓥ to keep company; to be in accord or agreement **consort with** …와 어울려 지내다
회개의, 참회의	ⓐ feeling regret and sorrow for one's sins or offenses **a contrite apology[manner]** 깊이 뉘우치며 하는 사과/깊이 뉘우치는 태도
난제	ⓝ a problem or puzzle which is difficult or impossible to solve
소집(환)하다	ⓥ to arrange for it to take place **convene an assembly** 회의를 소집하다 **convene [hold] a congress** 회의를 열다

☐ compress _____ ☐ confidant _____ ☐ congeal _____ ☐ congenial _____

NO.	Entry Word	Example Sentence	
583 ☐☐	**copious** [kóupiəs]	The documentation is copious. 증거 서류는 풍부하다. We had a copious rainfall this summer. 금년 여름에는 비가 많았다.	
584 ☐☐	**corollary** [kɔ́rəlèri]	Good health is a corollary of having good habits. 건강은 좋은 습관을 가진 데서 오는 필연적인 결과이다. The corollary of that argument is that they want to spend less on everything else. 그러한 논쟁의 필연적인 결과는 그들이 그 밖의 모든 것에서 덜 소비하기 원한다는 것이다.	
585 ☐☐	**corroborate** [kɔrɑ́bɔrèit]	Recent research in this field seems to corroborate the theory. 이 분야의 최근 조사는 그 이론을 확증하는 것처럼 보인다. Unless we find a witness to corroborate your evidence, it will not stand up in court. 우리가 당신의 증거를 확증해 줄 목격자를 찾지 못한다면 그것은 법정에서 유효하지 못할 것이다.	
586 ☐☐	**countenance** [káuntənəns]	Her countenance fell. 그녀는 침통한 표정을 지었다. He was of noble countenance. 그는 고상한 용모를 지녔었다.	
587 ☐☐	**coup** [kuː]	He never formally retracted the statement about the military coup of 1961. 그는 1961년 군사 쿠데타에 관한 성명을 정식으로 철회하지 않았다. Yesterday's coup brought further upheaval to a country already struggling with famine. 어제의 쿠데타는 이미 기근에 시달리고 있는 나라에 더욱 큰 격변을 가져왔다.	
588 ☐☐	**covert** [kʌ́vəːrt]	He had no knowledge of covert activities. 그는 은밀한 활동에 관해서는 몰랐다. The United States alleges that the program has a covert weapons component. 미국은 그 프로그램이 비밀스럽게 무기를 만든다고 주장한다.	
589 ☐☐	**crescendo** [kriʃéndou]	Her life is a swift crescendo of waste and destruction ending in ruin and collapse. 그녀의 인생은 낭비와 파괴가 갑자기 심해져서 타락과 붕괴로 끝난다. There has been a rising crescendo of violence which started last year and is now reaching a climax. 작년부터 시작된 폭력이 점점 심해져서 이제는 절정에 달하고 있다.	

☐ connoisseur _____ ☐ consecrate _____ ☐ console _____

Definition	Meaning/Relation
풍부한; 많은	ⓐ yielding or containing plenty; affording ample supply **contain copious annotations** 상세한(풍부한) 주석이 들어 있다
필연적인 결과	ⓝ a natural consequence or effect
확증하다	ⓥ to strengthen or support with other evidence **corroborate (the) evidence** 증거를 제시하다(보완하다)
표정; 용모	ⓝ the expression of the face; appearance **a forbidding[stern] countenance** 성서 무서운 표정(얼굴) **a radiant[shining] countenance** 환한 얼굴
쿠데타	ⓝ a masterstroke; a coup d'état **pull off[score] a coup** 성공을 이뤄내다
은밀한, 비밀의	ⓐ not openly practiced, avowed, engaged in, accumulated, or shown **covert operations** 비밀 작전(공작) **a covert threat** 은밀한 협박
점점 세어지기	ⓝ A steady increase in intensity or force **reach[rise to] a crescendo** 최고조에 달하다 **a deafening crescendo** 귀청을 찢는 듯한 음의 고조

□ consort _____ □ contrite _____ □ conundrum _____ □ convene _____

NO.	Entry Word	Example Sentence
590 □□	**cull** [kʌl]	Deer are culled by hunters. 사슴은 사냥꾼들이 추려낸다. Every month the farmer culls the nonlaying hens from his flock and sells them to the local butcher. 매 달 그 농부는 무리에서 알을 낳지 못하는 닭을 추려내어 도살장에 판다.
591 □□	**cursory** [kə́ːrsəri]	The book is cursory in its treatment of his early life. 그 책은 그의 유년시절을 대강 다루고 있다. "I was so pressed for time that I couldn't give the lengthy report more than a cursory reading", the busy executive confessed. "시간이 너무 촉박해서 대강 읽는 정도 이상의 자세한 보고를 드릴 수 없었습니다."라고 바쁜 중역이 고백했다.
592 □□	**debase** [dibéis]	You debase yourself by telling such lies. 너는 그런 거짓말을 해서 너의 격을 떨어뜨리고 있어. Do not debase yourself by becoming maudlin. 감상에 젖어서 너 자신의 품위를 떨어뜨리지 마라.
593 □□	**decimate** [désəmèit]	Disease has decimated the population. 질병이 수많은 생명을 앗아갔다. We do more to decimate our population in automobile accidents than we do in war. 우리는 전쟁에서보다 자동차 사고에서 많은 인구를 죽이기 위해 더 많은 것을 한다.
594 □□	**definitive** [difínətiv]	There are no definitive answers to this problem. 이 문제에는 결정적인 답이 없다. It's a good study, no one study is definitive. 그것은 훌륭한 연구이지만, 어떤 한 연구가 결정적일 수는 없다.
595 □□	**defunct** [difʌ́ŋkt]	They used to be members of a now defunct communist organization. 그들은 현재는 존재하지 않는 공산당 당원이었다. Cambodia's comprehensive peace plan is defunct, and war with the Khmer Rouge is inevitable. 캄보디아의 일괄 평화안은 폐기되었으며, 크메르 루즈와의 전쟁이 불가피하다.
596 □□	**demur** [dimə́ːr]	I suggested putting the matter to a vote, but the chairwoman demurred. 나는 그 문제를 표결에 부칠 것을 제안했지만 의장이 이의를 제기했다. They accepted my proposal without demur. 그들은 내 제안을 이의 없이 받아들였다.

□ copious _____   □ corollary _____   □ corroborate _____

PART 1

PART 2

PART 3

PART 4

PART 5

PART 6

Definition	Meaning/Relation
추려내다	ⓥ to pick out from others **cull from** …에서 골라 모으다
대강의	ⓐ performed with haste and scant attention to detail
떨어뜨리다	ⓥ to lower in character, quality, or value
많은 사람을 죽이다	ⓥ to destroy or kill a large part of (a group) **decimate an army** 군대를 섬멸하다
결정적인	ⓐ supplying or being a final settlement or decision **a definitive answer** 결정적인 대답 **a definitive solution** 확실한 해답 **a definitive statement** 확고한 진술
현존하지 않는; 폐지된	ⓐ having ceased to exist or live; no longer in use
이의를 제기하다; 이의	ⓥ to voice opposition ⓝ an objection **without demur** 이의없이

☐ countenance _____ ☐ coup _____ ☐ covert _____ ☐ crescendo _____

NO.	Entry Word	Example Sentence	
597 ☐☐	**deplete** [diplíːt]	It's an energy-depleting job. 그것은 정력을 소모시키는 일이다. We must wait until we deplete our present inventory before we order replacements. 우리는 대체물들을 주문하기 전에 현재의 재고품들을 소모시킬 때까지 기다려야만 한다.	
598 ☐☐	**desolate** [désəlit]	There was a desolate plain ahead of us. 우리 앞에는 황량한 벌판이 펼쳐져 있었다. The house looked out over a bleak and desolate landscape. 그 집은 황량하고 쓸쓸한 풍경에 면해 있었다.	
599 ☐☐	**deviate** [díːvièit]	Her behavior deviated from the rules. 그녀의 행동은 규칙에서 벗어났다. Do not deviate from the truth, you must face the facts. 진실에서 벗어나지 말라, 사실을 직시하라.	
600 ☐☐	**dirge** [dəːrdʒ]	He accurately described as "suicide music," a series of pulseless love dirges. 그는 "자살 음악"을 일련의 무기력한 애가로 정확하게 묘사했다. The music in the piece is a mix of diverse genres including jazz, rock, paso doble and Macedonian dirge. 악보에 있는 그 음악은 재즈, 락, 파소 도블레, 그리고 마케도니아식 애가를 포함하여 다양한 장르가 섞여 있다.	
601 ☐☐	**discrete** [diskríːt]	Occupations are grouped into discrete categories. 각각의 직업들은 서로 관련이 없는 여러 범주로 분류된다. The mind divides the continuity of the world around us into discrete units. 정신은 우리 주위를 둘러싼 세계의 연속성을 별개의 단위들로 나누어 놓는다.	
602 ☐☐	**disgruntle** [disgrʌ́nyl]	He succeeded in mollifying a disgruntled public. 그는 불만을 품은 대중들을 달래는데 성공했다. They say their effort will send a loud political signal to disgruntled U.S. voters. 그들은 그들의 노력이 화난 미국의 유권자에게 큰 정치적인 신호를 보낼 것이라고 말한다.	
603 ☐☐	**disparate** [díspərit]	He is trying to bring together the disparate elements of three cultural viewpoints. 그는 세 가지 문화적 견해의 이질적인 요소들을 규합하기 위해 애쓰고 있다. It is difficult, if not impossible, to organize these disparate elements into a coherent whole. 불가능하지 않다 하더라도 이러한 본질적으로 다른 요소를 하나의 응집성이 있는 전체로 조직하는 것은 어렵다.	

☐ cull _____   ☐ cursory _____   ☐ debase _____   ☐ decimate _____

Definition	Meaning/Relation
소모시키다	ⓥ to decrease the fullness of, use up or empty out **deplete of** …을 고갈시키다
황량한	ⓐ devoid of inhabitants (a) **desolate[barren] wasteland** 황무지 a **desolate wilderness** 황폐한 땅
벗어나다	ⓥ to turn aside from a course or way **deviate sharply** 심하게 일탈하다 **deviate slightly** 다소 벗어나다
장송가	ⓝ a funeral hymn or lament a **funeral dirge** 만가; 장송곡 a **mournful dirge** 애도가
서로 관련이 없는, 별개의	ⓐ constituting of separate things, distinct
불만을 품게 하다	ⓥ to make discontented
이질적인; 본질적으로 다른	ⓐ fundamentally distinct or different in kind; entirely dissimilar

PART 1

PART 2

PART 3

PART 4

PART 5

PART 6

☐ definitive _____ ☐ defunct _____ ☐ demur _____

NO.	Entry Word	Example Sentence	
604 ☐☐	**disperse** [dispə́:rs]	When the rain came down the crowds started to disperse. 비가 내리자 군중은 흩어지기 시작했다. Cut the remaining butter into cubes and disperse among the shrimp. 남아 있는 버터를 주사위꼴로 자른 다음 새우 사이에 흩뿌려 준다.	
605 ☐☐	**dour** [duər]	The man was dour and taciturn. 그 사람은 뚱하고 무뚝뚝 하였다. The dour old man of 79 shuffles in his heelless to the rooftop and waves apathetically to crowds. 뚱한 79세의 노인은 옥상에 뒷꿈치 없는 신발을 질질 끌고 가서 아무 생각 없이 대중들에게 손을 흔든다.	
606 ☐☐	**duplicity** [dju:plísəti]	I suspect him of duplicity. 그가 이심을 품고 있지 않은지 의심스럽다. People were shocked and dismayed when they learned of his duplicity in this affair. 이번 사건에서 사람들은 그의 대한 이중성을 알았을 때 충격이 컸다.	
607 ☐☐	**ebb** [eb]	The tide was on the ebb. 조수는 썰물이 되어 있었다. The tide is now at[or on] the lowest ebb. 지금이 조수가 가장 많이 빠진 때이다.	
608 ☐☐	**efface** [iféis]	The whole country had tried to efface the memory of the old dictatorship. 나라 전체가 옛 독재의 기억을 지우려고 노력했다. The coin had been handled so many times that its date had been effaced. 그 동전은 여러 차례 유통되었기 때문에 날짜가 지워졌다.	
609 ☐☐	**egoism** [í:gouìzəm]	His egoism was nourished by his mother. 그의 이기주의는 그의 어머니가 길러준 것이다. Asking its trade partner to defer further for its own benefits is simply a manifestation of excessive national egoism. 자국의 이익을 위해 무역 상대국에 계속 미룰 것을 요청하는 것은 단순히 과잉적인 국가 이기주의 표명이다.	
610 ☐☐	**egregious** [igrí:dʒəs]	She was an egregious liar and we could never believe her. 그녀는 터무니없는 거짓말쟁이여서 믿을 수 없었다. It was an egregious error for a statesman to show such ignorance. 정치인이 그런 무지를 보여주었다는 것은 터무니없는 실수이다.	

☐ deplete _____ ☐ desolate _____ ☐ deviate _____ ☐ dirge _____

Definition	Meaning/Relation
흩어지게 하다	ⓥ to drive off or scatter in different directions **disperse clouds** 구름을 흩트리다 **disperse a crowd** 군중을 해산시키다 **disperse a mob** 군중을 해산시키다
뚱한	ⓐ silently ill-humored **a dour expression** 뚱한 표정 **the dour Edinburgh sky** 음침한 에든버러의 하늘
이중성	ⓝ deliberate deceptiveness in behavior or speech **duplicity in** …의 이중성
썰물	ⓝ ebb tide **at a low ebb** 조수가 빠지는, 쇠퇴하는 **on the ebb** 간조에
지우다	ⓥ to rub or wipe out
이기주의	ⓝ the ethical doctrine that morality has its foundations in self-interest
터무니없는	ⓐ conspicuously bad or offensive **an egregious blunder** 돌이킬 수 없는〔치명적인〕 실수 **an egregious breach** 엄청난〔터무니없는〕 위반

☐ discrete _____   ☐ disgruntle _____   ☐ disparate _____

NO.	Entry Word	Example Sentence
611 ☐☐	**elation** [iléiʃən]	The life of an artist may be full of elation and disappointment in alternating cycles. 예술가 삶은 자신감과 실망감이 순환하여 가득차 있을지도 모른다. There's a sense of elation at having completed a race of such length. 그렇게 긴 경주를 완주했다는 것에 대해 매우 의기양양했다.
612 ☐☐	**emissary** [éməsèri]	The government appointed him President's special emissary to China. 정부는 그를 대중국 대통령 특사로 임명했다. The secretary of State was sent as the President's special emissary to the conference on disarmament. 국무 장관은 무장 해제를 토의할 회담에 대통령 특사로 보내졌다.
613 ☐☐	**endemic** [endémik]	Malaria is endemic in many of the hotter regions of the world. 말라리아는 세계의 많은 열대 지방에서 풍토병이다. Some suggest that violence is endemic to American society. 폭력은 미국 사회특유의 것이라고 말하는 사람이 있다.
614 ☐☐	**engender** [endʒéndər]	Pity often engenders love. 동정은 흔히 사랑이 된다. Her latest book has engendered a lot of controversy. 그녀의 최근 저서는 많은 논란을 일으켰다.
615 ☐☐	**entity** [éntiti]	The state is often an artificial entity. 국가는 때로 인공적 실체이다. Each creature is a separate entity. 모든 생물은 저마다 독립된 실체다.
616 ☐☐	**entreat** [entríːt]	I entreat you to let me go. 제발 보내주십시오. We would spend every meal time entreating the child to eat her vegetables. 우리는 아이가 야채를 먹도록 간청하며 매 식사시간을 보내곤 했다.
617 ☐☐	**entrepreneur** [àːntrəprənə́ːr]	There's no magic formula for running your own business, or being an entrepreneur. 자신의 사업을 운영하는, 즉 기업가가 되는 데 마술 같은 공식은 없습니다. Any successful entrepreneur knows that marketing is the key to building your business. 성공한 기업가라면 누구나 사업을 일으키는 열쇠는 마케팅이라는 사실을 알고 있다.

☐ disperse _____ ☐ dour _____ ☐ duplicity _____

Definition	Meaning/Relation
자신감, 의기양양함	ⓝ the state of being filled with excited pride and joy
특사	ⓝ an agent sent on a mission to represent or advance the interests of another **a peace emissary** 평화의 밀사 **a personal emissary** 개인 밀사 **an emissary to** …에의 사절
풍토병의, 어떤 지방 특유의	ⓐ prevalent in or peculiar to a particular locality, region, or people **endemic among [in, to]** …에서 풍토적인, … 사이에서 고질적인
생기게 하다	ⓥ to bring into existence
실체	ⓝ something that exists as a particular and discrete unit
간청하다	ⓥ to make an earnest request of
기업가	ⓝ a person who organizes, operates, and assumes the risk for a business venture **an independent entrepreneur** 독립 기업가 **a private entrepreneur** 개인 기업가

☐ ebb _____   ☐ efface _____   ☐ egoism _____   ☐ egregious _____

NO.	Entry Word	Example Sentence	
618 ☐☐	**epitome** [ipítəmi]	Her parents regard flying first-class as the epitome of extravagance, even though they can afford it. 지불할 여유가 있음에도 불구하고 그녀의 부모는 일등석으로 비행기 여행하는 것을 사치의 전형으로 여긴다. The book in epitome was interesting. 요약된 형태의 책은 흥미로웠다.	
619 ☐☐	**equanimity** [ì:kwəníməti]	He received the news of his mother's death with remarkable equanimity. 그는 어머니의 사망 소식을 매우 침착하게 받아들였다. Three years after the tragedy she has only just begun to regain her equanimity. 그 비극적인 사건이 일어난 지 3년이 지나서야 그녀는 겨우 평정을 되찾기 시작했다.	
620 ☐☐	**euphemism** [júːfəmìzəm]	The expression "he passed away" is a euphemism for "he died." "그는 세상을 떴다"라는 표현은 "그는 죽었다"라는 표현의 완곡어법이다. The article made so much use of euphemism that often its meaning was unclear. 그 논문은 완곡어법을 너무 많이 써서 때로 그 의미가 분명치 않았다.	
621 ☐☐	**execute** [éksikjù:t]	John makes the plans and Dick executes them. John은 계획을 짜고 Dick은 실행한다. Now that we have approval, we execute the scheme as previously agreed. 이제 승인을 받았으므로 우리는 예전에 합의한 대로 계획을 실행에 옮긴다.	
622 ☐☐	**expedient** [ikspí:diənt]	You'll find it expedient to see him. 그를 만나보는 것이 적절하다는 것을 알게 될 것이다. It is expedient that you (should) change the plan. 그 계획을 바꾸는 것이 적절하다.	
623 ☐☐	**expedite** [ékspədàit]	The government plans to expedite the emergency relief plan. 정부는 긴급 구호계획을 신속히 실시할 계획이다. I will expedite the processing to get you your check without further delay. 신속히 처리하여 빠른 시일 내에 지출 경비를 상환할 것이다.	
624 ☐☐	**extraneous** [ikstréiniəs]	Cut out all extraneous information. 관계없는 정보를 모두 삭제해라. His point was extraneous to the argument. 그의 논지는 그 주장과는 관계가 없다.	

☐ elation _____ ☐ emissary _____ ☐ endemic _____ ☐ engender _____

Definition	Meaning/Relation
전형; 요약	ⓝ a representative or an example of a class or type; a brief summary, as of a book or an artick
침착; 평정	ⓝ the quality of being calm and even-tempered; composure **maintain sb's equanimity** 평정[냉정]을 유지하다 **regain sb's equanimity** 평정[침착, 냉정]을 되찾다 **disturb[upset]** *sb's* **equanimity** …의 마음을 어지럽히다 **with equanimity** 침착하게, 태연하게
완곡어법	ⓝ the act or an example of substituting a mild, indirect, or vague term for one considered harsh, blunt, or offensive **a euphemism for** …의 완곡어
실행하다	ⓥ to put into effect **execute as** …으로서 처형하다 **execute for** …한 죄로 사형에 처하다 **execute a plan** 계획을 수행하다 **execute an order** 주문을 처리하다
적절한	ⓐ appropriate to a purpose
신속히 처리하다	ⓥ to speed up the progress of
(본질과) 관계없는	ⓐ not constituting a vital element or part **extraneous to** …와는 관계없는

☐ entity _____ ☐ entreat _____ ☐ entrepreneur _____

NO.	Entry Word	Example Sentence	
625 ☐☐	**extricate** [èkstrəkèit]	It took hours to extricate the car from the sand. 그 차를 모래 밖으로 빼내는 데 여러 시간이 걸렸다. He found that he could not extricate himself from the trap. 그는 덫에서 벗어날 수 없음을 알았다.	
626 ☐☐	**extrovert** [ékstrouvə̀:rt]	Her sister is extrovert and fun-loving, while she is ascetic and strict. 그녀가 금욕적이고 엄격한 반면, 그녀의 언니는 외향적이고 장난기가 있다. A good salesman is usually an extrovert, who likes to mingle with people. 훌륭한 외판원은 사람들과 어울리기를 좋아하는 외향적인 사람이다.	
627 ☐☐	**facade** [fəsáːd]	The building has nine large arches along the length of its facade. 그 건물 정면을 따라 아홉 개의 아치가 있다. A stock indicating screen is displayed on the facade of the Bombay Stock Exchange in Mumbai, India. 주식 시황판은 인도 Mumbai에 Bombay증권거래소 정면에 전시되었다.	
628 ☐☐	**facile** [fǽsil]	He is facile in device. 그는 책략이 뛰어나다. It is facile of reviewers to point out every misprint in a book. 검열자가 책의 모든 오식(誤植)을 지적하는 것은 쉬운 일이다.	
629 ☐☐	**faction** [fǽkʃən]	He unified the factions of a political party. 그는 정당의 파벌들을 통합했다. A two-week armistice has been declared between the rival factions. 경쟁적인 파벌 사이에 2주간의 휴전이 선언되었다.	
630 ☐☐	**feasible** [fíːzəbəl]	Without a larger federal income, none of these is feasible. 연방 정부의 세입 증대 없이는 이것들은 모두 불가능하다. Now that we have the extra resources, the scheme seems politically feasible. 이제 우리는 여분의 자원이 있으므로, 그 계획은 정치적으로 실현 가능해 보인다.	
631 ☐☐	**fetter** [fétər]	I hate being fettered by petty rules and regulations. 나는 사소한 법칙과 규정들에 구속받는 것이 싫다. Fettered by convention, we sometimes find it hard to go our own way. 인습에 사로잡혀 마음대로 하기가 어려운 경우가 있다.	

☐ epitome _____ ☐ equanimity _____ ☐ euphemism _____ ☐ execute _____

Definition	Meaning/Relation
빼내다, 벗어나다	ⓥ to release from an entanglement or difficulty **extricate from** …에서 구해내다
외향적인	ⓝ marked by interest in others or in the environment as opposed to or to the exclusion of self
정면	ⓝ the face of a building, especially the principal face.
손쉬운	ⓐ done or achieved with little effort or difficulty
파벌	ⓝ a group of persons forming a cohesive, usually contentious minority within a larger group **a contending faction** 경합 파벌 **an extremist faction** 극단주의 당파 **an opposing faction** 반대 파벌 **a rebel faction** 반란 파벌 **warring factions** 서로 싸우는〔교전 중인〕 파벌
실현 가능한; 가능성이 있는	ⓐ capable of being accomplished or brought about; possible
구속하다, 사로잡히다	ⓝ to restrict the freedom of

PART 1

PART 2

PART 3

PART 4

PART 5

PART 6

☐ expedient _____ ☐ expedite _____ ☐ extraneous _____

NO.	Entry Word	Example Sentence
632 ☐☐	**fodder** [fádər]	His lecture today concerns getting the most out of farm animals with regular fodder. 오늘 그는 일반 사료를 농장 가축에 최대한 활용할 수 있는 내용을 가지고 강의를 해 주실 겁니다. One of Nancy's chores at the ranch was to put fresh supplies of fodder in the hores' stalls. 목장에서 Nancy가 해야할 허드렛일 중에서는 하는 마굿간에 있는 말에게 신선한 사료를 공급하는 것이다.
633 ☐☐	**foresight** [fɔ́ːrsàit]	Foresight is better than hindsight. 선경지명(先見之明)이 때늦은 지혜보다 낫다. She'd had the foresight to sell her house just before house prices came down. 그녀는 선견지명이 있어서 집값이 떨어지기 직전에 집을 팔았다.
634 ☐☐	**forestall** [fɔːrstɔ́ːl]	I started to object, but she forestalled me. 내가 반대의 말을 시작하려고 했지만 그녀가 나를 앞질렀다. His plans to retire were forestalled by events. 그가 은퇴를 하려던 계획은 여러가지 사건들이 앞질러 방해했다.
635 ☐☐	**forsake** [fərséik]	They were forced to forsake their wounded soldiers. 그들은 부상병들을 버리고 떠나야 했다. No one expected Foster to forsake his wife and children and run off with another woman. 어느 누구도 Foster가 그의 아내와 아이들을 버리고 다른 여자와 도망치리라고 예상치 못했다.
636 ☐☐	**forthright** [fɔ́ːrθràit]	He has a reputation for being a forthright critic. 그는 직설적인 비판가로 유명하다. I prefer Jill's forthright approach to Jack's tendency to beat around the bush. 나는 Jack의 말을 돌리는 경향보다 직설적으로 말하는 Jill의 접근법을 선호한다.
637 ☐☐	**furtive** [fə́ːrtiv]	I saw him cast a furtive glance at the woman at the table. 나는 그가 테이블에 앉아 있는 여자에게 은밀한 시선을 던지는 것을 보았다. Pyongyang has a furtive program to produce highly enriched uranium. 북한 정부는 고농축 우라늄을 생산하기 위한 비밀 프로그램을 갖고 있다.
638 ☐☐	**gaffe** [gǽf]	He didn't realize what a gaffe he'd made. 그는 자신이 어떤 실언을 했는지 깨닫지 못했다. According to Miss Manners, to call your husband by your lover's name is worse than a mere gaffe. 미혼 여성의 예절에 따르면, 연인의 이름으로 당신 남편을 부르는 것은 단순한 실수 이상이다.

☐ extricate _____   ☐ extrovert _____   ☐ facade _____

PART 1

PART 2

PART 3

PART 4

PART 5

PART 6

Definition	Meaning/Relation
사료	ⓝ feed for livestock, especially coarsely chopped hay or straw **cannon fodder** 총알받이(전투에서 총알밥이 되는 군인들) **fodder for** …의 밥
선견지명	ⓝ perception of the significance and nature of events before they have occurred
앞지르다	ⓥ to delay, hinder, or prevent by taking precautionary measures beforehand **forestall a crisis** 위기를 미연에 방지하다
(사랑을) 버리다	ⓥ to give up (something formerly held dear) **forsake[disavow] one's allegiance to** …에의 충성을 거부하다
직설적인	ⓐ direct and without evasion
은밀한; 비밀의	ⓐ characterized by stealth; surreptitious **a furtive glance** 몰래 살피는 눈초리 **a furtive[shifty, sinister] look** 몰래 살피는[은밀한] 눈길
(교제상의) 실수	ⓝ a clumsy social error **commit[make] a gaffe** 결례를 범하다

☐ facile _____   ☐ faction _____   ☐ feasible _____   ☐ fetter _____

NO.	Entry Word	Example Sentence	
639 ☐☐	**galvanize** [gǽlvənàiz]	Ben has a special ability to galvanize me into life. Ben은 나에게 활력을 넣어주는 특별한 능력을 가졌다. Indignation and sympathy over the assult could galvanize voter support for opposition candidates. 그 피습사건은 지방선거에 출마한 야당 후보 지지자들의 분노와 동정을 자극했습니다.	
640 ☐☐	**goad** [goud]	Greed goaded him to steal. 탐욕 탓으로 그는 도둑질을 하게 되었다. He was goaded by his friends until he yielded to their wishes. 그는 그들의 소망에 양보를 할 때까지 친구들에 의해 선동되었다.	
641 ☐☐	**gratify** [grǽtəfài]	Please gratify my curiosity and tell me what it is. 제발 내 호기심을 채울 수 있게 그것이 무언지 말해줘요. I was most gratified by at/with the outcome of the meeting. 나는 그 회의의 결과에 대단히 만족했다.	
642 ☐☐	**gregarious** [grigɛ́əriəs]	He has an outgoing and gregarious personality. 그는 외향적이고 사교적인 성격이다. The human beings are naturally gregarious. 인간은 본래 군집성이다.	
643 ☐☐	**guile** [gail]	The President will need to use all her political guile to stay in power. 대통령은 권력을 유지하기 위해 자신의 모든 정치적 술책을 사용하려 할 것이다. He persuaded her to sign the document by guile. 그는 간사한 꾀로 그녀가 서명을 하도록 설득했다.	
644 ☐☐	**harass** [hǽrəs]	She harassed me for days about my mistake. 그녀는 내가 실수한 것에 대해 며칠 동안 괴롭혔다. Stop harassing the child with so many difficult questions. 그 아이를 그렇게 많은 어려운 질문으로 그만 괴롭혀라.	
645 ☐☐	**hedonism** [hí:dənìzəm]	A culture devoted to hedonism is in danger of becoming soft. 쾌락주의에 빠진 문화는 나약해질 위험이 있다. Hedonism and asceticism are opposing philosophies of human behavior. 쾌락주의와 금욕주의는 인간 행동에 대해 서로 대립되는 철학이다.	

☐ fodder _____ ☐ foresight _____ ☐ forestall _____

Definition	Meaning/Relation
···을 활기띄게 하다; 자극하다	ⓥ to arouse to awareness or action; to stimulate or shock **galvanize into** ···에 활기를 불어넣다
선동하다	ⓥ to prod or urge with or as if with a long pointed stick **goad into** 신경을 긁어 ···하게 하다 **goad with** ···로 신경을 긁다
채워주다, 만족시키다	ⓥ to please or satisfy **gratify one's hunger** ((비유)) 욕망을 채우다 **gratify[satisfy] one's lust** 욕망을 채우다 **gratify[satisfy] one's passion** 열정을 만족시키다
사교적인; 군집성인	ⓐ tending to move in or form a group with others of the same kind; seeking and enjoying the company of other
술책, 간사한 꾀	ⓝ treacherous cunning and skillful deceit
괴롭히다	ⓥ to irritate or torment persistently
쾌락주의	ⓝ pursuit of or devotion to pleasure, especially to the pleasures of the senses

369_645 205

PART 1

PART 2

PART 3

PART 4

PART 5

PART 6

□ forsake _____ □ forthright _____ □ furtive _____ □ gaffe _____

NO.	Entry Word	Example Sentence	
646 ☐☐	**heinous** [héinəs]	I cannot express the odium I feel at your heinous actions. 나는 너의 괘씸한 행위에서 느꼈던 반감을 표현할 수 없다. The judge felt that the criminal had shown no compunction for his heinous crime. 판사는 범죄자가 자기의 흉악한 범죄에 대해 양심의 가책을 느끼지 않았다고 생각했다.	
647 ☐☐	**hierarchy** [háiərɑ̀ːrki]	She's high up in the management hierarchy. 그녀는 관리직 계급에서 고위층이다. There's a very rigid social hierarchy in their society. 그들의 사회에는 매우 엄격한 사회 계급 제도가 있다.	
648 ☐☐	**homogeneous** [hòumədʒíːniəs]	It's a dull city of homogeneous buildings. 그곳은 동종(같은 모양)의 건물들로 이루어진 따분한 도시이다. The population of the village has remained remarkably homogeneous. 그 마을의 전 주민은 눈에 띄게 동질적인 상태로 남아 있었다.	
649 ☐☐	**hubris** [hjúːbris]	It is such political hubris that has plagued mankind. 그것은 인류를 괴롭히는 매우 정치적인 자만이다. Russia's new hubris and military activity is funded by recent oil wealth. 러시아의 새로운 자만과 군사적인 행동은 최근의 석유를 팔아서 얻은 부에 의해 재원이 공급되고 있다.	
650 ☐☐	**husbandry** [hʌ́zbəndri]	He holds a PH.D. in animal husbandry from Michigan State University. 그는 미시간 주립 대학에서 축산학 박사 학위를 취득했다. The clubs trained young men in animal husbandry skills. 그 동아리들은 젊은 남자들에게 축산 기술을 훈련시켰다.	
651 ☐☐	**illicit** [ilísit]	They were all prosecuted for illicit liquor selling. 그들은 모두 불법 주류판매죄로 기소됐다. Those found guilty of illicit funding would be given prison sentences. 불법 자금을 제공한 것으로 판명된 사람들은 징역형을 선고 받을 것이다.	
652 ☐☐	**impair** [impέər]	This arrest will impair her reputation in the community. 이러한 체포가 마을에서 그녀의 평판을 손상시킬 것이다. The accident has significantly impaired several of her cognitive functions. 그 사고는 그녀의 몇몇 인지 기능을 중대하게 손상시켰다.	

☐ galvanize _____   ☐ goad _____   ☐ gratify _____   ☐ gregarious _____

Definition	Meaning/Relation
괘씸한; 흉악한	ⓐ abominable; grossly wicked or reprehensible a heinous[dreadful, grisly, gruesome, horrible, horrid, monstrous, revolting, vile] atrocity 무시무시한 잔학 행위 an heinous[atrocious, brutal, horrendous, horrible, infamous, outrageous, unspeakable, vicious, violent] crime 극악 무도한(잔인한, 사악한) 범죄 a heinous[brutal, cold- blooded, grisly] murder 잔인(극악)한 살인
계급[제]	ⓝ categorization of a group of people according to ability or status rise in the hierarchy 계급이 높아지다 an academic hierarchy 학문상 (분류) 체계 a church hierarchy 교회의 위계 조직 a corporate hierarchy 법인의 위계 제도 a military hierarchy 군대의 계급 a ruling hierarchy 지배 계급
동종의, 동질의	ⓐ of the same or similar nature or kind
자만	ⓝ overbearing pride or presumption
농업, 축산	ⓝ the act or practice of cultivating crops and breeding and raising livestock animal husbandry 축산업
불법의	ⓐ not sanctioned by custom or law an illicit[illegal] act 불법(위법) 행위 an illicit[extramarital] affair 혼외 정사, 간통 illicit[illegal] drugs 불법 마약 illicit sex 간통, 부정(不貞) illicit trade 부정 거래 illicit[illegal] traffic 불법 거래
손상시키다	ⓥ to cause to diminish, as in strength, value, or quality impair efficiency 능률을 떨어뜨리다

□ guile _____   □ harass _____   □ hedonism _____

NO.	Entry Word	Example Sentence	
653 ☐☐	**impeach** [impíːtʃ]	The prime minister was impeached for taking a bribe. 총리는 뇌물을 받아서 탄핵되었다. The angry congressman wanted to impeach the President for his misdeeds. 성난 하원의원은 죄를 범한 대통령을 탄핵하려고 했다.	
654 ☐☐	**impotent** [ímpətənt]	Without the chairman's support, the committee is impotent. 회장의 후원이 없이는 그 위원회는 무력하다. Violent behavior is a result of feeling powerless and impotent. 폭력적인 행동은 힘이 없거나 무력하게 느끼는 결과이다.	
655 ☐☐	**impregnable** [imprégnəbəl]	Until the development of the airplane as a military weapon, the fort was considered impregnable. 군사 무기로서 비행기가 개발되기 전까지 그 요새는 난공불락으로 여겨졌다. The automaker will be able to recapture the seemingly impregnable Japanese market. 그 자동차 회사는 난공불락으로 보였던 일본 시장을 재탈환할 수 있을 것이다.	
656 ☐☐	**impromptu** [imprámptjuː]	Sara unexpectedly announced that she was pregnant so we had a little impromptu party. Sara가 예상치 않게 자신의 임신을 알려서 우리는 작은 즉흥 파티를 열었다. Her listeners were amazed that such a thorough presentation could be made in an impromptu speech. 그녀의 청취자들은 그런 완전한 발표가 즉흥 연설에 의한 것이라는 사실에 놀랐다.	
657 ☐☐	**impute** [impjúːt]	Don't impute me with it. 그 일을 내 탓으로 돌리지 마라. The police impute the accident to the bus driver's carelessness. 경찰은 사고의 원인을 버스 운전사의 부주의로 돌리고 있다.	
658 ☐☐	**inane** [inéin]	These are two of the most popular inane questions amongst the staff. 이것은 직원들 중에서 가장 많이 나오는 어리석은 질문들 중 두 개이다. Why does Korea have such an inane law that prevents sitting presidents from making political statements? 왜 한국에는 현직 대통령이 정치적인 발언을 막는 이런 어리석은 법이 있을까요?	
659 ☐☐	**inanimate** [inǽnəmit]	A rock is an inanimate object. 바위는 생명이 없는 물체이다. They see the whole world, animate and inanimate, as God's creation. 그들은 생물이든 무생물이든 전 세계를 신의 창조물로 본다.	

☐ heinous _____ ☐ hierarchy _____ ☐ homogeneous _____

Definition	Meaning/Relation
탄핵하다	ⓥ to make an accusation against **impeach for** …에 대해서 탄핵하다
무력한	ⓐ lacking physical strength or vigor
난공불락의	ⓐ impossible to capture or enter by force **an impenetrable[impregnable, strong] fortress** 난공불락의 요새 **an impregnable position** 난공불락 지대
즉흥의	ⓐ prompted by the occasion rather than being planned in advance **an impromptu[unrehearsed] speech** 즉흥 연설
(죄 등을) …에게 돌리다	ⓥ to charge with the fault or responsibility for **impute to** …의 탓으로 돌리다
어리석은	ⓐ lacking sense or substance **an inane remark** 멍청한 말
생명 없는, 무생물의	ⓐ not having the qualities associated with active, living organisms

☐ hubris _____ ☐ husbandry _____ ☐ illicit _____ ☐ impair _____

NO.	Entry Word	Example Sentence
660 ☐☐	**incandescent** [ìnkəndésənt]	She was incandescent with rage. 그녀는 성이 나서 빛나(달아올라) 있었다. If you leave on an incandescent light bulb, it quickly grows too hot to touch. 백열전구를 켜둔 채로 둔다면 너무 빨리 뜨거워져 손댈 수 없게 된다.
661 ☐☐	**incantation** [ìnkæntéiʃən]	The witch muttered a diabolical incantation. 그 마녀는 악마의 주문을 중얼거렸다. By incantation and prayer, the medicine man sought to exorcise the evil spirits. 주문과 기도로서 마법사는 악령들을 몰아내고자 하였다.
662 ☐☐	**incentive** [inséntiv]	I gave him an incentive to[or to do] the work. 나는 그를 자극하여 일을 하게 하였다. The promise of a bonus acted as an incentive to greater efforts. 보너스 지급에 대한 약속은 더 열심히 노력하게 하는 자극제가 되었다.
663 ☐☐	**incessant** [insésənt]	We had incessant rain last month. 지난 달에는 끊임없이 비가 왔었다. His feverish and incessant activity cannot hide the fact that he doesn't know what he is doing. 그의 열성적이고 끊임없는 활동이 자기가 무엇을 하고 있는지 모른다는 사실을 감출 수 없다.
664 ☐☐	**influx** [ínflʌks]	Tourism has brought a huge influx of wealth into the country. 관광산업으로 그 나라에 많은 부(돈)가 유입되었다. Turkey is expecting an influx of refugees running into several thousands. 터키는 수천 명에 이르는 난민이 유입될 것으로 내다보고 있다.
665 ☐☐	**insinuate** [insínjuèit]	He insinuates (to me) that you are a liar. 그는 (나에게) 네가 거짓말쟁이라고 넌지시 비추고 있다. Why don't you say openly what is on your mind instead of insinuating such vile charges against me? 나에 대한 그런 나쁜 비난을 빗대어 말하는 대신 왜 마음속에 있는 것을 공개적으로 말하지 않습니까?
666 ☐☐	**insolent** [ínsələnt]	I resent your insolent manner. 나는 당신의 무례한 태도에 불쾌하다. At school he was the sort of child that teachers would describe as insolent. 학교에서 그는 교사들이 건방지다고 했던 아이였다.

☐ impeach _____   ☐ impotent _____   ☐ impregnable _____

Definition	Meaning/Relation
빛나는, 백열의	ⓐ emitting visible light as a result of being heated **an incandescent bulb** 백열등
주문	ⓝ ritual recitation of verbal charms or spells to produce a magic effect
자극[제]	ⓝ something, such as the fear of punishment or the expectation of reward, that induces action or motivates effort **give[offer, provide] an incentive** 장려금을 주다 **have an incentive** 장려금을 받다
끊임없는	ⓐ continuing without interruption **incessant babble** 끊임없는 주절거림 **incessant[constant] bickering** 끊임없는 언쟁
유입	ⓝ a mass arrival or incoming **an influx from** …로부터의 유입 **an influx into** …로의 유입
넌지시 비치다, 빗대어 말하다	ⓥ to introduce or otherwise convey (a thought, for example) gradually and insidiously (=ingratiate) **insinuate into** 교묘히…의 환심을 사다
무례한, 건방진	ⓐ presumptuous and insulting in manner or speech, arrogant **insolent in** …이 건방진

660_666 211

PART 1
PART 2
PART 3
PART 4
PART 5
PART 6

☐ impromptu _____ ☐ impute _____ ☐ inane _____ ☐ inanimate _____

NO.	Entry Word	Example Sentence
667	**insurrection** [ìnsərékʃən]	Insurrection was seen as the only way of changing the government. 반란은 정부를 바꾸는 유일한 방법으로 보였다. Given the current state of affairs in South Africa, an insurrection seems unavoidable. 남아프리카의 현재 사정으로 보아 폭동은 피할 수 없을 것 같다.
668	**interminable** [intə́ːrmənəbəl]	Although his speech lasted for only twenty minutes, it seemed interminable to his bored audience. 그의 연설은 단지 20분 동안이었지만 지루함을 느꼈던 청중들에게는 끝없이 느껴졌다. When we are having fun, time rushes by, but even five minutes in the dentist's waiting room may seem interminable. 재미가 있을 때 시간은 빨리 지나가지만 치과병원 대기실에서는 5분도 지루하게 길 수 있다.
669	**intervene** [ìntərvíːn]	I tried to intervene between the two friends. 나는 두 친구 사이를 중재하려고 애썼다. The Bank of Korea is aggressively intervening in the foreign exchange markets. 한국 은행은 외환 시장에 적극 개입하고 있다.
670	**intimate** [íntəmit]	We are intimate friends. 우리는 절친한 친구이다. He was on intimate terms with them. 그는 그들과 가까운 사이다.
671	**intransigent** [intrǽnsədʒənt]	Owing to their intransigent attitude we were unable to reach an agreement. 그들의 비타협적인 태도 때문에 우리는 협정에 도달할 수 없었다. The strike settlement has collapsed because both sides are intransigent. 파업 타결은 양측이 비타협적이기 때문에 결렬되었다.
672	**introspective** [ìntrəspéktiv]	She is famous for her introspective songs about failed relationships. 그녀는 실패한 관계에 대한 자기 성찰적인 노래로 유명하다. We all have our introspective moments during which we examine our souls. 우리 모두는 우리의 마음을 점검해 보는 자기 성찰의 시기를 갖는다.
673	**itinerant** [aitínərənt]	The country's itinerant masses, as many as 100 million people, are adrift in China. 중국내 무려 1억 명에 달하는 유랑민들이 떠돌아 다닌다. There were itinerant lecturers going round the country demonstrating scientific findings. 시골을 돌면서 과학적 발견을 설명해 보이 순회 강연이 있었다.

☐ incandescent _____ ☐ incantation _____ ☐ incentive _____

PART 1

PART 2

PART 3

PART 4

PART 5

PART 6

Definition	Meaning/Relation
반란, 폭동	ⓝ the act or an instance of open revolt against civil authority or a constituted government **foment[stir up] an insurrection** 반란을 선동하다 **crush[put down, quell, suppress] an insurrection** 반란을 진압하다
끝없는, 지루하게 긴	ⓐ being or seeming to be without an end; tiresomely long **an interminable[long] delay** 지루하게 오래 계속되는 지체
중재하다; 개입하다	ⓥ to interrupt, especially in order to prevent a bad result **intervene between** …사이를 중재하다 **intervene in** …에 개입하다
절친한, 가까운	ⓐ marked by close acquaintance, association, or familiarity **intimate with** …와 친밀한
비타협적인	ⓐ refusing to moderate a position, especially an extreme position **intransigent about** …에 대해 비타협적인
자기 성찰의	ⓝ tending to think deeply about oneself
순방(순회)하는	ⓐ traveling from place to place, especially to perform work or a duty **an itinerant judge** 순회 재판관 **an itinerant laborer** 순회 노동자 **an itinerant peddler** 행상인

☐ incessant _____ ☐ influx _____ ☐ insinuate _____ ☐ insolent _____

NO.	Entry Word	Example Sentence	
674 ☐☐	**jocular** [dʒɑ́kjələr]	Our next-door neighbor is a very cheerful, jocular man 우리 옆집 사는 사람은 매우 유쾌하고 재미있는 사람이다. In the subways of New York are the ads for 'Roach Motel' with the jocular slogan, "Roaches check in. They never check out." "바퀴벌레는 체크인은 하지만 결코 체크아웃은 하지 않는다"라는 재미있는 표어가 있는 '바퀴벌레 모텔'에 대한 광고가 뉴욕의 지하철에 있다.	
675 ☐☐	**jubilation** [dʒùːbəléiʃən]	There was jubilation in the crowd as the winning goal was scored. 결승 골이 들어가자 군중들 사이에는 환호가 넘쳤다. The nationwide jubilation offers a ray of hope for reunifying the country. 그러한 전국적인 환호는 나라의 재통일에 대한 한 줄기의 빛을 비춰준다.	
676 ☐☐	**judicious** [dʒuːdíʃəs]	She is always ready to give judicious parental advice. 그녀는 언제든지 부모로서의 현명한 조언을 해줄 준비가 되어 있다. If the policies are judicious and farsighted, they can help a lot. 그 정책들이 판단력 있고 선견지명이 있는 것들이라면 상당한 도움이 될 것이다.	
677 ☐☐	**laconic** [ləkɑ́nik]	She had a laconic sense of humor. 그녀는 간결한 유머감각을 지니고 있다. Americans in another time were supposed to be a people that made cool, laconic and collected responses to crises. 또 다른 시기에 미국인들은 위기에 멋지고 간결하며 합쳐진 반응을 했던 사람이어야 했다.	
678 ☐☐	**languid** [lǽŋgwid]	A hot day makes me feel languid. 더운 날에는 몸이 나른해진다. I felt too languid to work. 나는 너무 기운이 없어서 일하기가 싫었다.	
679 ☐☐	**languish** [lǽŋgwiʃ]	He has been languishing in jail for the past 20 years. 그는 지난 20년간 감옥에서 기운을 잃어가고 있었다. The project would provide new impetus to a languishing R&D program of South Korea. 그 사업은 한국의 부진한 연구개발 계획에 새로운 활력을 불어넣을 것이다.	
680 ☐☐	**larceny** [lɑ́ːrsəni]	In this his second trial Kozlowski faces 25 years in prison if convicted on grand larceny charges. 이 두번째 재판에서 큰 절도죄가 확정된다면 Kozlowski는 25년 형에 직면하게 된다. The site contains rules to follow when committing acts of larceny, including: "Do not kill or rape while stealing." 그 사이트는 "도둑질을 하는 동안 사람을 죽이거나 강간하지 말라"와 같은 절도를 할 때 따라야 할 규칙을 담고 있다.	

☐ insurrection _____ ☐ interminable _____ ☐ intervene _____ ☐ intimate _____

PART 1

PART 2

PART 3

PART 4

PART 5

PART 6

Definition	Meaning/Relation
재미있는	ⓐ characterized by joking
환호	ⓝ a celebration or other expression of joy **express jubilation** 환호하다 **feel jubilation** 기뻐하다
현명한; 판단력이 있는	ⓐ wise and tactful; having or exhibiting sound judgment
간결한	ⓐ terse or concise
나른한;기운이 없는	ⓐ lacking energy or vitality; weak **feel languid** 나른하다
기운을 잃다	ⓥ to be or become weak or feeble **conversation languishes** 대화에 맥이 빠지다 **languish for** …을 못내 그리워하다
절도(죄), 도둑질	ⓝ the unlawful taking and removing of another's personal property with the intent of permanently depriving the owner **commit larceny** 도둑질하다 **aggravated larceny** 가중절도

☐ intransigent _____ ☐ introspective _____ ☐ itinerant _____

NO.	Entry Word	Example Sentence	
681 ☐☐	**limber** [límbər]	She's as limber as a cat. 그녀는 몸이 정말 유연하다. I always do stretching and yoga exercises to make my body limber. 나는 몸을 유연하게 하기 위해서 스트레칭이나 요가를 항상 합니다.	
682 ☐☐	**livid** [lívid]	She'll be livid if she finds out. 그녀가 알게 된다면 격분할 것이다. His face was so livid with rage that we were afraid that he might have an attack of apoplexy. 그의 얼굴은 분노로 화가 너무 나서 우리는 그가 뇌졸중으로 쓰러지지 않을까 걱정되었다.	
683 ☐☐	**loiter** [lɔ́itər]	Tom always loiters on his way home from school. 톰은 학교에서 귀가할 때 항상 빈둥거린다. The men were loitering near the bank. 그 사람들은 은행 근처에서 빈둥거리고 있었다.	
684 ☐☐	**lugubrious** [lugjú:briəs]	The lugubrious howling of the dogs added to our sadness. 개들의 애처로운 울부짖음이 우리의 슬픔을 더하였다. He has been set adrift into this lugubrious sea, without a rudder or compass. 그는 키나 나침반도 없이 이 애처로운 바다에 표류해오고 있다.	
685 ☐☐	**magnanimous** [məgnǽniməs]	He assumed a magnanimous attitude toward a conquered enemy. 그는 정복당한 적에게 관대한 태도를 취했다. He was magnanimous to everybody. 그는 모든 사람에게 관대했다.	
686 ☐☐	**magnitude** [mǽgnətjù:d]	We simply don't have the resources to take on a project of that magnitude. 우린 그 정도 크기의 프로젝트를 맡을 자금력이 없어요. The war brought problems of very great magnitude to many nations. 그 전쟁은 여러 나라에 대단히 중대한 문제들을 안겨주었다.	
687 ☐☐	**malleable** [mǽliəbəl]	The young are more malleable than the old. 나이가 적은 사람들이 많은 사람들보다 더 적응성이 있다. As Breitz paradoxically suggests, mass culture can be both monolithic and malleable. Breitz가 역설적으로 제안을 하는 것처럼, 대중문화는 획일적이고 적응성이 있을 수 있다.	

☐ jocular _____ ☐ jubilation _____ ☐ judicious _____

Definition	Meaning/Relation
유연한	ⓐ bending or flexing readily; pliable
격분한	ⓐ extremely angry **livid with** …로 흙빛이 된
빈둥거리다	ⓥ to stand idly about
애처로운	ⓐ mournful, dismal, or gloomy, especially to an exaggerated or ludicrous degree **have a lugubrious expression** 슬픈 표정을 짓다
관대한	ⓐ courageously noble in mind and heart **magnanimous towards** …에 관대한
크기; 중요성	ⓝ greatness of rank or position; greatness in significance or influence **considerable[great] magnitude** 엄청난 크기
적응성 있는	ⓐ easily controlled or influenced **malleable iron** 단철

☐ laconic _____ ☐ languid _____ ☐ languish _____ ☐ larceny _____

NO.	Entry Word	Example Sentence
688 □□	**manifesto** [mæ̀nəféstou]	The government have described their manifesto as a blueprint for the future. 정부는 그들의 선언을 미래의 청사진이라고 묘사했다. The results will be rounded up at the final meeting on June 18, which will produce a joint manifesto. 결과는 공동선언문을 작성하게 될 6월 18일 마지막 모임에서 도출될 것이다.
689 □□	**martial** [máːrʃəl]	I'll teach him martial arts. 그에게 무술 한 수 가르쳐줘야겠어. Martial law has been proclaimed in Seoul. 서울에 계엄령이 선포되었다.
690 □□	**melee** [méilei]	We lost sight of each other in the melee. 우리는 난투의 와중에 서로를 시야에서 놓쳤다. The captain tried to ascertain the cause of the melee. 선장은 난투의 원인을 밝히려고 노력했다.
691 □□	**mendicant** [méndikənt]	From the moment we left the ship, we were surrounded by mendicants and peddlers. 우리가 배를 떠난 그 순간부터 우리는 거지와 잡상인으로부터 둘러싸였다. At that time, a mendicant monk visited the rich man and told him that giving is important. 그 순간, 한 탁발 스님이 그 부자를 방문하고 그에게 주는 것이 중요하다고 말했다.
692 □□	**mercenary** [máːrsənèri]	He has a mercenary scheme to merry a wealthy widow. 그는 돈을 위해 부유한 과부와 결혼할 계획이다. That doesn't mean that she's mercenary and indifferent to doing good work. 이것이 그녀가 돈만 좋아하고 좋은 일을 하는 데 무관심하다는 뜻은 아니다.
693 □□	**millennium** [miléniəm]	Big celebrations are planned for the arrival of the next millennium. 다음 1,000년의 도래를 맞는 큰 축하 행사가 계획되고 있다. The Christian Era is more than two millenniums old. 서력 기원은 2천 년이 넘었다.
694 □□	**mirth** [məːrθ]	His sides shook with mirth. 하도 유쾌한 나머지 그의 양 옆구리가 흔들렸다. Performers in the play are drawing on the mirth and sorrow of ordinary Korean people. 연극에서 배우들은 보통 한국 사람들의 기쁨과 슬픔을 그려내고 있다.

□ limber _____ □ livid _____ □ loiter _____ □ lugubrious _____

Definition	Meaning/Relation
선언(문)	ⓝ a public declaration of principles, policies, or intentions, especially of a political nature **draft[draw up] a manifesto** 선언서〔성명서〕를 작성하다 **issue a manifesto** 성명을 발표하다
무(武)의, 전쟁의	ⓐ relating to or connected with the armed forces or the profession of arms **a martial air** 군악 **(the) martial arts** 무술(武術) **court martial** 군법 회의
난투	ⓝ confused, hand-to-hand fighting in a pitched battle
거지, 탁발수도사	ⓐ a beggar **a mendicant order** 탁발 수도회
돈을 위한	ⓐ motivated solely by a desire for monetary or material gain **a foreign mercenary** 외국인 용병
천 년	ⓝ a span of one thousand years
유쾌함, 기쁨	ⓝ gladness and gaiety, especially when expressed by laughter **provoke mirth** 흥겨움을 자아내다 **general mirth** 모두가 웃으며 흥겨워함

☐ magnanimous _____　☐ magnitude _____　☐ malleable _____

NO.	Entry Word	Example Sentence	
695 ☐☐	**mitigate** [mítəgèit]	Being polite now is not going to mitigate his earlier rudeness. 지금 공손하게 군다고 그가 이전에 무례하게 행동한 것에 대한 처벌이 완화될 수는 없을 것이다. Nothing he did could mitigate her wrath. 그가 한 어떤 것도 그녀의 화를 누그러뜨리지 못했다.	
696 ☐☐	**motley** [mátli]	His freidns were a motley crew. 그녀의 친구들은 다양하다. The people she'd invited were a pretty motley crew. 그녀가 초대한 사람들은 상당히 잡다한 무리였다.	
697 ☐☐	**nebulous** [nébjələs]	They had quite nebulous tasks in front of them. 그들은 매우 모호한 임무를 띄게 되었다. He sacrified the lives of people in the name of some nebulous future purpose. 그는 다소 막연한 미래의 목적이라는 미명하에 사람들의 목숨을 희생시켰다.	
698 ☐☐	**nemesis** [néməsis]	I decided to play the nemesis one day. 언젠가는 복수하리라 나는 맘먹었다. The tax increase proved to be the President's political nemesis at the following election. 세금 증가는 그 다음 선거에서 대통령의 정치적 재앙이었음이 증명됐다.	
699 ☐☐	**nepotism** [népətìzəm]	So, he says, nepotism was not involved. 따라서 그의 말대로 하면 어떤 연줄도 작용하지 않은 거지요. He felt that advancement was based on nepotism rather than ability. 그는 승진이 능력보다 연줄에 의해서 된다는 것을 느꼈다.	
700 ☐☐	**nomenclature** [nóumənklèitʃər]	He even ordered the nomenclature of a "war against terror" dropped. 그는 심지어 "테러와의 전쟁"이라는 명칭을 폐지하도록 명령했다. Swedish scientist Linnaeus laid the foundations for the modern scheme of nomenclature and is the father of taxonomy. 스웨덴 과학자 Linnaeus는 용어법의 현대적인 체계에 대한 기반을 세웠고 분류학의 아버지이다.	
701 ☐☐	**nominal** [námənl]	His position as chairman is purely nominal. 회장으로서 그의 지위는 순전히 명목뿐이다. The Queen is the nominal head of the British state. 여왕은 영국에서 명목상의 우두머리이다.	

☐ manifesto _____   ☐ martial _____   ☐ melee _____

Definition	Meaning/Relation
완화시키다, 누그러뜨리다	ⓥ to moderate (a quality or condition) in force or intensity, alleviate **mitigate against** (비표준적으로 쓰여) …을 방해하다(＝militate against)
다양한, 잡다한	ⓐ having elements of great variety or incongruity, heterogeneous **a motley crew** 오합지졸(＝a disparate group)
모호한, 막연한	ⓐ lacking definite form or limits, vague **a nebulous line between** …사이의 작은 차이
복수, 재앙	ⓝ one that inflicts retribution or vengeance **meet one's nemesis** 천벌을 받다
연줄	ⓝ favoritism shown or patronage granted to relatives, as in business
명칭; 용어법	ⓝ a list or set of names; a system of names used in an art or a science
명목상의	ⓐ existing in name only **a nominal clause** 명사절 **nominal damages** 명목상의 피해 보상금 **a nominal fee** 명목상의 요금

☐ mendicant _____　☐ mercenary _____　☐ millennium _____　☐ mirth _____

702 ☐☐	**nuance** [njúːɑːns]	The painter has managed to capture every nuance of the woman's expression. 그 화가는 그녀의 표정에 나타나는 온갖 미묘한 차이를 가까스로 잡아낼 수 있었다. Get a sense of some of the nuances of that organization. 해당 기업의 미묘한 문화를 감지하라.	
703 ☐☐	**obdurate** [ábdʒurit]	The President remains obdurate on the question of cutting taxes. 대통령은 세금 삭감 문제에 대해 완고한 입장을 고수하고 있다. He was obdurate in his refusal to listen to our complaints. 그는 고집이 세서 우리의 충고를 들으려고 하지 않았다.	
704 ☐☐	**oblique** [əblíːk]	In through the window came the last few oblique rays of evening sunshine. 창을 통해서 저녁 햇빛의 마지막 몇 줄기가 비스듬히 들어왔다. Putin expressed this stance in a more oblique way. Putin은 더욱 간접적인 방식으로 이러한 입장을 표현했다.	
705 ☐☐	**obsequious** [əbsíːkwiəs]	She is almost embarrassingly obsequious to anyone in authority. 그녀는 권력자라면 아무한테나 거의 당황스러울 정도로 아부한다. Nothing is more disgusting to me than the obsequious demeanor of the people who wait upon you. 당신에게 시중드는 사람들의 아부하는 행동보다 더 구역질 나는 것은 없다.	
706 ☐☐	**obtrusive** [əbtrúːsiv]	I find the music in the bar very obtrusive. 그 바의 음악은 너무 귀에 거슬리더군. The soldiers were in civilian clothes, to make their presence less obtrusive. 그 군인들은 자신들의 존재를 눈에 덜 띄게 하려고 민간인 복장을 했다.	
707 ☐☐	**odyssey** [ádəsiː]	The refugee's journey from Cambodia was a terrifying odyssey. 캄보디아 난민들은 끔찍한 여행이였다. In the course of his odyssey he visited his family's native village in Italy. 그는 이 여행을 하면서 이탈리아에 있는 자기 가족의 고향 마을을 방문했습니다.	
708 ☐☐	**officious** [əfíʃəs]	He's an officious little man and widely disliked in the company. 그는 참견하기 좋아하는 유치한 남자로 회사에서 널리 미움을 받았다. An officious little guard came and told me not to whistle in the museum garden. 참견하기 좋아하는 작은 체구의 가드가 내게와서는 박물관의 앞뜰에서는 휘파람을 불지 말라고 하였다.	

☐ mitigate _____ ☐ motley _____ ☐ nebulous _____

Definition	Meaning/Relation
미묘한 차이	ⓝ a subtle or slight degree of difference, as in meaning, feeling, or tone a delicate[fine, subtle] nuance 미묘한 뉘앙스
완고한; 고집이 센	ⓐ hardened in wrongdoing or wickedness; stubbornly impenitent
비스듬히; 간접적인	ⓐ having a slanting or sloping direction, course, or position; indirect or evasive the oblique case 사격 an oblique[indirect] reference 간접적 언급, 돌려서 말함
아부하는	ⓐ full of or exhibiting servile compliance obsequious behavior 비굴한 행동
거슬리는; 눈에 띄는	ⓐ tending to push self-assertively forward; undesirably noticeable
(장기간의 방랑 모험) 여행	ⓝ an extended adventurous voyage or trip
참견하기 좋아하는	ⓐ marked by excessive eagerness in offering unwanted services or advice to others

PART 1
PART 2
PART 3
PART 4
PART 5
PART 6

☐ nemesis _____ ☐ nepotism _____ ☐ nomenclature _____ ☐ nominal _____

NO.	Entry Word	Example Sentence
709 ☐☐	**ominous** [ámənəs]	Ominous clouds have begun to gather over Eastern Europe. 동유럽에 암운이 감돌기 시작했다.
		Most ominous for South Korea are statistics that show wage gains starting to outpace labor productivity increases. 한국에 있어 가장 불길한 것은 임금 상승이 노동 생산성 증가를 앞지르기 시작했음을 보여주는 통계이다.
710 ☐☐	**ordeal** [ɔːrdíːəl]	He described the rest of his terrible ordeal. 그는 자신이 겪은 끔찍한 시련의 나머지 부분을 묘사했다.
		It was the worst ordeal I have ever experienced, worse than the death of my parents. 그 시련이 내 부모님이 돌아가셨을 때보다 더 고통스러운 경험이었다.
711 ☐☐	**ordinance** [ɔːrdənəns]	We'll fight this zoning ordinance tooth and nail. 우리는 이 용도별 지역지정 법령에는 결사반대로 싸우겠습니다.
		Some cities have ordinances forbidding the use of soft coal. 일부 도시들은 역청탄 사용을 금지하는 법령을 시행하고 있다.
712 ☐☐	**ostentatious** [àstentéiʃəs]	They criticized the ostentatious lifestyle of their leaders. 그들은 자기 지도자들의 허세부리는 삶의 방식을 비난했다.
		Isn't it rather ostentatious to wear a Phi Beta Kappa key on a chain around your neck? 당신 목걸이에 Phi Beta Kappa 열쇠를 달고 있는 것은 꽤 허세를 부리는게 아닐까요?
713 ☐☐	**paradigm** [pǽrədim]	This gives way to a simple paradigm. 이것은 단순한 예를 보여준다.
		Preparation is urgently required as the nation is going through a drastic paradigm shift. 국가가 격렬한 패러다임의 이동을 겪고 있기 때문에 긴급하게 준비할 것을 요구된다.
714 ☐☐	**paragon** [pǽrəgàn]	The author seems to view the British system as a paragon of democracy. 저자는 영국 체제를 민주주의의 모범으로 보는 것 같다.
		My parents set up my older brother as such a paragon that I despaired of ever being able to follow in his footsteps. 부모님들이 나의 형을 모범으로 너무나 추켜세웠기 때문에 나는 형을 따르기를 단념했다.
715 ☐☐	**paramount** [pǽrəmàunt]	That is a matter of paramount importance. 그것이 가장 중요한 일이다.
		In automation feedback is of paramount concern. 자동화에 있어 자동 제어가 중요 관건이다.

☐ nuance _____ ☐ obdurate _____ ☐ oblique _____

Definition	Meaning/Relation
불길한	ⓐ menacing; threatening (an) ominous silence 불길한 침묵
시련[체험]	ⓝ a difficult or painful experience, especially one that severely tests character or endurance go through[undergo] an ordeal 시련을 겪다 a dreadful[terrible, terrifying, trying]ordeal 괴로운(끔찍한) 시련
법령	ⓝ a statute or regulation, especially one enacted by a city adopt[enact, pass] an ordinance 법령을 채택(가결)하다 issue an ordinance 법령을 발표하다
허세부리는	ⓐ characterized by or given to ostentation a ostentatious[lavish, spectacular] display 지나친 과시 an ostentatious lifestyle 과시적인 생활 방식
예, 패러다임	ⓝ an example that serves as pattern or model a paradigm for others to copy 다른 사람들이 모방할 범례 shifting paradigms of morality 변하는 도덕의 범례 verb paradigms 동사 어형 변화표
모범	ⓝ a model of excellence or perfection of a kind a paragon of virtue 미덕의 귀감
중(주)요한	ⓐ of chief concern or importance paramount over …보다 주요한

☐ obsequious _____ ☐ obtrusive _____ ☐ odyssey _____ ☐ officious _____

NO.	Entry Word	Example Sentence	
716 ☐☐	**paranoia** [pÆrənɔ́iə]	Next there is the issue of paranoia. 다음으로 (하나의 주장을 병적으로 고집하는) 편집증의 이슈가 있다. The psychiatrists analyzed his ailment as paranoia when he claimed that everyone hated him. 정신과 의사들은 모든 사람들이 자기를 미워한다고 주장하는 그의 병을 편집증으로 분석했다.	
717 ☐☐	**parody** [pÆrədi]	She has a gift for parody. 그녀는 모방을 하는 재능이 있다. We enjoyed the clever parodies of popular songs which the chorus sang. 우리는 합창 단원이 인기있는 노래를 재치있게 풍자해서 부르는 것을 즐겼다.	
718 ☐☐	**paroxysm** [pÆrəksìzəm]	He went into a paroxysm of rage. 그는 발작적으로 화를 냈다. A paroxysm of indignation passed through the community, and the streets were filled with angry people ready to flight. 분노의 발작이 그 지역을 스쳐갔고 거리는 당장 싸우기라도 할 것 같은 화난 사람들로 가득 찼다.	
719 ☐☐	**patriarch** [péitrià:rk]	To his people, the patriarch had been the heart and sword of their revolution. 그 족장은 그의 부족들에게는 그들의 혁명의 심장이며 칼이었다. As well as having many privileges, the patriarch of each family unit has many responsibilities. 각 가족 단위의 가장들은 많은 특권을 가지고 있는 것만큼이나 많은 책임 또한 지니고 있다.	
720 ☐☐	**paucity** [pɔ́:səti]	They closed the restaurant because the paucity of customers made it uneconomical to operate. 손님이 적어 운영할 수 없었기 때문에 그들은 식당의 문을 닫았다. The paucity in volitional movement and lack of response to sensory stimuli was followed by death within a week. 운동욕구의 결핍과 자극에 대한 반응의 결핍이 일주일 내에 죽음으로 이어졌다.	
721 ☐☐	**periphery** [pərí:fəri]	The debate touched only the periphery of the issue. 그 토론은 문제의 주변적인 것들만 다루었다. He sensed that there was something just beyond the periphery of his vision. 그는 시야가 미치지 못하는 곳에 무엇인가 있음을 느꼈다.	
722 ☐☐	**perquisite** [pə́:rkwəzit]	The perquisites attached to this job make it even more attractive than the salary indicates. 이 직업에서 생기는 부수입은 봉급보다 더 낫다. With all the perquisites, such free meals and a car, she's really earning over $150,000 a year. 무료 식사와 차 같은 부수입을 합치면 그녀는 1년에 15만 달러 이상을 번다.	

☐ ominous _____ ☐ ordeal _____ ☐ ordinance _____ ☐ ostentatious _____

Definition	Meaning/Relation
편집증	ⓝ a psychotic disorder characterized by delusions of persecution or grandeur, often strenuously defended with apparent logic and reason
모방, 풍자	ⓝ a literary or artistic work that imitates the characteristic style of an author or a work for comic effect or ridicule **compose[write] a parody** 패러디를 쓰다 **a parody of[on] a poem** 어떤 시를 패러디한 것
발작	ⓝ a sudden outburst of emotion or action **paroxysms of coughing/giggling** 발작적인 기침/킥킥거림
족장, 가장	ⓝ a man who rules a family, clan, or tribe
소량; 결핍	ⓝ smallness of number; a scarcity or lack **a paucity of evidence** 증거 부족
주변	ⓝ a line that forms the boundary of an area **on the periphery** 주변에
부수입	ⓝ a payment or profit received in addition to a regular wage or salary, especially a benefit expected as one's due

☐ paradigm _____ ☐ paragon _____ ☐ paramount _____

NO.	Entry Word	Example Sentence	
723 ☐☐	**perverse** [pərvə́:rs]	The perverse child did just what we told him not to do. 고집불통의 그 아이는 우리가 하지 말라고 한 일만 골라 했다. Jack was being perverse and refused to do anything the rest of us wanted to do. Jack은 고집불통이라서 우리 나머지 사람들이 하고 싶어 하는 것은 무엇이든 하지 않겠다고 했다.	
724 ☐☐	**petulant** [pétʃələnt]	Come on. Don't be petulant. Just pick up the stupid can. 왜 이래, 화내지 말고 그냥 주우면 되잖아. Take the reaction of a petulant child, for example. 예를 들어, 화를 잘 내는 아이의 반응을 보자.	
725 ☐☐	**pivotal** [pívətl]	The year was pivotal and messy. 매우 중요하면서도 혼란스러웠던 한 해였다. It was a pivotal event in the country's struggle for independence. 그것은 그 나라의 독립 투쟁에 중요한 사건이었다.	
726 ☐☐	**placebo** [plətʃéibou]	In a controlled experiment, fifty volunteers were given erythromycin tablets; the control group received only placebos. 통제된 실험에서 50명의 자원자에게 에르스마이신이 주어졌다. 대조군은 단지 위양이 주어졌다. In the most comprehensive female trial of Viagra to date, released this week, the drug proved no more effective than a placebo. 이번 주에 발표된 사상 대규모의 여성 비아그라 실험 결과에 따르면, 위약 효과 외에 별다른 효력이 없는 것으로 입증되었다.	
727 ☐☐	**plaintive** [pléintiv]	The dove has a plaintive and melancholy call. 그 비둘기는 구슬프고 슬픈 울음소리를 가지고 있다. We heard a plaintive whimpering coming from the kitchen. 우리는 부엌에서 구슬프게 울먹이는 소리를 들었다.	
728 ☐☐	**polarize** [póuləràiz]	Public opinion has polarized on this issue. 이 쟁점에 대해서는 여론이 양극화되어 왔다. The issue has polarized public opinion. 그 쟁점이 여론을 양극화시켜 왔다.	
729 ☐☐	**porous** [pɔ́:rəs]	The liquid drained through a porous layer. 그 액체는 기공층을 통해 빠져나갔다. He added sand to the soil to make it more porous. 그는 토양의 다공성을 더 좋게 하려고 모래를 섞었다.	

☐ paranoia _____   ☐ parody _____   ☐ paroxysm _____

Definition	Meaning/Relation
고집불통인	ⓐ obstinately persisting in an error or a fault
화를 잘 내는	ⓐ unreasonably irritable or ill-tempered **a petulant and jealous wife** 잘 토라지고 질투심 많은 아내 **petulant children** 잘 토라지는 아이들
중요한	ⓐ of, relating to, or serving as a pivot
위약	ⓝ a substance containing no medication and prescribed or given to reinforce a patient's expetation to get well **administer[give] a placebo** 가짜 약을 투여하다 **a placebo effect** 위약 효과(가짜 약이지만 약을 복용하고 있다는 데 대한 심리효과 따위로 실제 환자의 상태가 좋아지는 것)
구슬픈	ⓐ expressing sorrow **a plaintive cry / voice** 애처로운 울음 / 목소리
양극화 시키다	ⓥ to induce polarization in **polarize into** …으로 양극화하다
작은 구멍이 많은, 다공성의	ⓐ full of or having pores **porous soil** 기공(氣孔)토

□ patriarch _____ □ paucity _____ □ periphery _____ □ perquisite _____

NO.	Entry Word	Example Sentence	
730 □□	**posture** [pástʃər]	Humans have a naturally erect posture. 인간은 날 때부터 곧추 선 자세를 가지고 있다. Should South Korea adopt a tougher, more adversarial posture toward North Korea? 한국은 북한에 대해 보다 강경하고 적대적인 입장을 취해야 하는가?	
731 □□	**precept** [prí:sépt]	Practice is better than precept. 실행은 교훈보다 낫다. The policy contravenes international law and common precepts of decency. 그 정책은 국제법과 품위에 대한 일반적 가르침에 부합하지 않는다.	
732 □□	**precipitous** [prisípətəs]	If a slope is precipitous, it is very steep. 비탈이 험하다는 말은 매우 가파르다는 것을 뜻한다. The Indonesian economic crisis was triggered by the precipitous devaluation of the rupiah. 인도네시아의 경제위기는 루피아화의 가파른 가치하락에 의해 촉발되었다.	
733 □□	**predilection** [prì:dəlékʃən]	Ever since she was a child, she has had a predilection for spicy food. 어린 시절 이후 내내 그녀는 양념맛이 강한 음식을 편식해 왔다. Although the artist used various media from time to time, she had a predilection for watercolors. 그 미술가는 때때로 여러 가지 매체를 사용했지만 수채화 그림 물감을 선호했다.	
734 □□	**preempt** [priémpt]	I was preparing to speak when she pre-empted me. 내가 연설을 하려고 준비하고 있었는데 그녀가 선수를 쳤다. Her departure pre-empted any further questions. 그녀의 출발로 더 이상의 어떤 질문도 무산되었다.	
735 □□	**prodigy** [prádədʒi]	Mozart was a musical prodigy. 모차르트는 음악의 천재였다. At just 15 years old, the child prodigy enrolled as a freshman at the University of Denver. 그 천재 아이는 겨우 15세의 나이에 덴버 대학에 입학했습니다.	
736 □□	**profane** [prəféin]	He uses too much profane language. 그는 불경스러운 말을 지나치게 많이 쓴다. What was once a church is now a profane museum of the village's history. 예전에 교회였던 건물이 이제는 마을 역사를 보여 주는 세속적인 박물관이 되었다.	

□ perverse _____   □ petulant _____   □ pivotal _____   □ placebo _____

Definition	Meaning/Relation

730_736 231

PART 1

PART 2

PART 3

PART 4

PART 5

PART 6

Definition	Meaning/Relation
자세;입장	ⓝ a position of the body or of body parts; a stance or disposition with regard to something **adopt[assume] a posture** 자세를 취하다 **an erect[upright] posture** 직립 자세
교훈, 가르침	ⓝ a rule or principle prescribing a particular course of action or conduct
가파른	ⓐ extremely steep **a precipitous[dizzy, vertiginous] height** 아찔한 높이
편애[식], 선호	ⓝ a partiality or disposition in favor of something **a predilection for** ···에 대한 편애
선수를 치다, 무산되다	ⓥ to appropriate, seize, or take for oneself before others
천재	ⓝ a person with exceptional talents or powers **a child [infant] prodigy** 신동 **prodigygies of nature** 자연의 경이
불경스러운, 세속적인	ⓐ marked by contempt or irreverence for what is sacred

☐ plaintive _____ ☐ polarize _____ ☐ porous _____

NO.	Entry Word	Example Sentence	
737 ☐☐	**profligate** [práfligit]	They are thoroughly fed-up with the budget deficit and the profligate Congress. 그들은 예산 적자와 방탕한 의회에 대해 전적으로 싫증을 느끼고 있다. He was so profligate that he consumed in a few years the fortune it had taken his parents a lifetime to accumulate. 그는 부모가 모으는 데 걸린 평생 걸린 재산을 단지 몇 년에 다 써 버렸다.	
738 ☐☐	**progeny** [prádʒəni]	His numerous progeny are scattered all over the country. 그의 수많은 자손들이 이 나라 방방곡곡에 흩어져 산다. I expect they will produce progeny very soon. 나는 그들이 곧 아이를 가질 것을 기대한다.	
739 ☐☐	**promulgate** [práməlgèit]	The American Declaration of Independence was promulgated in January 1776. 미국 독립 선언은 1776년 1월에 공표되었다. The new law was finally promulgated in the autumn of last year. 새 법이 작년 가을에 드디어 발표되었다.	
740 ☐☐	**prone** [proun]	He is prone to act without thinking. 그는 생각하지 않고 행동하는 경향이 있다. Elderly people are prone to pneumonia. 나이 지긋한 사람들은 폐렴에 걸리기 쉽다.	
741 ☐☐	**propagate** [prápəgèit]	Most plants propagate by seed. 대부분의 식물들은 씨로 번식한다. The weeds propagate themselves rapidly. 잡초는 재빨리 퍼진다.	
742 ☐☐	**propensity** [prəpénsəti]	I dislike your propensity to belittle every contribution she makes to our organization. 나는 우리 조직에 대한 그녀의 모든 기여를 헐뜯는 당신의 성향을 싫어한다. The economists studied the public's propensity to save. 경제학자들이 국민의 저축성향을 알아보았다.	
743 ☐☐	**propriety** [prəpráiəti]	I doubt the propriety of making use of the method. 그 방법을 이용하는 것이 적절한지 어떤지 의문이다. These essays were then evaluated according to the criteria of purity, truthfulness, elegance, and propriety. 이 글은 순수성, 진실성, 우아함, 타당성의 기준에 의해서 평가되었다.	

☐ posture _____ ☐ precept _____ ☐ precipitous _____

Definition	Meaning/Relation
방탕한; 낭비하는	ⓐ given over to dissipation; recklessly wasteful **profligate spending** 낭비가 심한 씀씀이 **a profligate lifestyle** 낭비벽이 있는 생활방식
자손, 아이	ⓝ one born fo, begotten by, or derived from another
공표하다, 발표하다	ⓥ to make known (a decree, for example) by public declaration **promulgate a law** 법률을 공표하다 **promulgate a belief/an idea/a theory** 신념/생각/이론을 널리 알리다
(…하기) 쉬운; (…의) 경향이 있는	ⓐ inclined; having a tendency **prone to** …을 잘하는, …의 경향이 있는
번식하다, 퍼지다	ⓥ to cause (an organism) to multiply or breed
성향	ⓝ an innate inclination and a tendency **a propensity for** …의 버릇
적절함, 타당함	ⓝ the quality of being proper **doubt the propriety of** *sth* …의 타당성을 의심하다 **with propriety** 예법에 따라 적절히

☐ predilection _____ ☐ preempt _____ ☐ prodigy _____ ☐ profane _____

NO.	Entry Word	Example Sentence
744 ☐☐	**punctilious** [pʌŋktíliəs]	We must be punctilious in our planing of this affair. 우리는 이번 사건에서 계획을 세울 때 꼼꼼해야만 한다. My uncle is punctilious about using the right tool for each job. 나의 삼촌께서는 모든 일에 적당한 도구를 사용하는데 까다로우시다.
745 ☐☐	**pundit** [pándit]	The pundit discussed the presidental elections. 그 전문가는 대통령 선거를 토론했다. Even though he discourses on the matter like a pundit, he is actually rather ignorant about this topic. 그가 전문가처럼 그 문제에 대해 논의를 하지만 그는 실제로는 이 주제에 대해 다소 문외한이다.
746 ☐☐	**punitive** [pjúːnətiv]	He asked for punitive measures against the offender. 그는 공격자에 대해 형벌을 요구했다. The defendant's behavior must be egregious before punitive damages can be imposed. 징벌적 손해 배상이 부과되기 전에 그 피고의 행동은 과도한 것이임에 틀림없다.
747 ☐☐	**quandary** [kwándəri]	I was in a quandary about whether to go. 나는 가야 할지 말아야 할지 곤란한 상황에 처해 있다. The government has placed itself in a quandary as to how it should deal with the problem. 정부는 그 문제를 다루는 방법에 대해 스스로 곤란한 상황에 처하게 했다.
748 ☐☐	**quiver** [kwívər]	Her lips quivered with anger. 성이 나서 그녀의 입술이 바르르 떨렸다. She quivered at the sight. 그녀는 그 광경을 보고 떨었다.
749 ☐☐	**quixotic** [kwiksátik]	Quixotic goals of creating democracy in Iraq is conversely disheartening them. 이라크에 민주주의를 도입한다는 비현실적인 목표가 도리어 이라크인들을 낙심시키고 있다. The boys embarked on a quixotic voyage. 그 소년들은 공상적인 여행을 시작했다.
750 ☐☐	**ramification** [ræ̀məfikéiʃən]	The ramifications for drivers seem obvious. 운전자들에 대해 미치는 결과는 명백하다. She says that her organization is holding seminars all across the United States to explain the ramifications of the new law. 그녀가 속한 조직이 새 법의 세부 조항들을 설명하기 위한 세미나를 미국 전역에서 개최하고 있다고 합니다.

☐ profligate _____   ☐ progeny _____   ☐ promulgate _____

744_750 235

PART 1

PART 2

PART 3

PART 4

PART 5

PART 6

Definition	Meaning/Relation
꼼꼼한	ⓐ strictly attentive to minute details of form in action or conduct **punctilious about** …에 대해 꼼꼼한
전문가	ⓝ a learned person **a political pundit** 정치 전문가
형벌의, 징벌의	ⓐ Inflicting or aiming to inflict punishment **a punitive action** 토벌 전투 **punitive[exemplary] damages** (실제 손해액 이상으로 과하는) 징계적 피해 보상금 **a punitive expedition** 토벌대 **punitive measures** 징벌[보복] 조치
곤란한 상황[입장]	ⓝ a state of uncertainty or perplexity **a hopeless quandary** 대책 없는 곤경 **in a quandary** 곤경에 처한 **a quandary about[over]** …에 대한 곤경
떨(리게)다	ⓥ to shake with a slight, rapid, tremulous movement **quiver with** …로 떨다
비현실적인, 공상적인	ⓐ caught up in the romance of noble deeds and the pursuit of unreachable goals
결과; 세분화	ⓝ a development or consequence growing out of and sometimes complicating a problem, plan, or statement; a subordinate part extending from a main body

☐ prone _____ ☐ propagate _____ ☐ propensity _____ ☐ propriety _____

NO.	Entry Word	Example Sentence	
751 ☐☐	**redress** [ríːdres]	The bank has carried out its plans by redressing organizational bureaucracy and inefficiency. 그 은행은 관료 주의와 비효율적인 면을 바로 잡음으로써 계획을 실행했다. The company offered her a large sum of money to redress the harm that their product had done to her. 그 회사는 자사의 제품이 그녀에게 끼친 손해를 보상하고자 그녀에게 거액의 돈을 지불하였다.	
752 ☐☐	**relegate** [réləgèit]	The chairman has decided to relegate the North Korean project to a lower priority. 의장은 북한 프로젝트를 후순의 의제로 결정했다. She was relegated to a post at the fringes of the sales department. 그녀는 판매부의 한직으로 밀려났다.	
753 ☐☐	**reserve** [rizɔ́ːrv]	They reserve some money for the future. 그들은 장래를 대비해 약간의 돈을 비축하고 있다. I'd like to reserve a table for two for eight o'clock. 8시에 두 사람 자리를 예약하고 싶은데요.	
754 ☐☐	**resplendent** [rispléndənt]	The toreador wore a resplendent costume. 기마 투우사는 화려한 복장을 했다. The queen's resplendent purple robes and crown were on display in the museum. 여왕이 입었던 화려한 보라색 예복과 왕관이 박물관에 전시되었다.	
755 ☐☐	**reticent** [rétəsənt]	He is naturally reticent. 그는 천성이 과묵하다. She is a reticent woman. 그녀는 말이 적은 여자다.	
756 ☐☐	**rigid** [rídʒid]	The old man is rigid. 그 노인은 완고하다. He was rigid with fear. 그는 두려움으로 굳어 있었다.	
757 ☐☐	**robust** [roubʌ́st]	You need to be robust to go rock climbing. 암벽 등반을 하려면 건강해야 한다. Robust growth abroad will help keep the U.S. economy on track. 해외에서의 활발한 성장은 미국 경제가 순조롭게 성장하도록 기여할 것이다.	

☐ punctilious _____   ☐ pundit _____   ☐ punitive _____   ☐ quandary _____

PART 1

PART 2

PART 3

PART 4

PART 5

PART 6

Definition	Meaning/Relation
바로잡다; 보상하다	ⓥ to set right; to remedy or rectify
밀려나다	ⓥ to put into a lower or worse place **relegate to** …로 격하시키다
비축하다; 예약하다	ⓥ to keep back, as for future use or for a special purpose; to set or cause to be set apart for a particular person or use **reserve for** …을 위해 따로 두다 **reserve for** …을 위해 예약하다
화려한	ⓐ splendid or dazzling in appearance **resplendent in** … 속에서 빛나는
과묵한, 말이 적은	ⓐ inclined to keep one's thoughts, feelings, and personal affairs to oneself **reticent about** …에 대해 말하려고 하지 않는
완고한; 굳은	ⓐ stiff; not flexible or pliant **rigid about[in, on]** …에 관해 엄격한
건강한; 활발한	ⓐ full of health and strength; vigorous **a robust[iron, rugged, strong, very healthy, wiry] constitution** 강건한 체질 **robust[good] health** 양호한 건강

□ quiver _____   □ quixotic _____   □ ramification _____

NO.	Entry Word	Example Sentence
758 ☐☐	**rustic** [rʌ́stik]	The village has a certain rustic charm. 그 마을은 뭔가 시골풍의 매력이 있다. The landlord had tried to give the pub a rustic appearance by putting horseshoes and old guns on the walls. 집주인은 벽에 편자와 오래된 총 등을 걸어 놓음으로써 술집의 겉모양을 시골풍으로 만들려고 했다.
759 ☐☐	**sagacious** [səgéiʃəs]	He is a sagacious person. 그는 현명한 사람이다. He is much too sagacious to be fooled by a trick like that. 그는 너무 현명해서 그와 같은 속임수에는 속지 않는다.
760 ☐☐	**salient** [séiliənt]	Remind me of the salient features of the proposal. 그 제안의 중요한 점이 무엇인지 알려주십시오. The 2000 election campaign was the first since 1936 in which foreign policy was not a salient issue. 2000년 선거운동에서는 1936년 이래 처음으로 외교 정책이 중요한 이슈로 대두되지 않았다.
761 ☐☐	**salutary** [sǽljətèri]	The war is a salutary reminder of how dangerous the world has become. 그 전쟁은 세계가 얼마나 위험해 는지를 생각하게 하는 유익한 지표이다. The punishment had a salutary effect on the boy. 그 처벌은 그 소년에게 유익한 영향을 끼쳤던 것 같다.
762 ☐☐	**sanction** [sǽŋkʃən]	At long last the sanction came through. 마침내 인가가 났다. He tried to get official sanction for his scheme. 그는 자신의 계획에 대해 공식적인 인가를 얻으려 했다.
763 ☐☐	**serendipity** [sèrəndípəti]	I landed a great job when I bumped into an old friend at the grocery store—talk about serendipity! 우연히 수퍼에서 옛친구를 만나게 되어 좋은 직장을 얻게 되었다. 얼마나 운수좋은 기회였는지 모르겠네! Many couples think that their meeting and coming together was pure serendipity. 많은 커플들은 그들의 만남과 함께함이 순수하게 운수가 좋은 일이었다고 생각한다.
764 ☐☐	**serpentine** [sə́ːrpəntàin]	We followed the serpentine course of the river. 우리는 그 강의 꾸불꾸불한 행로를 따라갔다. In the south of this area, there is a serpentine river. 이 지역의 남쪽에는 꾸불꾸불한 강이 있다.

☐ redress _____   ☐ relegate _____   ☐ reserve _____   ☐ resplendent _____

Definition	Meaning/Relation
시골(풍)의	ⓐ of, relating to, or typical of country life or country people
현명한	ⓐ having or showing keen discernment, sound judgment, and farsightedness
중요한	ⓐ projecting or jutting beyond a line or surface **form a salient** 전선 돌출부를 형성하다
유익한	ⓐ effecting or designed to effect an improvement **a salutary[beneficial, good] effect** 바람직한[유익한] 효과 **salutary[beneficial, good, positive] influence** 긍정적인[유익한] 영향
인가	ⓝ authoritative permission or approval that makes a course of action valid **give sanction to** …을 인가하다 **receive sanction** 승인받다 **legal sanction** 법률상의 인가
우연히 찾아내는 능력(것)	ⓝ the lucky tendency to find interesting or valuable things by chance
꾸불꾸불한	ⓐ of or resembling a serpent(a snake), as in form or movement

☐ reticent _____ ☐ rigid _____ ☐ robust _____

NO.	Entry Word	Example Sentence	
765 ☐☐	**shrewd** [ʃruːd]	He is shrewd in business. 그는 장삿속이 밝다. My brother is shrewd in business. 나의 형은 사업에 빈틈이 없다.	
766 ☐☐	**solvent** [sálvənt]	The court was told that the firm was barely solvent. 법원은 그 회사가 지불 능력이 거의 없다는 말을 들었다. He was finally able to become solvent and avoid bankruptcy proceedings. 그는 마침내 채무를 지불할 수 있었고 파산절차를 피할 수 있었다.	
767 ☐☐	**sophomoric** [sàfəmɔ́ːrik]	The growing complaints about U.S. diplomacy these days seem more serious than sophomoric. 요즘 미국 외교에 관해 불평이 증가하는 상황은 미숙하다기보다 심각해 보인다. The new supervisor must learn to deal with these sophomoric employees in whatever way he deems most effective. 그 새로운 감독관은 그가 가장 효율적인 방법을 갖고 있더라도 이러한 미숙한 노동자를 다루는 방법을 배워야 한다.	
768 ☐☐	**soporific** [sàpərífik]	Her soporific voice made it difficult to stay awake in the lecture. 그녀의 졸리는 목소리 때문에 강의 시간에 깨어 있기가 어려웠다. The alcohol is known to have the soporific effect. 알코올은 졸리는 효과가 있다고 알려져 있다.	
769 ☐☐	**spectrum** [spéktrəm]	A rainbow may be regarded as a spectrum of the Sun. 무지개는 태양의 스펙트럼이라 볼 수도 있다. There's a wide spectrum of opinion on this question. 이 문제에 관해 다양한 의견이 있다.	
770 ☐☐	**sporadic** [spərǽdik]	More than 100 people have been killed this year in sporadic outbursts of ethnic violence. 100명이 넘는 사람들이 올해 산발적으로 터진 종족간 폭력사태에서 목숨을 잃었다. There still seems to be sporadic fighting in the streets of the city. 시내에서는 아직도 산발적으로 전투가 벌어지고 있는 것으로 보인다.	
771 ☐☐	**spurious** [spjúəriəs]	They were spurious claims. 그것들은 허위주장이었다. He claimed a spurious argument. 그는 잘못된 추론에 의한 주장을 하고 있다.	

☐ rustic _____ ☐ sagacious _____ ☐ salient _____ ☐ salutary _____

PART 1
PART 2
PART 3
PART 4
PART 5
PART 6

Definition	Meaning/Relation
영리한, 빈틈없는	ⓐ characterized by keen awareness, sharp intelligence, and often a sense of the practical **shrewd at[in]** …에 빈틈없는
지불 능력이 있는	ⓐ capable of meeting financial obligations
미숙한	ⓐ exhibiting great immaturity and lack of judgment
졸리는	ⓐ inducing or tending to induce sleep
스펙트럼; 다양함	ⓝ the distribution of energy emitted by a radiant source; a range of values of a quantity or set of related quantities **a broad [wide] spectrum** 넓은 범위
산발적인	ⓐ occurring at irregular intervals **a sporadic outbreak** 산발적인 발발 **sporadic rioting** 산발적으로 일어나는 폭동 **sporadic violence** 산발적인 폭동
허위의, 비논리적인	ⓐ lacking authenticity or validity in essence or origin **false[specious, spurious] logic** 그럴듯한〔진짜 같은〕논리

☐ sanction _____ ☐ serendipity _____ ☐ serpentine _____

NO.	Entry Word	Example Sentence	
772 ☐☐	**stagnant** [stǽgnənt]	There is a stagnant pool at the bottom of the garden. 정원 아래쪽에는 물이 고여있는 웅덩이가 있다. A stagnant construction business in the first half resulted mainly from a decrease of public construction order. 상반기 건설업 정체는 공공부문 발주공사 감소에서 비롯됐다.	
773 ☐☐	**stolid** [stálid]	They sat in stolid silence. 그들은 둔감하게 말없이 앉아 있었다. She cannot believe that her quiet routine with a stolid, unambitious man represents the happiness she has dreamed of. 그녀는 따분해지며, 둔감하고 야심이 없는 남자와 조용한 일상생활을 하는 것이 그녀가 꿈꾸었던 행복이라고 믿을 수 없었다.	
774 ☐☐	**stringent** [stríndʒənt]	We shall need more stringent laws against pollution. 우리에게는 공해 방지를 위한 보다 엄격한 법이 필요하다. Some of the conditions in the contract are too stringent. 계약상의 어떤 조건들은 너무 가혹하다.	
775 ☐☐	**substantive** [sʌ́bstəntiv]	Substantive research on the subject needs to be carrried out. 그 문제에 대한 실질적인 조사가 수행될 필요가 있다. Although the delegates were aware of the importance of the problem, they could not agree on the substantive issues. 대의원들은 그 문제의 중요성을 알고 있었지만 실질적인 논쟁점에 대해서 합의를 볼 수 없었다.	
776 ☐☐	**subterfuge** [sʌ́btərfjùːdʒ]	It was clear that they must have obtained the information by subterfuge. 그들은 틀림없이 속임수를 써서 정보를 얻었음이 분명하다. We realized that you had won our support by a subterfuge. 당신이 속임수를 써서 우리의 지지를 얻었다는 것을 알았다.	
777 ☐☐	**supersede** [sùːpərsíːd]	This regulation will supersede all previous rules. 이 규정이 이전의 모든 규칙들을 대신할 것이다. The following old manuals can no longer be probvided gratis because they have been superseded by new editions. 아래의 구매뉴얼들은 신판으로 바뀐 관계로 무료로 제공할 수 없게 되었습니다.	
778 ☐☐	**sycophant** [síkəfənt]	The President surrounded himself with sycophants. 대통령은 아첨꾼들로 둘러 싸여 있다. He argues that there were many officials who were just like him, or even more sycophant to the Japanese than Yi Wan-yong was. 그는 그와 같이 혹은 이완용 보다 훨씬 더 일본에 아첨꾼이었던 많은 관리들이 있었다고 주장한다.	

☐ shrewd _____   ☐ solvent _____   ☐ sophomoric _____   ☐ soporific _____

PART 1

PART 2

PART 3

PART 4

PART 5

PART 6

Definition	Meaning/Relation
고여있는, 정체된	ⓐ not moving or flowing **a stagnant pond** 물이 괴어 썩은 연못 **a stagnant economy** 정체된 경제
둔감한	ⓐ having or revealing little emotion or sensibility
엄격한, 가혹한	ⓐ imposing rigorous standards of performance; severe **stringent[rigid, strict] enforcement** 엄격한 시행 **a stringent law** 엄중한 법률 **stringent[drastic, harsh, stern, tough] measures** 가혹한(철저한) 조치
실질적인	ⓐ relating to the essential nature of something **a substantive issue** 본질적인 사안
속임수	ⓝ a deceptive stratagem or device **use[resort to] a subterfuge** 속임수를 쓰다
대신하다, 대체하다	ⓥ to take the place of; replace
아첨꾼	ⓝ a servile self-seeker who attempts to win favor by flattering influential people

☐ spectrum _____   ☐ sporadic _____   ☐ spurious _____

NO.	Entry Word	Example Sentence	
779 ☐☐	**synthesis** [sínθəsis]	Rubber is produced from petroleum by synthesis. 고무는 석유를 합성해서 만들어진다. He describes his latest record as 'a synthesis of African and Latin rhythms.' 그는 자신의 최신 앨범의 특징이 '아프리카와 라틴 리듬의 만남'이라고 설명했다.	
780 ☐☐	**temerity** [təmérəti]	He had the temerity to file a grievance. 그는 무모하게도 불평을 제기했다. He ran the company like a dictator and no one had the temerity to question his judgement. 그는 회사를 독재자처럼 경영했는데 아무도 그의 판단에 의문을 제기하는 만용을 부리지 못했다.	
781 ☐☐	**temporal** [témpərəl]	'When' and 'while' are temporal conjunctions. when과 while은 시간 접속사이다. Temporal power and wealth are more important to many people than a spiritual promise of life after death. 많은 사람들에게 사후(死後) 영생(永生)에 대한 영적인 확신보다 순간적인 부와 권력이 더 중요하다.	
782 ☐☐	**temporize** [témpəràiz]	The peace plan is merely a temporizing device. 그 평화안은 일시적 미봉책일 뿐이다. Management temporized with labor to gain time. 경영자측은 시간을 벌기 위해 노동자측에 우물쭈물 대응했다	
783 ☐☐	**tentative** [téntətiv]	I have made tentative plans to take a trip to Seattle in July. 나는 7월에 시애틀 여행을 하기로 잠정적인 계획을 세워 놓았다. United Airlines and its pilots' union have reached a tentative agreement on a new contract. 유나이티드 항공과 운항승무원 노조간에 새 계약 체결에 대한 잠정적인 합의가 이루어졌다.	
784 ☐☐	**tenuous** [ténjuəs]	I found an excuse to phone her, but it was rather tenuous. 그녀에게 전화할 구실을 찾긴 했지만 좀 빈약했다. The connection between the film and the book is fairly tenuous. 영화와 책 사이의 연결은 매우 희박하다.	
785 ☐☐	**terse** [təːrs]	His remarks are always terse and pointed. 그의 표현은 항상 간결하다. My monther is remembered to have been a terse person. 나의 어머니는 무뚝뚝한 사람으로 기억된다.	

☐ stagnant _____   ☐ stolid _____   ☐ stringent _____   ☐ substantive _____

Definition	Meaning/Relation
합성	ⓝ the combining of separate elements or substances to form a coherent whole **make a synthesis** 합성하다
무모; 만용	ⓝ recklessness; foolhardy disregard of danger
시간의; 순간적인	ⓐ relating to, or limited by time; lasting only for a time **a temporal label** 시제 표시
일시적 미봉책을 쓰다, 우물쭈물하다	ⓥ to act evasively in order to gain time, avoid argument, or postpone a decision
잠정적인	ⓐ not fully worked out, concluded, or agreed on **a tentative plan** 시안(試案) **a tentative theory** 가설(說)
빈약한, 희박한	ⓐ with little strength or substance **a tenuous[weak] argument** 근거가 약한 논증 **a tenuous[loose] connection** 느슨한(미약한) 관계 **a tenuous relationship** 심드렁한 관계
간결한; 무뚝뚝한	ⓐ brief and to the point; abrupt and rude **a terse reply** 퉁명스러운 대답

☐ subterfuge _____   ☐ supersede _____   ☐ sycophant _____

NO.	Entry Word	Example Sentence	
786 ☐☐	**titular** [títʃulər]	Until 1989 the presidential post was merely titular. 1989년까지 그 회장직은 단지 명목뿐이었다. Kim Yong-nam, the North's second-most senior official, serves as its titular head of state. 북한 권력 서열 2위인 김영남은 명목상 국가 수반으로서 역할을 한다.	
787 ☐☐	**touchstone** [tʌ́tʃstòun]	This work was the touchstone of his ability for leadership. 이 일은 그의 지도력에 대한 시험대가 되었다. This opera is a touchstone by/against which later operas were judged. 이 오페라는 그 후에 나온 오페라들의 판단 기준이 된 선전한다.	
788 ☐☐	**tout** [taut]	He was touted as the next middleweight champion. 그는 다음 미들급 챔피언으로 칭찬받고 있었다. They are always touting statistics about the safety of their product. 그들은 자기네 상품의 안전성에 대해 항상 통계를 들먹인다.	
789 ☐☐	**transport** [trænspɔ́ːrt]	We need some containers to transport our goods. 우리는 상품을 수송할 컨테이너가 필요하다. Heavy items are expensive to transport by air. 무거운 물품은 항공편으로 수송하면 비용이 많이 든다.	
790 ☐☐	**trenchant** [tréntʃənt]	I am afraid of his trenchant wit for it is so often sarcastic. 나는 그의 신랄한 위트가 너무 자주 남을 비꼬는 것이라 걱정스럽다. He wrote a series of trenchant articles on the state of the British theater. 그는 연속으로 영국 연극계의 현 상황에 대한 신랄한 기사를 썼다.	
791 ☐☐	**tryst** [trist]	Taking comfort in each other's misery, they elected to engage in an alcohol-fueled tryst. 서로의 불행에 위로를 한 후, 그들은 술 마시는 모임에 참가하기로 결정했다. How completely he fulfilled the idea of a man who is keeping a secret tryst? 그는 비밀스런 모임 장소를 가지고 있는 남자라는 생각을 어떻게 완벽하게 실행했을까?	
792 ☐☐	**turpitude** [tə́ːrpitjùːd]	She was charged with moral turpitude. 그녀는 도덕적으로 타락했다는 비난을 받았다. Filling in a false tax return is not in itself a crime of gross moral turpitude. 거짓 납세 신고서를 작성하는 것은 그 자체로는 도덕적으로 엄청나게 비열한 범죄행위는 아니다.	

☐ synthesis _____   ☐ temerity _____   ☐ temporal _____

Definition	Meaning/Relation
명목상	ⓐ existing in name only **a titular head** 이름뿐인 지도자
시험대, 시금석	ⓝ a hard black stone, such as jasper or basalt, formerly used to test the quality of gold or silver by comparing the streak left on the stone by one of these metals with that of a standard alloy
칭찬하다; 선전하다	ⓥ to solicit customers, votes, or patronage, especially in a brazen way; to promote **tout as** …라고 칭찬하다
운송(수송)하다	ⓥ to carry from one place to another **transport bodily** 송두리째 나르다 **transport from** …에서 수송하다
신랄한	ⓐ keen and incisive **a trenchant argument** 신랄한 주장 **a trenchant comment** 통렬한(신랄한) 말
모임 장소	ⓝ an agreement, as between lovers, to meet at a certain time and place
타락; 비열	ⓝ depravity; baseness **moral turpitude** 도덕적으로 비열한 행위

☐ temporize _____ ☐ tentative _____ ☐ tenuous _____ ☐ terse _____

NO.	Entry Word	Example Sentence	
793 ☐☐	**uncanny** [ʌnkǽni]	It's uncanny how much you and Elizabeth look like sisters. 너하고 엘리자베스가 얼마나 자매처럼 보이는지 참 불가사의한 일이다. They've an uncanny ability to understand what they're good at and then go find experts in other areas. 자신이 어떤 분야에서 뛰어난지 파악하는 비상한 능력이 있고, 그렇지 않은 분야는 전문가를 찾아간다는 겁니다.	
794 ☐☐	**unwitting** [ʌnwítiŋ]	Her unwitting insight made him uncomfortable. 그녀의 무의식적인 통찰력이 그를 불안하게 했다. She was the unwitting tool of the swindlers. 그녀는 고의 아니게 사기꾼들의 똘마니가 되었다.	
795 ☐☐	**vagary** [véigəri]	She has her own style and is not influenced by the vagaries of fashion. 그녀는 자기만의 스타일이 있어서 유행의 변덕에 영향을 받지 않는다. For centuries, the paths of planets and vagaries of weather have been scrutinized by astrologers. 수세기 동안, 점성가들은 행성의 경로와 날씨 변화를 연구해왔다.	
796 ☐☐	**venal** [ví:nl]	They are accused of being involved in venal practices. 그들은 뇌물을 받고 매수되는 관행에 연루된 혐의로 기소된 상태이다. The venal policeman accepted the bribe offered him by the speeding motorist whom he had stopped. 부패한 경찰관은 그가 멈춰 세웠던 과속한 운전자가 준 뇌물을 받았다.	
799 ☐☐	**verdant** [və́ːrdənt]	Much of the region's verdant countryside has been destroyed in the hurricane. 그 지역의 녹지대 대부분이 허리케인 때문에 파괴됐다. The verdant meadows in the spring are always an inspiring sight. 봄에 잎이 무성한 초지는 항상 고무적인 광경이다.	
800 ☐☐	**verisimilitude** [vèrəsimílətjùːd]	His sculptures are famous for their verisimilitude. 그의 조각은 그 사실성으로 유명하다. To add verisimilitude, the stage is covered with sand for the desert scene. 사실성을 더하기 위해 사막 장면을 위해서는 무대에 모래를 깔았다.	
801 ☐☐	**verity** [vérəti]	No one can deny the verity of that research. 그 연구의 진실성은 아무도 부인할 수 없다. In the film, he plays a spy whose mission is to confirm the verity of a secret military document. 그 영화에서 그는 비밀 군사 서류의 진실성을 확인하는 임무를 띤 첩자역을 한다.	

☐ titular _____ ☐ touchstone _____ ☐ tout _____ ☐ transport _____

Definition	Meaning/Relation
불가사의한; 비상한	ⓐ peculiarly unsettling, as if of supernatural origin or nature **positively uncanny** 정말 <u>으스스한</u>
무의식적인, 고의가 아닌	ⓐ not knowing; done without being matended **an unwitting accomplice** 부지불식간에 연루된 공범자
변덕, 변화	ⓝ an extravagant or erratic notion or action
매수되기 쉬운; 부패한	ⓐ open to bribery; corrupt
초록의, 푸른잎이 무성한	ⓐ green with vegetation
사실성	ⓝ the quality of appearing to be true or real
진실(성)	ⓝ the quality or condition of being true, factual, or real

☐ trenchant _____　☐ tryst _____　☐ turpitude _____

NO.	Entry Word	Example Sentence	
802 ☐☐	**vindicate** [víndəkèit]	The witness tried very hard to vindicate three police officers accused of beating a woman coed. 그 증인은 한 여대생을 때린 혐의를 받고 있는 3명의 경찰관의 정당함을 입증하려고 무척 애썼다.	
		The report fully vindicated the unions. 그 보고서는 노조의 정당함을 입증해 주었다.	
803 ☐☐	**volatile** [válətil]	Last winter's price upswing in the volatile oil and food sector is subsiding. 지난 겨울의 휘발유와 식품부문의 가격 상승이 진정되고 있다.	
		Like many actors, he had a rather volatile temper and can't have been easy to live with. 많은 배우와 마찬가지로 그도 다소 변덕스러운 성미여서 함께 살기가 쉬웠을 리 없다.	
804 ☐☐	**voluminous** [vəlú:mənəs]	Despite her family burdens, she kept up a voluminous correspondence with her friends. 가족에 대한 부담에도 불구하고 그녀는 친구들과 많은 서신 왕래를 지속했다.	
		Thomas Jefferson kept up a voluminous correspondence with important people in America and abroad. Thomas Jefferson은 미국과 해외의 저명 인사들과 많은 서신 교환을 계속했다.	
805 ☐☐	**wily** [wáili]	I can see through your wily machinations. 나는 너의 교활한 음모를 꿰뚫어 볼 수 있다.	
		The wily president saved her position by calling on the support of thousands of town and city mayors. 그 교활한 대통령은 수천 명의 마을과 도시의 시장의 지지를 요구함으로써 그녀의 자리를 보존했다.	
806 ☐☐	**wither** [wíðər]	The flowers withered away[up]. 꽃이 시들었다.	
		Negro slaves had been seared in the flames of withering injustice. 시들어가는 수백만의 흑인 노예들은이 중대한 포고령은 파괴적인 불의의 불길 속에서 신음했다.	

☐ uncanny _____ ☐ unwitting _____ ☐ vagary _____ ☐ venal _____

Definition	Meaning/Relation
…의 정당함 입증하다	ⓥ to clear of accusation, blame, suspicion, or doubt with wupporting arguments or proof
휘발성의, 변덕스러운	ⓐ tending to vary often or widely, as in price **highly volatile** 매우 휘발성이 강한(변덕스러운)
많은	ⓐ filling or capable of filling a large volume or many volumes **voluminous literature** (규모가) 방대한 문학 작품
교활한	ⓐ full of wiles
시들다	ⓥ to dry up or shrivel from or as if from loss of moisture. **flowers wither** 꽃이 시들다

☐ verdant _____ ☐ verisimilitude _____ ☐ verity _____

레벨업 영단어

☆

A

NO.	Entry Word	Meaning	Definition
1 ☐☐	**abase** [əbéis]	ⓥ to lower in rank, prestige, or esteem	떨어뜨리다
2 ☐☐	**abdicate** [ǽbdikèit]	ⓥ to relinquish (power or responsibility) formally	(왕위 · 권리를) 버리다
3 ☐☐	**abeyance** [əbéiəns]	ⓝ the condition of being temporarily set aside	중지
4 ☐☐	**abject** [ǽbdʒekt]	ⓐ brought low in condition or status being of the most contemptible kind	비참한, 비열한
5 ☐☐	**abjure** [əbdʒúər]	ⓥ abjure to rebounce under oath; to recant solemnly	부인하다; 포기하다
6 ☐☐	**abolish** [əbáliʃ]	ⓥ to do away with; to destroy completely	폐지하다; 파괴하다
7 ☐☐	**abortive** [əbɔ́ːrtiv]	ⓐ failing to accomplish an intended objective	성공하지 못한
8 ☐☐	**abridge** [əbrídʒ]	ⓥ to reduce the length of (a written text); to cut short	요약(축약)하다; 단축하다
9 ☐☐	**abrogate** [ǽbrəgèit]	ⓥ to abolish, do away with, or annul, especially by authority	폐기하다
10 ☐☐	**abysmal** [əbízməl]	ⓐ resembling an abyss in depth	심연의
11 ☐☐	**accede** [æksíːd]	ⓥ to give one's consent, often at the insistence of another	동의하다
12 ☐☐	**accolade** [ǽkəlèid]	ⓝ an expression of approval; ceremonial bestowal of knighthood	칭찬; 작위 수여
13 ☐☐	**accrue** [əkrúː]	ⓥ to come to one as a gain, addition, or increment; to accumulate over time	생기다, 축적하다
14 ☐☐	**acrid** [ǽkrid]	ⓐ unpleasantly sharp, pungent, or bitter to the taste or smell; caustic in language or tone	얼얼한; 신랄한

NO.	Entry Word	Meaning	Definition
15 ☐☐	**adage** [ǽdidʒ]	ⓝ a saying that sets forth a general truth and that has gained credit through long use	격언
16 ☐☐	**adamant** [ǽdəmənt]	ⓐ impervious to pleas, appeals, or reason; stubbornly unyielding	단호한
17 ☐☐	**adduce** [ədjúːs]	ⓥ to cite as an example or means of proof in an argument	증거를 제시하다
18 ☐☐	**adherent** [ædhíərənt]	ⓐ sticking or holding fast	접착성의
19 ☐☐	**adjunct** [ǽdʒʌŋkt]	ⓝ something attached to another in a dependent or subordinate position; a person associated with another in a subordinate or auxiliary capacity	부가물; 조수
20 ☐☐	**adulterate** [ədʌ́ltərèit]	ⓥ to make impure by adding extraneous, improper, or inferior ingredients	불순물을 섞다
21 ☐☐	**adventitious** [ædvəntíʃəs]	ⓐ not inherent but added extrinsically	우연한
22 ☐☐	**affidavit** [æfədéivit]	ⓝ a written declaration made under oath before a notary public or other authorized officer	선서, 진술서
23 ☐☐	**affinity** [əfínəti]	ⓝ a natural attraction, liking, or feeling of	좋아함
24 ☐☐	**aggregate** [ǽgrigèit]	ⓥ to gather into a mass, sum, or whole	한데 모으다
25 ☐☐	**alchemy** [ǽlkəmi]	ⓝ a medieval chemical philosophy having as its asserted aims the transmutation of base metals into gold, the discovery of the panacea, and the preparation of the elixir of longevity	연금술
26 ☐☐	**allegory** [ǽləgɔ̀ːri]	ⓝ a literary, dramatic, or pictorial device in which characters and events stand for abstract ideas, principles, or forces, so that the literal sense has or suggests a parallel, deeper symbolic sense	풍유, 비유

PART 1

PART 2

PART 3

PART 4

PART 5

PART 6

NO.	Entry Word	Meaning	Definition
27 ☐☐	**alloy** [ǽlɔi]	ⓝ a homogeneous mixture or solid solution of two or more metals, the atoms of one replacing or occupying interstitial positions between the atoms of the other	합금
28 ☐☐	**altercation** [ɔ̀:ltərkéiʃən]	ⓝ a vehement quarrel	논쟁, 언쟁
29 ☐☐	**ambiance** [ǽmbiəns]	ⓝ the special atmosphere or mood created by a particular environment	분위기
30 ☐☐	**ameliorate** [əmíːljərèit]	ⓥ to make or become better; improve	개선하다[되다]
31 ☐☐	**amenable** [əmíːnəbəl]	ⓐ responsive to advice, authority, or suggestion	잘 따르는
32 ☐☐	**amnesty** [ǽmnəsti]	ⓝ a general pardon granted by a government, especially for political offenses	사면
33 ☐☐	**amoral** [eimɔ́:rəl]	ⓐ not admitting of moral distinctions or judgments	도덕과 관계없는
34 ☐☐	**anathema** [ənǽθəmə]	ⓝ a formal ecclesiastical ban, curse, or excommunication	저주
35 ☐☐	**anchor** [ǽŋkər]	ⓥ a heavy object attached to a vessel by a cable or rope and cast overboard to keep the vessel in place either by its weight or by its flukes, which grip the bottom	닻
36 ☐☐	**annihilate** [ənáiəlèit]	ⓥ to destroy completely	파괴하다
37 ☐☐	**annuity** [ənjúːəti]	ⓝ the annual payment of an allowance or income	연금
38 ☐☐	**antipathy** [æntípəθi]	ⓝ a strong feeling of aversion or repugnance	반감
39 ☐☐	**aperture** [ǽpərtʃùər]	ⓝ an opening, such as a hole, gap, or slit	구멍
40 ☐☐	**apex** [éipeks]	ⓝ the highest point	정점

NO.	Entry Word	Meaning	Definition
41 ☐☐	**aphorism** [ǽfərìzəm]	ⓝ a tersely phrased statement of a truth or opinion	금언, 격언
42 ☐☐	**apocryphal** [əpákrə]	ⓐ of questionable authorship or authenticity	진위가 의심스런
43 ☐☐	**apogee** [ǽpədʒì:]	ⓐ the highest point of power or success	최고점
44 ☐☐	**apoplexy** [ǽpəplèksi]	ⓝ sudden impairment of neurological function, especially that resulting from a cerebral hemorrhage	졸중
45 ☐☐	**apotheosis** [əpàθióusis]	ⓝ exaltation to divine rank or stature	신격화
46 ☐☐	**apparition** [æpəríʃən]	ⓝ a ghostly figure	유령
47 ☐☐	**apposite** [ǽpəzit]	ⓐ strikingly appropriate and relevant	적절한
48 ☐☐	**apprise** [əpráiz]	ⓥ to give notice to	통지하다
49 ☐☐	**approbation** [æproʊbéiʃən]	ⓝ an expression of warm approval	찬성
50 ☐☐	**apropos** [æprəpóu]	ⓐⓓ at an appropriate time	시의 적절하게
51 ☐☐	**arbiter** [á:rbitər]	ⓝ one chosen or appointed to judge or decide a disputed issue	중재자
52 ☐☐	**archetype** [á:rkitàip]	ⓝ an original model or type after which other similar things are patterned; an ideal example of a type	원형; 모범
53 ☐☐	**archipelago** [à:rkəpéləgòu]	ⓝ a large group of islands; a sea, such as the Aegean, containing a large number of scattered islands	군도; 다도해
54 ☐☐	**archive** [á:rkáiv]	ⓝ a place or collection containing records, documents, or other materials of historical interest	옛 기록
55 ☐☐	**ardor** [á:rdər]	ⓝ strong enthusiasm or devotion; fiery intensity of feeling	열정; 열의

PART 1 PART 2 PART 3 PART 4 PART 5 PART 6

NO.	Entry Word	Meaning	Definition
56 ☐☐	**arraign** [əréin]	ⓥ to call (an accused person) before a court to answer the charge made against him or her by indictment, information, or complaint	소환하다
57 ☐☐	**arrant** [ǽrənt]	ⓐ completely such	완전한
58 ☐☐	**arrears** [əríər]	ⓝ an unpaid, overdue debt or an unfulfilled obligation	지연, 지체
59 ☐☐	**artisan** [ɑ́ːrtəzən]	ⓝ a skilled manual worker; a craftsperson	장인(匠人); 기능공
60 ☐☐	**ascendancy** [əséndənsi]	ⓝ superiority or decisive advantage; domination	우세; 지배력
61 ☐☐	**askance** [əskǽns]	ⓐⓓ with disapproval, suspicion, or distrust	의심쩍은 마음[눈]으로
62 ☐☐	**assail** [əséil]	ⓥ to attack with or as if with violent blows	(맹렬하게) 공격하다
63 ☐☐	**assimilate** [əsíməlèit]	ⓥ to incorparate and absorb into the mind	동질화시키다
64 ☐☐	**assuage** [əswéidʒ]	ⓥ to make (something burdensome or painful) less intense or severe	완화시키다
65 ☐☐	**astringent** [əstríndʒənt]	ⓐ sharp and penetrating; pungent or severe	엄한, 가혹한
66 ☐☐	**atone** [ətóun]	ⓥ to make amends, as for a sin or fault	(죄를) 보상하다, 속죄하다
67 ☐☐	**atrophy**	ⓝ a wasting or decrease in size of a bodily organ, tissue, or part owing to disease, injury, or lack of use	위축, 쇠약
68 ☐☐	**attrition** [ətríʃən]	ⓝ a rubbing away or wearing down by friction; a gradual diminution in number or strength because of constant stress	마찰; 소모
69 ☐☐	**audacity** [ɔːdǽsəti]	ⓝ fearless daring	대담
70 ☐☐	**auxiliary** [ɔːgzíljəri]	ⓐ giving assistance or support	보조의

NO.	Entry Word	Meaning	Definition
71 ☐☐	**avert** [əvə́ːrt]	ⓥ to turn away; to ward off (something about to happen)	돌리다; 피하다
72 ☐☐	**avow** [əváu]	ⓥ to acknowledge openly, boldly, and unashamedly	솔직히 인정하다
73 ☐☐	**avuncular** [əvʌ́ŋkjulər]	ⓐ of or having to do with an uncle; regarded as characteristic of an uncle, especially in benevolence or tolerance	삼촌같은; 자상한
74 ☐☐	**awry** [ərái]	ⓐⓓ in a position that is turned or twisted toward one side; away from the correct course	구부러져; 이탈하여
75 ☐☐	**axiom** [ǽksiəm]	ⓝ a self-evident or universally recognized truth	자명한 이치

ß

NO.	Entry Word	Meaning	Definition
76 ☐☐	**baleful** [béilfəl]	ⓐ harmful or malignant in intent or effect; portending evil	해로운; 불길한
77 ☐☐	**balm** [bɑːm]	ⓝ any of various aromatic resins exuded from several trees and shrubs, especially the balm of Gilead and related plants	향유
78 ☐☐	**bandy** [bǽndi]	ⓥ to give and receive (words, for example); exchange	주고받다; 교환하다
79 ☐☐	**bane** [bein]	ⓝ fatal injury or ruin	파멸
80 ☐☐	**baroque** [bəróuk]	ⓐ of, relating to baroque; marked by rich and sometimes bizarre or incongruous ornamentation	바로크 양식의; 지나치게 장식한
81 ☐☐	**bastion** [bǽstʃən]	ⓝ a well-fortified position; one that is considered similar to a defensive stronghold	요새; 보루
82 ☐☐	**beget** [bigét]	ⓥ to father; to cause to exist or occur	(자식을) 보다, 초래하다
83 ☐☐	**begrudge** [bigrʌ́dʒ]	ⓥ to envy the possession or enjoyment of; to give or expend with reluctance	시기하다; 아까워하다

PART 1 PART 2 PART 3 PART 4 PART 5 PART 6

NO.	Entry Word	Meaning	Definition
84 ☐☐	**beleaguer** [bilíːgər]	ⓥ to harass; beset	괴롭히다
85 ☐☐	**bemuse** [bimjúːz]	ⓥ to cause to be bewildered; confuse	멍하게 하다
86 ☐☐	**benediction** [bènədíkʃən]	ⓝ a blessing; an invocation of divine blessing, usually at the end of a church service	축복; 축복의 기도
87 ☐☐	**bilious** [bíljəs]	ⓐ of, relating to, or containing bile; having a peevish disposition	담즙성의; 성을 잘 내는
88 ☐☐	**bivouac** [bívwæk]	ⓝ a temporary encampment often in an unsheltered area	야영지
89 ☐☐	**blanch** [blæntʃ]	ⓥ to take the color from; bleach	희게 하다
90 ☐☐	**blandishment** [blǽndiʃmənt]	ⓝ flattery intended to persuade or influence a person, especially to do something wrong	감언
91 ☐☐	**blithe** [blaið]	ⓐ carefree and lighthearted	쾌활한
92 ☐☐	**bovine** [bóuvain]	ⓐ of, relating to, or resembling a ruminant mammal of the genus Bos, such as an ox, cow, or buffalo; sluggish, dull, and stolid	소의; 둔한
93 ☐☐	**brawn** [brɔːn]	ⓝ solid and well-developed muscles, especially of the arms and legs; muscular strength and power	근육; 힘
94 ☐☐	**brazen** [bréizən]	ⓐ marked by flagrant and insolent audacity	뻔뻔스러운
95 ☐☐	**breach** [briːtʃ]	ⓝ an opening, a tear, or a rupture; a violation or infraction, as of a law, a legal obligation, or a promise	터진 구멍; 위반
96 ☐☐	**broach** [broutʃ]	ⓥ to bring up (a subject) for discussion or debate	(이야기를) 끄집어 내다
97 ☐☐	**brusque** [brʌsk]	ⓐ abrupt and curt in manner or speech; discourteously blunt	퉁명스러운

NO.	Entry Word	Meaning	Definition
98 ☐☐	**bucolic** [bjuːkálik]	ⓐ of or characteristic of the countryside or its people; rustic	전원적인
99 ☐☐	**bulwark** [búlwərk]	ⓝ a wall or embankment raised as a defensive fortification; a rampart	성채
100 ☐☐	**bureaucracy** [bjuərákrəsi]	ⓝ administration of a government chiefly through bureaus or departments staffed with nonelected officials	관료제

C

NO.	Entry Word	Meaning	Definition
101 ☐☐	**cabal** [kəbǽl]	ⓝ a conspiratorial group of plotters or intriguers	음모 집단
102 ☐☐	**cache** [kæʃ]	ⓝ a hiding place used especially for storing provisions	은닉처
103 ☐☐	**cadence** [kéidəns]	ⓝ balanced, rhythmic flow, as of poetry or oratory	운율
104 ☐☐	**callow** [kǽlou]	ⓐ lacking adult maturity or experience; immature	미숙한
105 ☐☐	**cant** [kænt]	ⓝ insincere talk, especially about moral or religious principles, intended to make yourself seem better than you are	위선적인 말
106 ☐☐	**canvass** [kǽnvəs]	ⓥ to examine carefully or discuss thoroughly; to go through (a region) or go to (persons) to solicit votes or orders	조사하다; 유세하다
107 ☐☐	**capitulate** [kəpítʃəlèit]	ⓥ to surrender under specified conditions	항복하다
108 ☐☐	**carcinogenic** [kùːrsənóudʒénik]	ⓐ causing cancer	발암성의
109 ☐☐	**cardinal** [káːrdənl]	ⓐ of foremost importance paramount	가장 중요한
110 ☐☐	**careen** [kəríːn]	ⓥ to lurch or swerve while in motion	기울이다

PART 1 PART 2 PART 3 PART 4 PART 5 PART 6

NO.	Entry Word	Meaning	Definition
111 ☐☐	**caricature** [kǽrikətʃùər]	ⓝ a representation, especially pictorial or literary, in which the subject's distinctive features or peculiarities are deliberately exaggerated to produce a comic or grotesque effect	풍자 만화
112 ☐☐	**cascade** [kæskéid]	ⓝ a waterfall or a series of small waterfalls over steep rocks	작은 폭포
113 ☐☐	**cavil** [kǽvəl]	ⓥ to find fault unnecessarily	트집잡다
114 ☐☐	**celestial** [siléstʃəl]	ⓐ of or relating to the sky or the heavens	하늘의
115 ☐☐	**chaff** [tʃæf]	ⓝ finely cut straw or hay used as fodder; trivial or worthless matter	왕겨; 가치 없는 것
116 ☐☐	**chagrin** [ʃəgrín]	ⓝ a keen feeling of mental unease, as of annoyance or embarrassment, caused by failure, disappointment, or a disconcerting event	억울함
117 ☐☐	**chameleon** [kəmíːliən]	ⓝ any of various tropical old world lizards of the family chamaeleonidae, characterized by their ability to change color; a changeable or inconstant person	카멜레온; 지조없는 사람
118 ☐☐	**charlatan** [tʃɑ́ːrlətən]	ⓝ a person who makes elaborate, fraudulent, and often voluble claims to skill or knowledge	허풍선이, 사기꾼
119 ☐☐	**chasm** [kǽzəm]	ⓝ a deep, steep-sided opening in the earth's surface; a sudden interruption of continuity	빈틈; 단절
120 ☐☐	**chaste** [tʃeist]	ⓐ morally pure in thought or conduct	순수한
121 ☐☐	**chastise** [tʃæstáiz]	ⓥ to criticize severely	호되게 비난하다
122 ☐☐	**chicanery** [ʃikéinəri]	ⓝ deception by trickery or sophistry	속임수
123 ☐☐	**choleric** [kɑ́lərik]	ⓐ easily angered, bad-tempered	화를 잘 내는

NO.	Entry Word	Meaning	Definition
124	**cleave** [kliːv]	ⓥ to split with or as if with a sharp instrument	쪼개다
125	**clemency** [klémənsi]	ⓝ a disposition to show mercy, especially toward an offender or enemy	(특히 재판이나 처벌 때의) 관용
126	**cloister** [klɔ́istər]	ⓝ a place, especially a monastery or convent, devoted to religious seclusion	종교적 은둔처 (수도원, 수녀원 등)
127	**clout** [klaut]	ⓝ influence	정치적 영향력, 권력
128	**coddle** [kάdl]	ⓥ to treat indulgently	부드럽게 다루다
129	**cogitate** [kάdʒətèit]	ⓥ to take careful thought or think carefully about	(…에 대하여) 숙고하다
130	**commensurate** [kəménʃrit]	ⓐ of the same size, extent, or duration as another; corresponding in size or degree	동등한; 적당한
131	**commiserate** [kəmízərèit]	ⓥ to feel or express sorrow or pity for	동정하다
132	**commodious** [kəmóudi]	ⓐ spacious, roomy	(집 방 등이) 넓은
133	**compendium** [kəmpéndiəm]	ⓝ a short, complete summary	개론
134	**compunction** [kəmpʌ́ŋkʃn]	ⓝ a strong uneasiness caused by a sense of guilt; a sting of conscience or a pang of doubt aroused by wrongdoing or the prospect of wrongdoing	후회; 양심의 가책
135	**concave** [kɑnkéiv]	ⓐ curved like the inner surface of a sphere	오목한
136	**concentric** [kənséntrik]	ⓐ having a common center	중심을 공유하는
137	**concomitant** [kɑnkάmətənt]	ⓝ one that occurs or exists concurrently with other	부수물

NO.	Entry Word	Meaning	Definition
138 □□	**concurrent** [kənkə́ːrənt]	ⓐ happening at the same time as something else	동시 발생의
139 □□	**confluence** [kánfluəns]	ⓝ a flowing together of two or more streams	합류
140 □□	**congenital** [kʌndʒénətl]	ⓐ existing at or before birth	선천적인
141 □□	**conjugal** [kándʒəgəl]	ⓐ of or relating to marriage or the relationship of spouses	부부(간)의
142 □□	**conservatory** [kənsə́ːrvətɔ̀ːri]	ⓝ a greenhouse, especially one in which plants are arranged aesthetically for display, as at a botanical garden; a school of music or dramatic art	온실; 음악(예술) 학교
143 □□	**consign** [kənsáin]	ⓥ to deliver (merchandise, for example) for custody or sale	탁송하다
144 □□	**construe** [kənstrúː]	ⓥ to adduce or explain the meaning of	해석하다
145 □□	**contentious** [kənténʃəs]	ⓐ given to contention; quarrelsome	논쟁적인
146 □□	**contiguous** [kəntígjuəs]	ⓐ sharing an edge or boundary	인접하는
147 □□	**contingent** [kəntíndʒənt]	ⓐ dependent on conditions or occurrences not yet established; conditional	~에 따라 결정되는
148 □□	**contraband** [kántrəbæ̀nd]	ⓝ goods prohibited by law or treaty from being imported or exported	밀수품
149 □□	**conversant** [kənvə́ːrsənt]	ⓐ familiar, as by study or experience	정통한
150 □□	**converse** [kənvə́ːrs]	ⓥ to engage in a spoken exchange of thoughts, ideas, or feelings	담화를 나누다
151 □□	**convivial** [kənvíviəl]	ⓐ fond of feasting, drinking, and good company	연회를 좋아하는
152 □□	**corporeal** [kɔːrpɔ́ːriəl]	ⓐ of, relating to, or characteristic of the body; of a material nature	육체의; 물질적인

NO.	Entry Word	Meaning	Definition
153 ☐☐	**correlation** [kɔ̀ːrəléiʃən]	ⓝ a structural, functional, or qualitative correspondence between two comparable entities	상관관계
154 ☐☐	**corrugate** [kɔ́ːrəgèit]	ⓥ to shape into folds or parallel and alternating ridges and grooves	주름지게 하다
155 ☐☐	**coterie** [kóutəri]	ⓝ a small, often select group of persons who associate with one another frequently	(공통의 취미를 가진) 친구
156 ☐☐	**covenant** [kʌ́vənənt]	ⓝ a binding agreement	계약
157 ☐☐	**cower** [káuər]	ⓥ to cringe in fear	움츠리다
158 ☐☐	**craven** [kréivən]	ⓐ characterized by abject fear	비겁한
159 ☐☐	**crestfallen** [kréstfɔ̀ːlən]	ⓐ dispirited and depressed	풀이 죽은
160 ☐☐	**cringe** [krindʒ]	ⓥ to shrink back, as in fear	움츠리다
161 ☐☐	**crux** [krʌks]	ⓝ the basic, central, or critical point or feature; a puzzling or apparently insoluble problem	요점; 수수께끼
162 ☐☐	**cuisine** [kwizíːn]	ⓝ a characteristic manner or style of preparing food	요리(법)
163 ☐☐	**culinary** [kʌ́lənèri]	ⓐ of or relating to a kitchen or to cookery	요리(용)의
164 ☐☐	**cumbersome** [kʌ́mbərsəm]	ⓐ difficult to handle because of weight or bulk	거추장스러운
165 ☐☐	**curmudgeon** [kərmʌ́dʒən]	ⓝ an ill-tempered person full of resentment and stubborn notions	심술궂은 사람
D			
166 ☐☐	**decadence** [dékədəns]	ⓝ a process, condition, or period of deterioration or decline, as in morals or art	타락

265

PART 1
PART 2
PART 3
PART 4
PART 5
PART 6

NO.	Entry Word	Meaning	Definition
167 ☐☐	**decry** [dikrái]	ⓥ to condemn openly	헐뜯다
168 ☐☐	**defile** [difáil]	ⓥ to make filthy or dirty	더럽히다
169 ☐☐	**degenerate** [didʒénərèit]	ⓥ to fall below a normal or desirable state, especially functionally or morally; to decline in quality	타락하다; 퇴보하다
170 ☐☐	**deign** [dein]	ⓥ to think it appropriate to one's dignity	황송하게도 (…)해 주시다
171 ☐☐	**delude** [dilú:d]	ⓥ to deceive the mind or judgment of	속이다
172 ☐☐	**delve** [delv]	ⓥ to search deeply and laboriously	깊이 파고들다
173 ☐☐	**demise** [dimáiz]	ⓝ the end of existence or activity	소멸, 활동 정지
174 ☐☐	**demure** [dimjúər]	ⓐ modest and reserved in manner or behavior	조심스러운
175 ☐☐	**denizen** [dénəzən]	ⓝ an inhabitant	주민
176 ☐☐	**deploy** [diplɔ́i]	ⓥ to position (troops) in readiness for combat, as along a front or line	배치하다
177 ☐☐	**depravity** [diprǽvəti]	ⓝ moral corruption or degradation	타락
178 ☐☐	**deprecate** [déprikèit]	ⓥ to express disapproval of; deplore	비난하다
179 ☐☐	**derogatory** [dirágətɔ̀:ri]	ⓐ disparaging	경멸적인
180 ☐☐	**desiccate** [désikèit]	ⓥ to dry out thoroughly	건조시키다
181 ☐☐	**despondent** [dispándənt]	ⓐ feeling or expressing despondency	낙심한

NO.	Entry Word	Meaning	Definition
182 ☐☐	**destitute** [déstətjùːt]	ⓐ utterly lacking	결핍한
183 ☐☐	**desultory** [désəltɔ̀ːri]	ⓐ moving or jumping from one thing to another	일관성 없는
184 ☐☐	**devout** [diváut]	ⓐ devoted to religion or to the fulfillment of religious obligations	독실한
185 ☐☐	**diatribe** [dáiətràib]	ⓝ a bitter, abusive denunciation	통렬한 비난
186 ☐☐	**dichotomy** [daikátəmi]	ⓝ division into two usually contradictory parts or opinions	양분, 이분법
187 ☐☐	**dictum** [díktəm]	ⓝ an authoritative, often formal, pronouncement	(공식적인) 선언
188 ☐☐	**dilapidated** [diltépədèitid]	ⓐ having fallen into a state of disrepair or deterioration, as through neglect	황폐한
189 ☐☐	**dilate** [dailéit]	ⓥ to become wider or larger; to speak or write at great length on a subject	팽창하다; 자세히 말하다 [쓰다]
190 ☐☐	**diminution** [dìmənjúːʃən]	ⓝ the act or process of diminishing	감소
191 ☐☐	**disarray** [dìsəréi]	ⓝ to throw into confusion	혼란시키다
192 ☐☐	**discursive** [diskə́ːrsiv]	ⓐ covering a wide field of subjects	광범위한
193 ☐☐	**dissident** [dísədənt]	ⓐ disagreeing, as in opinion or belief	의견을 달리하는
194 ☐☐	**dissolution** [dìsəlúːʃən]	ⓝ termination or extinction by disintegration or dispersion; indulgence in sensual pleasures	해산; 방탕
195 ☐☐	**dissuade** [diswéid]	ⓥ to deter (a person) from a course of action or a purpose by persuasion or exhortation	단념시키다
196 ☐☐	**distend** [disténd]	ⓥ to swell out or expand from or as if from internal pressure	팽창시키다[하다]

NO.	Entry Word	Meaning	Definition
197 ☐☐	**diurnal** [daiə́ːrnl]	ⓐ relating to or occurring in a 24-hour period; occurring or active during the daytime rather than at night	날마다의; 주간의
198 ☐☐	**divine** [diváin]	ⓐ having the nature of or being a deity	신의, 신성한
199 ☐☐	**doctrinaire** [dàktrənέər]	ⓐ adhering rigidly to theories or principles, often regardless of practicalities or appropriateness	비현실적인, 공론가의
200 ☐☐	**dogmatic** [dɔ(ː)gmǽtik]	ⓐ characterized by an authoritative, arrogant assertion of unproved or unprovable principles	독단적인
201 ☐☐	**doldrums** [dóuldrəmz]	ⓝ a period of stagnation or slump	침체, 부진
202 ☐☐	**dolt** [doult]	ⓝ a person regarded as stupid	바보
203 ☐☐	**dotage** [dóutidʒ]	ⓝ a deterioration of mental faculties	노망, 망령
204 ☐☐	**downcast** [dáunkæ̀st]	ⓐ directed downward; low in spirits	(눈을) 내리뜬; 의기소침한
205 ☐☐	**droll** [droul]	ⓐ amusingly odd or whimsically comical	까부는, 우스꽝스러운
206 ☐☐	**dross** [drɔːs]	ⓝ a waste product or an impurity, especially an oxide, formed on the surface of molten metal	(녹은 금속의) 불순물
207 ☐☐	**duress** [djuərés]	ⓝ constraint by threat	감금
E			
208 ☐☐	**eclipse** [iklíps]	ⓝ the partial or complete obscuring, relative to a designated observer, of one celestial body by another	일식
209 ☐☐	**edify** [édəfài]	ⓥ to instruct especially so as to encourage intellectual, moral, or spiritual improvement	교화하다

NO.	Entry Word	Meaning	Definition
210 ☐☐	**effectual** [ifékt∫uəl]	ⓐ producing or sufficient to produce a desired effect	효과적인
211 ☐☐	**efficacy** [éfəkəsi]	ⓝ power or capacity to produce a desired effect	유효성, 효험
212 ☐☐	**effigy** [éfədʒi]	ⓝ a likeness or image, especially of a person	조상(彫像), 초상
213 ☐☐	**effusion** [efjú:ʒən]	ⓝ the act or an instance of effusing	유출
214 ☐☐	**elegy** [élədʒi]	ⓝ a poem composed in elegiac couplets	애가
215 ☐☐	**elliptical** [ilíptikəl]	ⓐ of, relating to, or having the shape of, an ellipse	타원형의
216 ☐☐	**emanate** [émənèit]	ⓥ to come or send forth, as from a source	발산하다
217 ☐☐	**embargo** [embá:rgou]	ⓝ a government order prohibiting the movement of merchant ships into or out of its ports	입출항 금지 명령
218 ☐☐	**embed** [imbéd]	ⓥ to fix firmly in a surrounding mass	박아 넣다
219 ☐☐	**embroil** [embrɔ́il]	ⓥ to involve in argument, contention, or hostile actions	(분쟁 · 전쟁 등에) 휩쓸어 넣다
220 ☐☐	**embryonic** [èmbriánik]	ⓐ of, relating to, or being an embryo; rudimentary	태아의; 미발달한
221 ☐☐	**enervate** [énərvèit]	ⓥ to weaken or destroy the strength or vitality of	(…의) 힘을 약화시키다
222 ☐☐	**enfranchise** [enfrǽnt∫aiz]	ⓥ to bestow a franchise on	참정권을 주다
223 ☐☐	**enigma** [inígmə]	ⓝ one that is puzzling, ambiguous, or inexplicable	수수께끼
224 ☐☐	**ennui** [á:nwi:]	ⓝ listlessness and dissatisfaction resulting from lack of interest	권태감
225 ☐☐	**enormity** [inɔ́:rməti]	ⓝ the quality of passing all moral bounds	극악 행위

NO.	Entry Word	Meaning	Definition
226 ☐☐	**ensue** [ensú:]	ⓥ to follow as a consequence or result; to take place subsequently	잇따라 일어나다; (…의) 결과로서 일어나다
227 ☐☐	**enumerate** [injú:mərèit]	ⓥ to count off or name one by one	…을 차례로 들다
228 ☐☐	**epigram** [épigræm]	ⓝ a short, witty poem expressing a single thought or observation	경구
229 ☐☐	**epoch** [épək]	ⓝ a particular period of history, especially one considered remarkable or noteworthy	신기원
230 ☐☐	**equestrian** [ikwéstriən]	ⓐ of or relating to horseback riding or horseback riders	승마의
231 ☐☐	**erudite** [érjudàit]	ⓐ characterized by erudition	박식한
232 ☐☐	**ethereal** [iθíriəl]	ⓐ characterized by lightness and insubstantiality; highly refined	공기 같은; 영묘한
233 ☐☐	**evince** [ivíns]	ⓥ to show or demonstrate clearly	분명히 나타내다
234 ☐☐	**exasperate** [igzǽspərèit]	ⓥ to make very angry or impatient; annoy greatly	분개시키다
235 ☐☐	**excise** [éksaiz]	ⓝ an internal tax imposed on the production, sale, or consumption of a commodity or the use of a service within a country	소비세
236 ☐☐	**exhume** [igzjú:m]	ⓥ to remove from a grave	발굴하다
237 ☐☐	**exigency** [éksədʒənsi]	ⓝ the state or quality of requiring much effort or immediate action	긴급 (사태)
238 ☐☐	**existential** [ègzisténʃəl]	ⓐ of, relating to, or dealing with existence	존재의
239 ☐☐	**exodus** [éksədəs]	ⓝ a departure of a large number of people	대이동
240 ☐☐	**expiate** [ékspièit]	ⓥ to make amends or reparation for	보상하다

NO.	Entry Word	Meaning	Definition
241 ☐☐	**explicate** [éksplǝkèit]	ⓥ to make clear the meaning of	해설하다
242 ☐☐	**expunge** [ikspʌ́ndʒ]	ⓥ to erase or strike out	지우다
243 ☐☐	**extort** [ikstɔ́ːrt]	ⓥ to obtain from another by coercion or intimidation	빼앗다

F

NO.	Entry Word	Meaning	Definition
244 ☐☐	**fatuous** [fǽtʃuǝs]	ⓐ vacuously, smugly, and unconsciously foolish	어리석은
245 ☐☐	**fauna** [fɔ́ːnǝ]	ⓝ animals, especially the animals of a particular region or period, considered as a group	동물군
246 ☐☐	**fervent** [fɔ́ːrvǝnt]	ⓐ having or showing great emotion or zeal; ardent	열렬한
247 ☐☐	**fervor** [fɔ́ːrvǝr]	ⓝ great warmth and intensity of emotion	열정
248 ☐☐	**fester** [féstǝr]	ⓥ to generate pus	곪다
249 ☐☐	**fetish** [fétiʃ]	ⓝ an object of unreasonably excessive attention or reverence	맹목적 숭배물
250 ☐☐	**fiasco** [fiǽskou]	ⓝ a complete failure	대실패
251 ☐☐	**fiat** [fíːǝt]	ⓝ an arbitrary order or decree; authorization or sanction	명령; 허가
252 ☐☐	**figment** [fígmǝnt]	ⓝ something invented, made up, or fabricated	상상의 산물
253 ☐☐	**fledgling** [flédʒliŋ]	ⓝ a young or inexperienced person	풋내기
254 ☐☐	**foible** [fɔ́ibǝl]	ⓝ a minor weakness or failing of character	사소한 약점
255 ☐☐	**foment** [foumént]	ⓥ to promote the growth of	촉진하다, 조장하다

NO.	Entry Word	Meaning	Definition
256 □□	**foray** [fɔ́ːrei]	ⓝ a sudden raid or military advance; a venture or an initial attempt, especially outside one's usual area	급습; 진출
257 □□	**forensic** [fərénsik]	ⓐ relating to, used in, or appropriate for courts of law or for public discussion or argumentation	법정의
258 □□	**forswear** [fɔːrswέər]	ⓥ to renounce or repudiate under oath	맹세코 그만두다
259 □□	**forte** [fɔːrt]	ⓝ something in which a person excels	장점
260 □□	**fortuitous** [fɔːrtjúːətəs]	ⓐ happening by accident or chance	우발성의
261 □□	**frenetic** [frinétik]	ⓐ wildly excited or active; frantic	열광적인
262 □□	**fulminate** [fʌ́lmənèit]	ⓥ to explode or detonate	(큰 소리와 함께) 폭발하다

G

NO.	Entry Word	Meaning	Definition
263 □□	**gambit** [gǽmbit]	ⓝ a maneuver, stratagem, or ploy, especially one used at an initial stage	책략
264 □□	**gamut** [gǽmət]	ⓝ a complete range or extent	전 영역(全領域)
265 □□	**garrulous** [gǽrjələs]	ⓐ given to excessive and often trivial or rambling talk	수다스러운
266 □□	**gastronomy** [gæstrɑ́nəmi]	ⓝ the art or science of good eating; a style of cooking, as of a particular region	미식법; 요리법
267 □□	**genesis** [dʒénəsis]	ⓝ the coming into being of something	기원
268 □□	**genteel** [dʒentíːl]	ⓐ refined in manner	품위 있는
269 □□	**germane** [dʒəːrméin]	ⓐ being both pertinent and fitting	적절한

NO.	Entry Word	Meaning	Definition
270 ☐☐	**ghastly** [gǽstli]	ⓐ Inspiring shock, revulsion, or horror by or as if by suggesting death	무시무시한
271 ☐☐	**glut** [glʌt]	ⓥ to fill beyond capacity, especially with food	배불리 먹이다
272 ☐☐	**grandiloquent** [grændíləkwənt]	ⓐ pompous or bombastic speech or expression	호언장담; 허풍
273 ☐☐	**gratis** [grǽitis]	ⓐ without charge	무료로[의]
274 ☐☐	**grimace** [grímэs]	ⓝ a sharp contortion of the face expressive of pain, contempt, or disgust	찡그린 얼굴

H

NO.	Entry Word	Meaning	Definition
275 ☐☐	**halcyon** [hǽlsiэn]	ⓐ calm and peaceful	고요한
276 ☐☐	**hapless** [hǽplis]	ⓐ luckless	불운한
277 ☐☐	**harbinger** [háːrbindʒər]	ⓝ one that indicates or foreshadows what is to come	전조
278 ☐☐	**harry** [hǽri]	ⓥ to disturb or distress by or as if by repeated attacks	괴롭히다
279 ☐☐	**hegemony** [hidʒémэni]	ⓝ the predominant influence of one state over others	주도권
280 ☐☐	**heresy** [hérэsi]	ⓝ an opinion or a doctrine at variance with established religious beliefs, especially dissension from or denial of roman catholic dogma by a professed believer or baptized church member	이단
281 ☐☐	**hermetic** [həːrmétik]	ⓐ completely sealed, especially against the escape or entry of air	밀폐된
282 ☐☐	**heyday** [héidèi]	ⓝ the period of greatest popularity, success, or power; prime	전성기

273

PART 1

PART 2

PART 3

PART 4

PART 5

PART 6

NO.	Entry Word	Meaning	Definition
283 ☐☐	**hiatus** [haiéitəs]	ⓝ a gap or an interruption in space, time, or continuity	틈, 중단
284 ☐☐	**histrionic** [hìstriánik]	ⓐ of or relating to actors or acting	배우의, 연기의
285 ☐☐	**hoary** [hɔ́ːri]	ⓐ gray or white with or as if with age	흰, 백발인
286 ☐☐	**homage** [hámidʒ]	ⓝ special honor or respect shown or expressed publicly	경의
287 ☐☐	**homily** [háməli]	ⓝ a sermon, especially one intended to edify a congregation on a practical matter and not intended to be a theological discourse	설교
288 ☐☐	**hyperbole** [haipə́ːrbəlì]	ⓐ a figure of speech in which exaggeration is used for emphasis or effect	과장(법)

I

NO.	Entry Word	Meaning	Definition
289 ☐☐	**ideology** [àidiáələdʒi]	ⓝ the body of ideas reflecting the social needs and aspirations of an individual, a group, a class, or a culture	이데올로기
290 ☐☐	**idiosyncrasy** [ìdiəsíŋkrəsi]	ⓝ a structural or behavioral characteristic peculiar to an individual or a group	특질
291 ☐☐	**idyllic** [aidílik]	ⓐ of or having the nature of an idyll	목가적인
292 ☐☐	**ignoble** [ignóubəl]	ⓐ not noble in quality, character, or purpose	비열한
293 ☐☐	**imminent** [ímənənt]	ⓐ about to occur	긴박한
294 ☐☐	**impasse** [ímpæs]	ⓝ a situation that is so difficult that no progress can be made	막다른 상태
295 ☐☐	**impecunious** [ìmpikjúːniəs]	ⓐ lacking money	돈이 없는
296 ☐☐	**impede** [impíːd]	ⓥ to retard or obstruct the progress of	지체시키다

NO.	Entry Word	Meaning	Definition
297 ☐☐	**impervious** [impə́:rviəs]	ⓝ incapable of being affected	영향받지 않는
298 ☐☐	**implore** [implɔ́:r]	ⓥ to appeal to in supplication	간청하다
299 ☐☐	**importune** [ìmpərtjú:n]	ⓥ to beset with insistent or repeated requests	성가시게 졸라대다
300 ☐☐	**improvident** [imprάvədənt]	ⓐ not providing for the future; incautious	절약하지 않는; 경솔한
301 ☐☐	**improvise** [ímprəvàiz]	ⓥ to invent, compose, or recite without preparation	즉흥적으로 마련하다
302 ☐☐	**impunity** [impjú:nəti]	ⓝ exemption from punishment, penalty, or harm	형벌을 받지 않음
303 ☐☐	**inalienable** [inéiljənəbəl]	ⓐ cannot be taken away	양도할 수 없는
304 ☐☐	**inaugurate** [inɔ́:gjərèit]	ⓥ to induct into office by a formal ceremony; to cause to begin, especially officially or formally	취임시키다; 개시하다
305 ☐☐	**incarcerate** [inkɑ́:rsərèit]	ⓥ to put into jail; imprison	감금하다
306 ☐☐	**incarnation** [ìnkɑːrnéiʃən]	ⓝ someone or something that typifies a quality or idea	화신
307 ☐☐	**incendiary** [inséndièri]	ⓐ causing or capable of causing fire; causing, or likely to cause, trouble or violence	방화의; 선동적인
308 ☐☐	**incense** [ínsens]	ⓥ to make very angry	몹시 화나게하다
309 ☐☐	**incipient** [insípiənt]	ⓐ beginning to exist or appear	처음의, 초기의
310 ☐☐	**incite** [insáit]	ⓥ to provoke and urge on	자극하다
311 ☐☐	**incorrigible** [inkɔ́:ridʒəbəl]	ⓐ incapable of being corrected or reformed; difficult or impossible to control or manage	교정할 수 없는; 제멋대로 구는

PART 1
PART 2
PART 3
PART 4
PART 5
PART 6

NO.	Entry Word	Meaning	Definition
312 □□	**increment** [ínkrəmənt]	ⓝ the process of increasing in number, size, quantity, or extent	증가
313 □□	**inculcate** [inkʎlkeit]	ⓥ to teach an idea or opinion in someone's mind by repeating it until it is fixed in their mind	되풀이하여 가르치다
314 □□	**incursion** [inkə́:rʒən]	ⓝ an aggressive entrance into foreign territory	침략
315 □□	**indigent** [índidʒənt]	ⓐ experiencing want or need	궁핍한
316 □□	**indignity** [indígnəti]	ⓝ humiliating, degrading, or abusive treatment	모욕
317 □□	**ineluctable** [ìnilʎktəbəl]	ⓐ not to be avoided or escaped	불가피한
318 □□	**infamous** [ínfəməs]	ⓐ causing or deserving infamy	악명 높은
319 □□	**infinitesimal** [infìnitésəməl]	ⓐ immeasurably or incalculably minute	극소한
320 □□	**infraction** [infrǽkʃən]	ⓝ the act or an instance of infringing	위반
321 □□	**infringe** [infríndʒ]	ⓥ to transgress or exceed the limits of	어기다
322 □□	**ingratiate** [ingréiʃièit]	ⓥ to bring (oneself, for example) into the favor or good graces of another, especially by deliberate effort	환심사다
323 □□	**inimical** [inímikəl]	ⓝ injurious or harmful in effect; unfriendly	해로운; 비우호적인
324 □□	**inimitable** [inímitəbəl]	ⓐ defying imitation	모방할 수 없는
325 □□	**initiate** [iníʃièit]	ⓥ to set going by taking the first step	시작하다
326 □□	**innuendo** [ìnjuéndou]	ⓝ an indirect or subtle, usually derogatory implication in expression	풍자, 빈정대는 말

NO.	Entry Word	Meaning	Definition
327 ☐☐	**inordinate** [inɔ́ːrdənət]	ⓐ exceeding reasonable limits	지나친
328 ☐☐	**insatiable** [inséiʃəbəl]	ⓐ impossible to satiate or satisfy	만족할 줄 모르는
329 ☐☐	**insouciant** [insúːsiənt]	ⓐ marked by blithe unconcern	무관심한
330 ☐☐	**insuperable** [insúːpərəbəl]	ⓐ impossible to overcome	이겨내기 어려운
331 ☐☐	**insurgent** [insə́ːrdʒənt]	ⓝ people are who are fighting against the government or army of their own country	폭도
332 ☐☐	**integral** [íntigrəl]	ⓐ essential or necessary for completeness	없어서는 알될
333 ☐☐	**interim** [íntərim]	ⓝ an interval of time between one event, process, or period and another	잠시 (동안)
334 ☐☐	**interloper** [ìntərlóupər]	ⓝ one that interferes with the affairs of others, often for selfish reasons	남의 일에 참견하고 나서는 사람
335 ☐☐	**intractable** [inrǽktəbl]	ⓐ difficult to manage or govern	다루기 힘든
336 ☐☐	**invective** [invéktiv]	ⓝ denunciatory or abusive language	비난
337 ☐☐	**inveterate** [invétərit]	ⓐ firmly and long established; persisting in an ingrained habit	만성의; 상습적인
338 ☐☐	**invidious** [invídiəs]	ⓐ tending to rouse ill will, animosity, or resentment; discriminatory	화나게 만드는; 불공평한
339 ☐☐	**irascible** [irǽsəbəl]	ⓐ prone to outbursts of temper	성급한, 화를 잘 내는
340 ☐☐	**iridescent** [ìrədésənt]	ⓐ producing a display of lustrous, rainbowlike colors	무지개 빛깔[진주 빛깔]의
341 ☐☐	**irrevocable** [irévəkəbəl]	ⓐ impossible to retract or revoke	돌이킬 수 없는, 취소할 수 없는

PART 1

PART 2

PART 3

PART 4

PART 5

PART 6

NO.	Entry Word	Meaning	Definition

J

342 ☐☐	**jaunt** [dʒɔːnt]	ⓝ a short trip or excursion, usually for pleasure	짧은 여행
343 ☐☐	**jeopardy** [dʒépərdi]	ⓝ risk of loss or injury	위험
344 ☐☐	**jingoism** [dʒíŋgouìzəm]	ⓝ extreme nationalism characterized especially by a belligerent foreign policy	맹목적 애국주의
345 ☐☐	**junta** [hú(ː)ntə]	ⓝ a group of military officers ruling a country after seizing power	(쿠데타 직후의) 임시 정부

K

| 346 ☐☐ | **kindle** [kíndl] | ⓥ to build or fuel (a fire); to arouse (an emotion, for example) | 불붙이다; 부추기다 |
| 347 ☐☐ | **kinetic** [kinétik] | ⓐ of, relating to, or produced by motion | 운동의, 움직임의 |

L

348 ☐☐	**labyrinth** [lǽbərìnθ]	ⓝ an intricate structure of interconnecting passages through which it is difficult to find one's way; a maze	미궁
349 ☐☐	**lampoon** [læmpúːn]	ⓥ to criticize them very strongly, using humorous means	풍자하다
350 ☐☐	**largess** [lɑːrdʒés]	ⓝ liberality in bestowing gifts, especially in a lofty or condescending manner	아낌없이 선물함
351 ☐☐	**lascivious** [ləsíviəs]	ⓐ given to or expressing lust	음란한
352 ☐☐	**latent** [léitənt]	ⓐ present or potential but not evident or active	숨어있는, 잠재적인
353 ☐☐	**lax** [læks]	ⓐ lacking in rigor, strictness, or firmness	엄격하지 못한, 느슨한

NO.	Entry Word	Meaning	Definition
354 ☐☐	**levity** [lévəti]	ⓝ lightness of manner or speech, especially when inappropriate	경솔
355 ☐☐	**liaison** [líːəzɑ̀n]	ⓝ an instance or a means of communication between different groups or units of an organization, especially in the armed forces	연락, 접촉
356 ☐☐	**licentious** [laisénʃəs]	ⓐ lacking moral discipline or ignoring legal restraint, especially in sexual conduct	방탕한, 음탕한
357 ☐☐	**limpid** [límpid]	ⓐ characterized by transparent clearness	맑은, 투명한
358 ☐☐	**listless** [lístlis]	ⓐ lacking energy or disinclined to exert effort	무관심한, 생기 없는
359 ☐☐	**litany** [lítəni]	ⓝ a repetitive or incantatory recital	장황한 설명, 지루한 이야기
360 ☐☐	**loathe** [louð]	ⓥ to dislike (someone or something) greatly	몹시 싫어하다
361 ☐☐	**lofty** [lɔ́ːfti]	ⓐ of imposing height; arrogant	매우 높은; 거만한
362 ☐☐	**loquacious** [loukwéiʃəs]	ⓐ very talkative	수다스러운
363 ☐☐	**ludicrous** [lúːdəkrəs]	ⓐ laughable or hilarious because of obvious absurdity or incongruity	웃기는

M

NO.	Entry Word	Meaning	Definition
364 ☐☐	**magnate** [mǽgneit]	ⓝ a powerful or influential person, especially in business or industry	거물
365 ☐☐	**maladroit** [mælədrɔ́it]	ⓐ marked by a lack of adroitness	솜씨 없는, 재치[요령] 없는
366 ☐☐	**malaise** [mæléiz]	ⓝ a general sense of depression or unease	불안
367 ☐☐	**malapropism** [mǽləprɑ̀pizəm]	ⓝ ludicrous misuse of a word, especially by confusion with one of similar sound	말의 우스꽝스런 오용

279

PART 1

PART 2

PART 3

PART 4

PART 5

PART 6

NO.	Entry Word	Meaning	Definition
368 ☐☐	**malcontent** [mælkəntént]	ⓐ dissatisfied with existing conditions	불평을 품은
369 ☐☐	**malfeasance** [mælfíːzəns]	ⓝ misconduct or wrongdoing, especially by a public official	위법 행위
370 ☐☐	**mammoth** [mǽməθ]	ⓝ something of great size	거대한 것
371 ☐☐	**manifold** [mǽnəfòuld]	ⓐ many and varied	여러 가지의
372 ☐☐	**maudlin** [mɔ́ːdlin]	ⓐ effusively or tearfully sentimental	잘 우는, 감상적인
373 ☐☐	**mawkish** [mɔ́ːkiʃ]	ⓐ sickening or insipid in taste	구역질나게 하는
374 ☐☐	**meander** [miǽndər]	ⓥ to follow a winding and turning course	(강이) 꼬불꼬불[굽이쳐] 흐르다
375 ☐☐	**meddlesome** [médlsəm]	ⓐ inclined to meddle or interfere	쓸데없이 참견하는
376 ☐☐	**mellifluous** [məlífluəs]	ⓐ smooth and sweet	감미로운
377 ☐☐	**mendacious** [mendéiʃəs]	ⓐ lying	거짓인
378 ☐☐	**mercurial** [məːrkjúəriəl]	ⓐ quick and changeable in temperament	민활한
379 ☐☐	**metamorphosis** [mètəmɔ́ːrfəsis]	ⓝ a marked change in appearance, character, condition, or function	현저한 변화
380 ☐☐	**microcosm** [máikroukàzəm]	ⓝ a small, representative system having analogies to a larger system in constitution, configuration, or development	작은 세계, 소우주
381 ☐☐	**milieu** [míljəː]	ⓝ an environment or a setting	환경
382 ☐☐	**minuscule** [mínʌskjùːl]	ⓐ very small	아주 작은

NO.	Entry Word	Meaning	Definition
383 □□	**miserly** [máizərli]	ⓐ of, relating to, or characteristic of a miser	인색한
384 □□	**mollify** [málifài]	ⓥ to lessen in intensity; temper	누그러뜨리다
385 □□	**momentum** [mouméntəm]	ⓝ impetus of a physical object im motion; impetus of a nonphysical process	힘; 추진력
386 □□	**monolithic** [mànəliθik]	ⓐ constituting or acting as a single, often rigid, uniform whole	단일체의
387 □□	**moratorium** [mɔ̀(ː)rətɔ́riəm]	ⓝ an authorization to a debtor, such as a bank or nation, permitting temporary suspension of payments	지급유예(령)
388 □□	**mores** [mɔ́ːriːz]	ⓝ the accepted traditional customs and usages of a particular social group	관례, 관습
389 □□	**munificent** [mjuːnífəsənt]	ⓐ very liberal in giving	아낌없이 주는
390 □□	**muse** [mjuːz]	ⓥ to reflect or ponder silently	깊이[골똘히] 생각하다
391 □□	**muster** [mʌ́stər]	ⓥ to call (troops) together, as for inspection	소집하다

N

NO.	Entry Word	Meaning	Definition
392 □□	**neologism** [niːálədʒìzəm]	ⓝ a new word, expression, or usage	신조어, 새 표현
393 □□	**neophyte** [níːəfàit]	ⓝ a beginner or novice	초심자, 신출내기
394 □□	**nirvana** [nəːrvάːnə]	ⓝ the ineffable ultimate in which one has attained disinterested wisdom and compassion	열반(涅槃)
395 □□	**noisome** [nɔ́isəm]	ⓐ offensive to the point of arousing disgust; foul	불쾌한

PART 1

PART 2

PART 3

PART 4

PART 5

PART 6

NO.	Entry Word	Meaning	Definition
396 ☐☐	**nomad** [nóumæd]	ⓝ a member of a group of people who have no fixed home and move according to the seasons from place to place in search of food, water, and grazing land	유목민
397 ☐☐	**noxious** [nάkʃəs]	ⓐ harmful to living things	몸에 해로운
O			
398 ☐☐	**obeisance** [oʊbéisəns]	ⓝ a gesture or movement of the body, such as a curtsy, that expresses deference or homage	인사
399 ☐☐	**obfuscate** [abfʌ́skeit]	ⓥ to render indistinct or dim	(판단을) 흐리게 하다
400 ☐☐	**oblivion** [əblíviən]	ⓝ the condition or quality of being completely forgotten	잊혀져 있는 상태
401 ☐☐	**obtrude** [əbtrúːd]	ⓥ to impose (oneself or one's ideas) on others with undue insistence or without invitation	강요[강제]하다
402 ☐☐	**obtuse** [əbtʃúːs]	ⓐ lacking quickness of perception or intellect	둔감한
403 ☐☐	**obviate** [άbvièit]	ⓥ to anticipate and dispose of effectively	미연에 방지하다
404 ☐☐	**occult** [əkʌ́lt]	ⓐ of, relating to, or dealing with supernatural influences, agencies, or phenomena	초자연적인
405 ☐☐	**odious** [óudiəs]	ⓐ arousing or meriting strong dislike, aversion, or intense displeasure	증오할
406 ☐☐	**olfactory** [alfǽktəri]	ⓐ of, relating to, or contributing to the sense of smell	후각의
407 ☐☐	**oligarchy** [άləgàːrki]	ⓝ government by a few, especially by a small faction of persons or families	과두정치
408 ☐☐	**omnipresent** [àmnəprézənt]	ⓐ present everywhere simultaneously	어디에나 있는

NO.	Entry Word	Meaning	Definition
409 ☐☐	**omniscient** [ɑmníʃənt]	ⓐ having total knowledge	박식한
410 ☐☐	**opprobrious** [əpróubriəs]	ⓐ expressing contemptuous reproach	모욕적인
411 ☐☐	**oscillate** [ásəlèit]	ⓥ to waver, as between conflicting opinions or courses of action	동요하다
412 ☐☐	**ostracize** [ástrəsàiz]	ⓥ to exclude from a group	추방하다, 배척하다
413 ☐☐	**oust** [aust]	ⓥ to eject from a position or place	내쫓다
P			
414 ☐☐	**pacify** [pǽsəfài]	ⓥ to ease the anger or agitation of	진정시키다
415 ☐☐	**painstaking** [péinztèikiŋ]	ⓐ marked by or requiring great pains	힘이 드는, 애쓴
416 ☐☐	**palliate** [pǽlièit]	ⓥ to relieve the symptoms of a disease or disorder	(일시적으로) 완화시키다
417 ☐☐	**palpable** [pǽlpəbəl]	ⓐ capable of being handled, touched, or felt	손으로 만질 수 있는
418 ☐☐	**paltry** [pɔ́ːltri]	ⓐ lacking in importance or worth	시시한, 하찮은
419 ☐☐	**panacea** [pæ̀nəsíːə]	ⓝ a remedy for all diseases, evils, or difficulties	만병통치약
420 ☐☐	**pandemic** [pændémik]	ⓐ epidemic over a wide geographic area; widespread	전 지역에 걸치는; 일반적인
421 ☐☐	**panegyric** [pæ̀nədʒírik]	ⓝ a formal eulogistic composition intended as a public compliment	찬양의 연설[글]
422 ☐☐	**parable** [pǽrəbəl]	ⓝ a simple story illustrating a moral or religious lesson	우화
423 ☐☐	**parochial** [pəróukiəl]	ⓐ narrowly restricted in scope or	편협한

NO.	Entry Word	Meaning	Definition
424 ☐☐	**parsimonious** [pɑ̀ːrsəmóuniəs]	ⓐ excessively sparing or frugal	인색한
425 ☐☐	**pastoral** [pǽstərəl]	ⓐ of or relating to shepherds or herders; of or relating to the country or country life	양치기의; 전원 생활의
426 ☐☐	**patina** [pǽtənə]	ⓝ a thin greenish layer, usually basic copper sulfate, that forms on copper or copper alloys, such as bronze, as a result of corrosion	고색(古色)
427 ☐☐	**patrician** [pətríʃən]	ⓝ a member of an aristocracy	귀족
428 ☐☐	**patronize** [péitrənàiz]	ⓥ to act as a patron to; to support or sponsor	단골로 삼다; 후원하다
429 ☐☐	**pecuniary** [pikjúːnièri]	ⓐ of or relating to money	금전의
430 ☐☐	**pejorative** [pidʒárətiv]	ⓐ tending to make or become worse	가치를 떨어뜨리는
431 ☐☐	**pensive** [pénsiv]	ⓐ deeply, often wistfully or dreamily thoughtful	깊은 생각에 잠긴
432 ☐☐	**peregrination** [pèrəgrinéiʃən]	ⓝ a long and wandering journey, especially in foreign countries	여행
433 ☐☐	**peremptory** [pərémptəri]	ⓐ not allowing contradiction or refusal	불문곡직의
434 ☐☐	**perfidy** [pə́ːrfədi]	ⓝ deliberate breach of faith	배신행위
435 ☐☐	**perfunctory** [pərfʌ́ŋktəri]	ⓐ done routinely and with little interest or care	형식적인, 마지못해 하는
436 ☐☐	**peripatetic** [pèrəpətétik]	ⓐ walking about or from place to place	순회하는, 걸어 다니는
437 ☐☐	**perjury** [pə́ːrdʒəri]	ⓝ the deliberate, willful giving of false, misleading, or incomplete testimony under oath	위증(죄)
438 ☐☐	**pernicious** [pərníʃəs]	ⓐ tending to cause death or serious injury	파멸적인

NO.	Entry Word	Meaning	Definition
439 ☐☐	**perturb** [pərtə́ːrb]	ⓥ to disturb greatly	당황하게 하다
440 ☐☐	**pervade** [pərvéid]	ⓥ to be present throughout	널리 퍼지다
441 ☐☐	**piquant** [píːkənt]	ⓐ pleasantly pungent or tart in taste	얼얼한
442 ☐☐	**placate** [pléikeit]	ⓥ to allay the anger of, especially by making concessions	위로하다
443 ☐☐	**platitude** [plǽtətjùːd]	ⓝ a trite or banal remark or statement, especially one expressed as if it were original or significant	진부한 이야기
444 ☐☐	**platonic** [plətánik]	ⓐ speculative or theoretical	관념적인
445 ☐☐	**plebeian** [plibíːən]	ⓐ of or relating to the common people of ancient Rome ⓝ one of the common people of ancient Rome	평민의, 평민
446 ☐☐	**plethora** [pléθərə]	ⓐ excessive in quantity	과다한
447 ☐☐	**poignant** [pɔ́injənt]	ⓐ physically painful	통렬한
448 ☐☐	**polemic** [poulémik]	ⓝ a controversial argument, especially one refuting or attacking a specific opinion or doctrine	반론, 논쟁
449 ☐☐	**ponderous** [pándərəs]	ⓐ having great weight; lacking grace or fluency	크고 무거운; 답답한
450 ☐☐	**portent** [pɔ́ːrtənt]	ⓝ an indication of something important or calamitous about to occur	징후, 전조
451 ☐☐	**posterity** [pɑstérəti]	ⓝ future generations; all of a person's descendants	자손; 후대
452 ☐☐	**practicable** [prǽktikəbəl]	ⓐ capable of being effected, done, or put into practice	실행 가능한

PART 1

PART 2

PART 3

PART 4

PART 5

PART 6

NO.	Entry Word	Meaning	Definition
453 ☐☐	**prattle** [prǽtl]	ⓥ to talk or chatter idly or meaninglessly	쓸데없는 말을 하다
454 ☐☐	**prelude** [préljuːd]	ⓝ an introductory performance, event, or action preceding a more important one; a preliminary or preface	전조
455 ☐☐	**preponderance** [pripɑ́ndərəns]	ⓝ superiority in weight, force, importance, or influence	우세
456 ☐☐	**prerogative** [prirɑ́gətiv]	ⓝ an exclusive right or privilege held by a person or group, especially a hereditary or official right	특권
457 ☐☐	**presage** [présidʒ]	ⓝ an indication or a warning of a future occurrence; an omen	전조
458 ☐☐	**presentiment** [prizéntəmənt]	ⓝ a sense that something is about to occur	예감
459 ☐☐	**prodigal** [prɑ́digəl]	ⓐ rashly or wastefully extravagant	낭비하는
460 ☐☐	**prodigious** [prədídʒəs]	ⓐ impressively great in size, force, or extent	거대한
461 ☐☐	**propitious** [prəpíʃəs]	ⓐ presenting favorable circumstances	상서로운
462 ☐☐	**proscribe** [prouskráib]	ⓥ to prohibit	금지하다
463 ☐☐	**proselytize** [prɑ́sələtàiz]	ⓥ to induce someone to convert to one's own religious faith	개종시키다
464 ☐☐	**protocol** [próutəkɑ̀l]	ⓝ the forms of ceremony and etiquette observed by diplomats and heads of state	외교 의례
465 ☐☐	**protract** [proutrǽkt]	ⓥ to draw out or lengthen in time	연장하다
466 ☐☐	**provident** [prɑ́vədənt]	ⓐ providing for future needs or events; frugal	장래에 대한 대비가 있는; 검소한
467 ☐☐	**provisional** [prəvíʒənəl]	ⓐ provided or serving only for the time being	일시적인

NO.	Entry Word	Meaning	Definition
468 ☐☐	**provocation** [prɑ̀vəkéiʃən]	ⓝ the act of provoking or inciting	도발
469 ☐☐	**prurient** [prúəriənt]	ⓐ inordinately interested in matters of sex	호색[음란]한, 외설한
470 ☐☐	**psyche** [sáikiː]	ⓝ the spirit or soul	정신
471 ☐☐	**pummel** [pʌ́məl]	ⓥ to beat, as with the fists	주먹으로 때리다
472 ☐☐	**pungent** [pʌ́ndʒənt]	ⓐ affecting the organs of taste or smell with a sharp, acrid sensation	찌르듯이 자극하는
473 ☐☐	**purblind** [pə́ːrblàind]	ⓐ having poor vision; nearly or partly blind	눈이 침침한; 반소경의
474 ☐☐	**purge** [pəːrdʒ]	ⓥ to free from impurities	정화하다
475 ☐☐	**putative** [pjúːtətiv]	ⓐ generally regarded as such	추정의

Q

NO.	Entry Word	Meaning	Definition
476 ☐☐	**quay** [kiː]	ⓝ a wharf or reinforced bank where ships are loaded or unloaded	부두
477 ☐☐	**queue** [kju(ː)]	ⓝ a line of waiting people or vehicles	(차례를 기다리는 사람들이나 자동차 등의) 줄
478 ☐☐	**quiescent** [kwaiésənt]	ⓐ being quiet, still, or at rest	조용한
479 ☐☐	**quotidian** [kwoutídiən]	ⓐ recurring daily	매일 일어나는

R

NO.	Entry Word	Meaning	Definition
480 ☐☐	**rampant** [ræmpənt]	ⓐ extending unchecked; unrestrained	만연하는
481 ☐☐	**rapacious** [rəpéiʃəs]	ⓐ taking by force	약탈하는

PART 1 PART 2 PART 3 PART 4 PART 5 PART 6

NO.	Entry Word	Meaning	Definition
482 ☐☐	**rarefied** [rέərəfáid]	ⓐ belonging to or reserved for a small, select group	선발된
483 ☐☐	**ratiocination** [ræ̀ʃiɑ́sənéiʃən]	ⓝ exact and careful thinking	추론
484 ☐☐	**raucous** [rɔ́:kəs]	ⓐ rough-sounding and harsh	귀에 거슬리는
485 ☐☐	**recalcitrant** [rikǽlsətrənt]	ⓐ marked by stubborn resistance to and defiance of authority or guidance	저항하는
486 ☐☐	**recant** [rikǽnt]	ⓥ to make a formal retraction or disavowal of (a statement or belief to which one has previously committed oneself)	철회하다
487 ☐☐	**recidivism** [risídəvìzəm]	ⓝ a tendency to lapse into a previous pattern of behavior, especially a tendency to return to criminal habits	상습적인 비행
488 ☐☐	**reciprocal** [risíprəkəl]	ⓐ concerning each of two or more persons or things	상호간의
489 ☐☐	**recondite** [rékəndàit]	ⓐ not easily understood	이해하기 어려운
490 ☐☐	**refractory** [rifrǽktəri]	ⓐ obstinately resistant to authority or control	다루기 어려운
491 ☐☐	**remission** [rimíʃən]	ⓝ the act of remitting	면죄
492 ☐☐	**remonstrate** [rimánstreit]	ⓥ to say or plead in protest, objection, or reproof	항의하다
493 ☐☐	**rend** [rend]	ⓥ to tear or split apart or into pieces violently	찢다
494 ☐☐	**renounce** [rináuns]	ⓥ to give up (a title, for example), especially by formal announcement	포기하다
495 ☐☐	**reparation** [rèpəréiʃən]	ⓝ the act or process of repairing or the condition of being repaired	배상

NO.	Entry Word	Meaning	Definition
496 ☐☐	**repartee** [rèpɑːrtíː]	ⓝ a swift, witty reply	재치 있는 응답
497 ☐☐	**repercussion** [rìːpərkʌ́ʃən]	ⓝ an often indirect effect, influence, or result that is produced by an event or action	(간접적) 영향
498 ☐☐	**replenish** [riplέniʃ]	ⓥ to fill or make complete again	보충하다
499 ☐☐	**replete** [riplíːt]	ⓐ abundantly supplied	풍부한
500 ☐☐	**repress** [riprés]	ⓥ to hold back by an act of volition	억누르다
501 ☐☐	**reprisal** [ripráizəl]	ⓝ retaliation for an injury with the intent of inflicting at least as much injury in return	보복
502 ☐☐	**reprobate** [réprəbèit]	ⓝ a morally unprincipled person	타락한 사람
503 ☐☐	**reprove** [riprúːv]	ⓥ to voice or convey disapproval of	질책하다
504 ☐☐	**requisite** [rékwəzit]	ⓝ something that is indispensable	필수품
505 ☐☐	**respite** [réspit]	ⓝ a usually short interval of rest or relief	일시적 중단
506 ☐☐	**retaliate** [ritǽlièit]	ⓥ to return like for like, especially evil for evil	보복하다
507 ☐☐	**retort** [ritɔ́ːrt]	ⓥ to reply, especially to answer in a quick, caustic, or witty manner	응수하다
508 ☐☐	**revile** [riváil]	ⓥ to assail with abusive language	욕설을 퍼붓다
509 ☐☐	**revulsion** [rivʌ́lʃən]	ⓝ a sudden, strong change or reaction in feeling, especially a feeling of violent disgust or loathing	급변
510 ☐☐	**ribald** [ríbəld]	ⓐ characterized by or indulging in vulgar, lewd humor	상스러운

PART 1 PART 2 PART 3 PART 4 PART 5 PART 6

NO.	Entry Word	Meaning	Definition
511 ☐☐	**rife** [raif]	ⓐ in widespread existence, practice, or use	퍼져 있는
512 ☐☐	**rout** [raut]	ⓝ an overwhelming defeat	완패
513 ☐☐	**ruminate** [rúːmənèit]	ⓥ to turn a matter over and over in the mind	심사숙고하다
S			
514 ☐☐	**saccharine** [sǽkərin]	ⓐ of, relating to, or characteristic of sugar or saccharin	달콤한
515 ☐☐	**sacrosanct** [sǽkrousæ̀ŋkt]	ⓐ regarded as sacred and inviolable	신성한
516 ☐☐	**sanguinary** [sǽŋgwənèri]	ⓐ accompanied by bloodshed	피비린내 나는
517 ☐☐	**sanguine** [sǽŋgwin]	ⓐ cheerfully confident; optimistic	자신감이 넘치는
518 ☐☐	**sardonic** [sɑːrdánik]	ⓐ scornfully or cynically mocking	조소적인
519 ☐☐	**savant** [səvɑ́ːnt]	ⓝ a learned person	학식이 높은 사람
520 ☐☐	**scanty** [skǽnti]	ⓐ barely sufficient or adequate; insufficient, as in extent or degree	빈약한; 부족한
521 ☐☐	**schism** [sízəm]	ⓝ a separation or division into factions	분리
522 ☐☐	**scintillate** [síntəlèit]	ⓥ to throw off sparks	번쩍이다
523 ☐☐	**seclusion** [siklúːʒən]	ⓝ the state of being secluded	격리
524 ☐☐	**secular** [sékjələr]	ⓐ worldly rather than spiritual not connected with religion	세속의
525 ☐☐	**sedentary** [sédəntèri]	ⓐ done while sitting down, and giving one the chance to move about much	줄곧 앉아 있는

NO.	Entry Word	Meaning	Definition
526 ☐☐	**sedition** [sidíʃən]	ⓝ conduct or language inciting rebellion against the authority of a state	선동
527 ☐☐	**sententious** [senténʃəs]	ⓐ terse and energetic in expression	격언식의, 격언이 많은
528 ☐☐	**sequester** [sikwéstər]	ⓥ to remove or set apart	격리시키다
529 ☐☐	**servile** [sə́ːrvil]	ⓝ abjectly submissive; slavish	노예 근성의
530 ☐☐	**shackle** [ʃǽkəl]	ⓝ a metal fastening, usually one of a pair, for encircling and confining the ankle or wrist of a prisoner or captive; a fetter or manacle	수갑
531 ☐☐	**shibboleth** [ʃíbəliθ]	ⓝ a word or phrase identified with a particular group or cause	표어
532 ☐☐	**singular** [síŋgjələr]	ⓐ being beyond what is ordinary or usual; being the only one of a kind	뛰어난; 유일한
533 ☐☐	**skirmish** [skə́ːrmiʃ]	ⓝ a minor or preliminary conflict or dispute	작은 충돌
534 ☐☐	**skittish** [skítiʃ]	ⓐ restlessly active or nervous; shy	까부는; 수줍어하는
535 ☐☐	**slake** [sleik]	ⓥ to satisfy (a craving); to lessen the force or activity of	만족시키다; 약화시키다
536 ☐☐	**slander** [slǽndər]	ⓝ oral communication of false statements injurious to a person's reputation	명예훼손
537 ☐☐	**sloth** [slouθ]	ⓝ aversion to work or exertion	나태
538 ☐☐	**sobriety** [soubráiəti]	ⓝ moderation in or abstinence from consumption of alcoholic liquor or use of drugs	금주, 맑은 정신
539 ☐☐	**solicitous** [səlísətəs]	ⓐ anxious or concerned; full of desire	걱정하는; 열성적인
540 ☐☐	**sordid** [sɔ́ːrdid]	ⓐ filthy or dirty; morally degraded	더러운; 야비한

PART 1

PART 2

PART 3

PART 4

PART 5

PART 6

NO.	Entry Word	Meaning	Definition
541 ☐☐	**spawn** [spɔːn]	ⓥ to lay their eggs; to cause it to happen or to be created	알을 낳다; 유발하다
542 ☐☐	**spurn** [spəːrn]	ⓥ to reject disdainfully or contemptuously	일축하다
543 ☐☐	**stalwart** [stɔ́ːlwərt]	ⓐ firm and resolute	신념이 굳은
544 ☐☐	**stifle** [stáifəl]	ⓥ to interrupt or cut off(the voice, for example)	막다
545 ☐☐	**stigmatize** [stígmətàiz]	ⓥ to characterize or brand as disgraceful or ignominious	오명을 씌우다, 비난하다
546 ☐☐	**stint** [stint]	ⓥ to restrict or limit, as in amount or number	절약하다
547 ☐☐	**stipend** [stáipend]	ⓝ a fixed and regular payment, such as a salary for services rendered or an allowance	급료
548 ☐☐	**stipulate** [stípjəlèit]	ⓥ to lay down as a condition of an agreement	규정하다
549 ☐☐	**stratagem** [strǽtədʒəm]	ⓝ a military maneuver designed to deceive or surprise an enemy	전략
550 ☐☐	**stratum** [stréitəm]	ⓝ a horizontal layer of material, especially one of several parallel layers arranged one on top of another	지층
551 ☐☐	**stricture** [stríktʃər]	ⓝ a restraint, limit, or restriction; an adverse remark or criticism	제한; 비난
552 ☐☐	**stupor** [stjúːpər]	ⓝ a state of reduced or suspended sensibility; a state of mental numbness, as that resulting from shock	무감각; 인사불성
553 ☐☐	**stymie** [stáimi]	ⓥ to thwart	방해하다
554 ☐☐	**subjugate** [sʌ́bdʒugèit]	ⓥ to bring under control	정복하다
555 ☐☐	**sublime** [səbláim]	ⓐ characterized by nobility	고상한, 장엄한

NO.	Entry Word	Meaning	Definition
556 ☐☐	**subside** [səbsáid]	ⓥ to sink to a lower or normal level	가라앉다
557 ☐☐	**subsidiary** [səbsídièri]	ⓐ serving to assist or supplement	보조의
558 ☐☐	**succinct** [səksíŋkt]	ⓐ characterized by clear, precise expression in few words	간결한
559 ☐☐	**succumb** [səkʌ́m]	ⓥ to submit to an overpowering force or yield to an overwhelming desire	굴복하다
560 ☐☐	**suffuse** [səfjúːz]	ⓥ to spread through or over, as with liquid, color, or light	뒤덮다
561 ☐☐	**sumptuous** [sʌ́mptʃuəs]	ⓐ of a size or splendor suggesting great expense	값비싼
562 ☐☐	**supercilious** [sùːpərsíliəs]	ⓐ feeling or showing haughty disdain	거만한
563 ☐☐	**superfluous** [suːpərfluəs]	ⓐ being beyond what is required or sufficient	여분의
564 ☐☐	**supine** [suːpáin]	ⓐ lying on the back or having the face upward	반듯이 누운
565 ☐☐	**surmise** [sərmáiz]	ⓥ to infer (something) without sufficiently conclusive evidence	추측하다
566 ☐☐	**surpass** [sərpǽs]	ⓥ to be beyond the limit, powers, or capacity of	⋯보다 낫다
567 ☐☐	**surrogate** [sə́ːrəgèit]	ⓝ one that takes the place of another	대리인

T

NO.	Entry Word	Meaning	Definition
568 ☐☐	**tacit** [tǽsit]	ⓐ not spoken	무언의
569 ☐☐	**taciturn** [tǽsətəːrn]	ⓐ habitually untalkative	과묵한

PART 1

PART 2

PART 3

PART 4

PART 5

PART 6

NO.	Entry Word	Meaning	Definition
570 ☐☐	**tantamount** [tǽntəmàunt]	ⓐ equivalent in effect or value	동등한
571 ☐☐	**tautological** [tɔ̀ːtəládʒikəl]	ⓐ of the use of different words to say the same thing twice in the same statement	같은 말을 거듭하는
572 ☐☐	**tedium** [tíːdiəm]	ⓝ the quality or condition of being tedious	지루함
573 ☐☐	**tenet** [ténət]	ⓝ an opinion, doctrine, or principle held as being true by a person or especially by an organization	주의(主義)
574 ☐☐	**tepid** [tépid]	ⓐ moderately warm; lukewarm	미지근한
575 ☐☐	**throttle** [θrátl]	ⓥ to kill or injure them by squeezing their throat or tightening something around it and preventing them from breathing	목을 조르다
576 ☐☐	**thwart** [θwɔːrt]	ⓥ to prevent the occurrence, realization, or attainment of	방해하다
577 ☐☐	**tirade** [táireid]	ⓝ a long angry or violent speech, usually of a censorious or denunciatory nature	길고 신랄한 비난
578 ☐☐	**titillate** [títəlèit]	ⓥ to stimulate by touching lightly	기분좋게 자극하다
579 ☐☐	**torpor** [tɔ́ːrpər]	ⓝ a state of mental or physical inactivity or insensibility	무기력, 무감각
580 ☐☐	**tortuous** [tɔ́ːrtʃuəs]	ⓐ having or marked by repeated turns or bends; winding or twisting	꼬불꼬불한
581 ☐☐	**trepidation** [trèpidéiʃn]	ⓝ a state of alarm or dread	공포
582 ☐☐	**turbid** [tə́ːrbid]	ⓐ having sediment or foreign particles stirred up or suspended	흐린, 탁한
U			
583 ☐☐	**ubiquitous** [juːbíkwətəs]	ⓐ being or seeming to be everywhere at the same time	편재하는

NO.	Entry Word	Meaning	Definition
584 ☐☐	**unanimity** [jùːnəníməti]	ⓝ the condition of being unanimous	만장일치
585 ☐☐	**unconscionable** [ʌnkɑ́nʃənəbəl]	ⓐ beyond prudence or reason	터무니없는
586 ☐☐	**unctuous** [ʌ́ŋktʃuəs]	ⓐ having the quality or characteristics of oil or ointment	미끈미끈한
587 ☐☐	**unilateral** [jùːnəlǽtərəl]	ⓐ of, on, relating to, involving, or affecting only one side	일방적인
588 ☐☐	**usury** [júːʒəri]	ⓝ the practice of lending money and charging the borrower interest, especially at an exorbitant or illegally high rate	고리대금

V

NO.	Entry Word	Meaning	Definition
589 ☐☐	**vacuous** [vǽkjuəs]	ⓐ devoid of matter; laking intelligence	텅빈; 멍청한
590 ☐☐	**vagabond** [vǽgəbɑ̀nd]	ⓝ a person without a permanent home who moves from place to place	방랑자
591 ☐☐	**velocity** [vilɑ́səti]	ⓝ rapidity or speed of motion	속력
592 ☐☐	**veracity** [vərǽsəti]	ⓝ conformity to fact or truth	정확성, 진실성
593 ☐☐	**verbose** [vəːrbóus]	ⓐ using or containing a great and usually an excessive number of words	말이 많은
594 ☐☐	**vernacular** [vərnǽkjələr]	ⓝ the standard native language of a country or locality	자국어, 사투리
595 ☐☐	**vex** [veks]	ⓥ to annoy, as with petty importunities	초조하게 하다
596 ☐☐	**viable** [váiəbəl]	ⓐ capable of success or continuing effectiveness	성장[발전]할 수 있는
597 ☐☐	**vicissitude** [visísətjùːd]	ⓝ a change or variation	변화

295

PART 1
PART 2
PART 3
PART 4
PART 5
PART 6

NO.	Entry Word	Meaning	Definition
598 □□	**vie** [vai]	ⓥ to offer in competition	경쟁하다
599 □□	**vignette** [vinjét]	ⓝ a short, usually descriptive literary sketch	삽화
600 □□	**vilify** [víləfài]	ⓥ to make vicious and defamatory statements about	비방하다
601 □□	**virulent** [vírjulənt]	ⓐ extremely infectious, malignant, or poisonous	전염성이 강한
602 □□	**vitriolic** [vìtriálik]	ⓐ bitterly scathing	신랄한
603 □□	**vociferous** [vosífərəs]	ⓐ making, given to, or marked by noisy and vehement outcry	시끄러운
604 □□	**vogue** [voug]	ⓝ popular acceptance or favor	인기
605 □□	**volition** [voulíʃən]	ⓝ the act or an instance of making a conscious choice or decision	결단
606 □□	**voluptuous** [vəlʌ́ptʃuəs]	ⓐ devoted to or indulging in sensual pleasures	관능적인
607 □□	**voracious** [vɔːréiʃəs]	ⓐ consuming or eager to consume great amounts of food	식욕이 왕성한

W

NO.	Entry Word	Meaning	Definition
608 □□	**waft** [wæft]	ⓥ to cause to go gently and smoothly through the air or over water	떠돌게 하다
609 □□	**waive** [weiv]	ⓥ to give up (a claim or right) voluntarily	포기하다
610 □□	**wane** [wein]	ⓥ to decrease gradually in size, amount, intensity, or degree	약해지다
611 □□	**wanton** [wántən]	ⓐ having no just cause or no good reason	이유가 없는
612 □□	**willful** [wílfəl]	ⓐ said or done on purpose; deliberate	계획적인, 고의인

NO.	Entry Word	Meaning	Definition
613 ☐☐	**wizened** [wíznd]	ⓐ withered	시든
Z			
614 ☐☐	**zenith** [zíːniθ]	ⓝ the point of culmination	정상

PART 1

PART 2

PART 3

PART 4

PART 5

PART 6

부록

수학용어 정리

수학용어 정리

A

absolute value 절대값

acute angle 예각

acute triangle 예각 삼각형

addition property for inequality 부등식의 덧셈법칙

addition property of equality 등식의 덧셈법칙

addition or subtraction method 가감법

adjacent angle 접각

adjacent arcs 접호

algebraic expression 대수식

altitude 높이

altitude of a cone 원뿔의 높이

altitude of a cylinder 원기둥의 높이

altitude of a parallelogram 평행사변형의 높이

altitude of a prism 각기둥의 높이

altitude of a pyramid 각뿔의 높이

altitude of a triangle 삼각형의 높이

angle 각

angle bisector of a triangle 삼각형의 각의 이등분선

antecedent 전항

approximate 약, 대강

arc length 호의 길이

arc measure 호의 값

arc of a chord 현의 호

area 넓이, 면적

arithmetic 산수

(arithmetic) mean 산술평균

ascending order of power 오름차순

associative properties(axioms) 결합법칙

auxiliary line 보조선

average 평균

axes 좌표축

axioms 원리, 공리

B

bar graph 막대그래프

base 밑변

base angles of an isosceles triangle 이등변 삼각형의
밑각

base of an isosceles triangle 이등변 삼각형의
밑변(base)

between 사이

between and inclusive 같거나 크다, 같거나 작다

boundary(of half-plane) 경계선

braces 중괄호

brackets 대괄호

broken line graph 꺾은선 그래프

C

calculator 계산기

celsius temperature scale 섭씨온도계

center of a circle 중점

center of a regular polygon 정다각형의 중점

center of a sphere 구의 중점

chart 표 차트

chord 현

circle 원

circle graph 원 그래프

circumference 원주

circumscribed circle 외접원

coefficient 계수

common factor 공약수

common multiple 공배수

commutative property 교환법칙(=comparison
property)

complementary angles 보각

composite number 합성수

compound interest 복리

concentric 중심이 같은

concentric circles 동심원

conclusion 결론

conditional 조건문

conditional 조건명제

conditional equation 조건등식

cone 원뿔

conjecture 추측

consecutive even integers 연속적인 짝수

consecutive integers 연속적인 정수

consecutive odd integer 연속적인 홀수

consequent 후항

constant 상수

constant of variation 계수

converse 역

convex polygon 볼록다각형

coordinates 좌표

coordinate axis 좌표축

PART 1

PART 2

PART 3

PART 4

PART 5

PART 6

coordinate plane 좌표평면
coordinates of a point 점의 좌표
coordinate proof 좌표평면을 이용한 증명
cosine 코사인
cost 물건값 비용
counterexample 반증, 반례
cube 세제곱, 정육면체
cubic 삼차
cubic equation 삼차방정식
cylinder 원기둥

D

data 자료
decagon 십각형
decimal 소수의, 십진법의
deductive reasoning 연역법
definition 뜻, 정의
degree 도, 차수
degree of a polynomial 다항식의 차수
denominator 분모
density 밀도
density property 두 유리수
dependent variable 종속변수
diagonal 대각선의
diagrams 다이어그램(도표)
diameter 지름
difference 차, 나머지
differences of squares 두 완전제곱수의 차
distance between a point and a line 한 점과 선 사이 거리
distance between two parallel lines 평행한 두 선 사이의 거리
distance formula 두 점 사이의 거리공식
distributive property of multiplication 곱셈의 분배법칙
divide 나누다
dividing rational numbers 유리수의 나눗셈
division 나눗셈
division property for inequality 부등식의 분배법칙
division property of equality 등식의 분배 법칙
dodecagon 십이각형
domain 정의역(번역)

E

edge 모서리
element 원소

elimination 소거
empty set 공집합
equality 등식
equally likely(outcomes) 결과(그 결과가 나올 확률이 동등할 때를 말함)
equation 방정식
equation in two variables 이원방정식
equiangular triangle 정삼각형
equidistant 같은 거리의(등거리의)
equilateral triangle 정삼각형
equivalent equation 답이 같은 방정식
estimate 어림잡다
evaluate 값을 구하다
even numbers 짝수
example 보기
excluded value 극값
exponent 지수
exponential decay 감가상각
exponential function 지수함수
exponential growth 시간이 지남에 따라 원래보다 증가하는 것 (함수)
expression 식
exterior angles 외각
extreme values 극값

F

face 면
factor 인수
factorial 팩토리얼(계승)
factoring 인수분해
fahrenheit temperature scale 화씨온도
formula 공식
fraction 분수
fractional equation 분수식
frequency 도수, 빈도
frequency table 도수분포표
function 함수

G

GCF(greatest common factor) 최대공약수
geometric mean 기하평균
geometric probability 기하확률
geometric sequence 등비수열
geometry 기하학
graph 그래프, 그래프를 그리다

graphic method 그래프를 사용해서 푸는 방법(식)
graph theory 그래프 이론
graphing calculators 그래픽 캘큘레이터(계산기)
great circle 반구의 면
greater than symbol '~보다 크다'를 나타내는 부호
greater than or equal to symbol '~보다 같거나 크다'를 나타내는 부호

H

height 높이, 키
hemisphere 반구
heptagon 칠각형
hexagon 육각형
horizontal axis 수평축(x축)
hypotenuse 빗변
hypothesis 가정

I

if and only if 필요충분조건
identify 지적하다, 알아내다
identity 항등식
if–then statement 조건문
illustrated 그림으로 나타난, 그림으로 설명된
image 상
inch 인치
independent events 독립사건
independent (systems of equations) 일반적 연립방정식
independent variable (quantity) 독립변수
index 지수
inductive reasoning 귀납법
inequalities 부등식
inequality symbol 부등호
insert 대입하다
integers 정수
intercept 절편
interest 이자
interior angle sum theorem 내각의 합 정리
interior angles 내각
interquartile range 사분범위
intersection 교집합
interval 구간
inverse 역원
involving 포함하는
irrational numbers 무리수
isosceles trapezoid 등변사다리꼴

isosceles triangle 이등변삼각형
isosceles triangle theorem 이등변삼각형 정리
iteration 반복

L

law of cosines 코사인법칙
law of sines 사인법칙
least common denominator 최소공분모(lcd)
least common multiple(lcm) 최소공배수
length 세로(길이)
less than symbol '~보다 작다'를 나타내는 부호
less than or equal to symbol 같거나 작다
line 선
line graph 선 그래프
linear equation 일차방정식
linear function 일차함수
linear graphs 일차함수의 그래프
locus 자취
lower quartile 제1사분위

M

marked down 인하
marked up 인상
matrix 매트릭스(행렬)
maximun (point of function) 이차함수의 최대
mean 평균
means 내항
measurement 측정(값)
median 중앙값(중간값)
median 중선
midpoint(of line segment) 중점
midpoint formulas 중점공식
minimum (point of function) 이차함수의 최소
minus 뺄셈
mode 최빈값(모드)
multiple 배수
multiplication 곱하기
multiplicative property of equality 양변에 같은 수를 곱해도 그 결과는 같다.

N

natural numbers 자연수
negation 부정
negative correlation 음의 상관관계
negative exponents 음의 지수

PART 1

PART 2

PART 3

PART 4

PART 5

PART 6

negative integer 음의 정수
negative number 음수
negative sign(−) 음수부호
network 네트워크
nickel 5센트
nonagon 구각형
not equal to symbol 같지 않다는 부호
number line 수직선
number theory 수이론
numerals 숫자
numerator 분자
numerical coefficient 수계수
numerical expression 수식

O

oblique cone 빗원뿔
oblique cylinder 빗원기둥
oblique prism 빗각기둥
obtuse angle 둔각
obtuse triangle 둔각삼각형
octagon 팔각형
odd numbers 홀수
odds 경우의 수
omit 생략하다
operation 사칙연산
opposites 덧셈에 대한 역원
order of operations 연산의 순서
ordered pairs 순서쌍
organize data 자료를 정리하다
origin 0(원점)
outcomes 결과
outlier 아웃라이어

P

parabola 포물선
parallel lines 평행선
parallel postulate 평행정리
parallelogram 평행사변형
parallelogram law 평행사변형의 법칙
parent graph 기본 그래프
parentheses 소괄호
penny 1센트
pentagon 오각형
percent 퍼센트(%)
percent of decrease 몇 퍼센트 감소했는지

percent of increase 몇 퍼센트 증가했는지
percent proportion 퍼센트 비율
percentage 퍼센티지
perfect square 완전제곱
perimeter 둘레
perpendicular bisector 수직이등분선
perpendicular bisector of a triangle 삼각형의 수직이등분선
perpendicular lines 수(직)선
perpendicular segment 수직인 선분
pi 파이
pint 파인트 (액체의 단위)
plane 평면
plane euclidean geometry 유클리드기하학
plane figure 평면도형
platonic solid 플라톤의 입체
point 점
point of relection 중점
point of symmetry 대칭점
point of tangency 점점
polygons 다각형
polyhedron 다면체
polynomial 다항식
polynomial equation 다항방정식
positive 양수의
positive correlation 양의 삼관관계
positive integer 양의 정수
positive sign (+) 0보다 큰 수량을 말해 주는 부호
positive number 양수
postulate 공리
power 거듭제곱
prime factorization 소인수분해
prime number 소수
principal 자본
principal square root 양의 제곱근
prism 각기둥
probability 확률
problem-solving strategies(plan) 응용문제 푸는 법
product 곱
product of powers 거듭제곱수의 곱
product property of square roots 제곱근의 곱셈법칙
proof 증명
proportion 비례
protractor 각도기
pyramid 각뿔

pythagorean theorem 피타고라스 정리
pythagorean triple 피타고라스의 수

Q

quadrant 사분면
quadratic equation 이차방정식
quadratic formula 근의 공식
quadratic function 이차함수
quadrilateral 사각형
quart 쿼트(액체의 단위)
question 질문
questionnaire 질문지
quotient 몫
quatient of powers 거듭제곱수의 나눗셈

R

radical equation 무리방정식
radical expressions 무리식
radical sign 근호, 루트
radius 반지름
random 무작위
range 치역, 범위
rate 속도, 비율
ratio 비율
rational equations 분수방정식
rational expression 유리식(분수식)
rational number 유리수
ray 반직선
real numbers 실수(유리수와 무리수를 합한 수)
reciprocal 곱셈에 대한 역원
rectangle 직사각형
rectangular solid 직육면체
reflection 반사
regular polygon 정다각형
regular polyhedron 정다면체
regular prism 정각기둥
regular pyramid 정각뿔
regular tessellation 정다각형의 배열
relation 관계
remainder 나머지
remote interior angles 주어진 외각과 접해 있지 않은 두 내각
rhombus 마름모
right angle 직각
right circular cone 직원뿔

right cylinder 직기둥
right prism 직각기둥
right pyramid 직각뿔
right triangle 직각삼각형
rise y축 방향
roots 답, 근, 해
rotation 회전
round off 반올림

S

smaple space 표본공간
sampling 표본조사
scalar multiplication 행렬의 곱셈
scale 스케일
scalene triangle 부등변삼각형
scatter plot graph 점그래프
scientific notation 십진법의 표기법
segment 선분
semicircle 반원
sequence 수열
set 집합
side 변
sides of the equation 방정식의 변
similar figures 닮은꼴
similar polygons 닮은 다각형
similar solids 닮은 입체
similar triangles 닮은 삼각형
simple interest 단리
simplest form of expression 간단히 한 식
simplest radical form 간단히 한 무리식
simplify 정리하다, 간단히 하다
sine 사인
skew lines 비대칭선
slice of a solid 단면
slope 기울기
slope-intercept form of linear equations 일차방정식의 표준
solid 입체
solution 해, 답
solution of a system of equations 연립방정식의 해
solution set 해집합
solving a triangle 삼각형 풀기
space 공간
sphere 구
spreadsheets 컴퓨터용 회계처리장부

PART 1

PART 2

PART 3

PART 4

PART 5

PART 6

square 제곱, 정사각형
square root 제곱근
square root algorithm 제곱근표
standard form(of linear equations) 일차방정식의 일반형
statistics 통계
straight angle 평각
straightedge 직선자
strictly self-similar 위치와 크기에 상관없이 부분이 전체와 같은 모양이 되는 것
substitution 대입
subtraction 뺄셈
subtraction property for inequality 부등식의 뺄셈법칙
subtraction property of equality 등식의 뺄셈법칙
sum 합
supplementary angles 보각
surface area 겉넓이
symmetric property of equality 등식의 양변을 바꾸어도 결과는 같다
symmetry 대칭
systems of equations 연립방정식
systems of inequality 연립부등식

T

tables 표
tangent 탄젠트
tangent segment 접선
term 항
theorem 정리
times 곱하기
total 합계
transformation 변환
transitive property of equality 등식에서 a와 b가 같고, b와 c가 같으면 a와 c도 같다는 법칙
translation 평행이동
transversal 횡단선
trapezoid 사다리꼴
tree diagram 수형도
triangle 삼각형
triangular cylinder 삼각기둥
trigonometric ratios 삼각비

U

undefined term 무정의 용어
uniform 균등
union 합집합

unit cost 단위 값
upper quartile 제3사분위

value 값, 수치
variable 문자(변수)
venn diagrams 벤다이어그램
verbal expression 대수식을 말로 풀어 써놓은 것
vertex 꼭지점
vertex angle 꼭지각
vertical angles 맞꼭지각
vertical axis 수직축
vertical line test 수직선이 그래프의 한 점만 통과하는 관계는 함수이다
volume 부피

weight 무게
weighted average 하중평균
whole number 범자연수
working backward 거꾸로 풀기
width 가로

x-axis x축
x-coordinate x좌편
x-intercept x절편

Y

yard 야드
y-axis y축
y-coordinate y좌편
y-intercept y절편

Z

z-axis z축
zero exponent 0인 지수
zero product property 어느 수에 0을 곱해도 결과는 0이다
zeros(of a function) 함수를 0으로 만드는 값